Settling Ohio

SETTLING OHIO

First Peoples and Beyond

Edited by
Timothy G. Anderson and Brian Schoen

Foreword by M. Duane Nellis

Afterword by Chief Glenna J. Wallace

Ohio University Press
Athens

Ohio University Press, Athens, Ohio 45701

ohioswallow.com

Chapter 7 originally appeared in Gruenwald, Kim M. *River of Enterprise: The Commercial Origins of Regional Identity in the Ohio Valley, 1790–1850.* © 2002 Indiana University Press. Reprinted with permission of Indiana University Press.
Printed in the United States of America

Ohio University Press books are printed on acid-free paper ∞ ™

31 30 29 28 27 26 25 24 23   5 4 3 2 1

Library of Congress Cataloging-in-Publication Data
Names: Anderson, Timothy Gene, editor. | Schoen, Brian, editor.
Title: Settling Ohio : first peoples and beyond / edited by Timothy G. Anderson and Brian Schoen.
Other titles: First peoples and beyond
Description: Athens : Ohio University Press, [2023] | Series: New approaches to midwestern studies | "This collection of essays is an outgrowth of a conference entitled 'Settling Ohio: First Nations and Beyond' held in February 2020 at Ohio University"—Afterword. | Includes bibliographical references and index.
Identifiers: LCCN 2022057353 (print) | LCCN 2022057354 (ebook) | ISBN 9780821425275 (paperback) | ISBN 9780821425268 (hardcover) | ISBN 9780821447994 (pdf)
Subjects: LCSH: Ohio—History—To 1787. | Ohio—History—1787–1865. | Pioneers—Ohio. | Indians of North America—Ohio—History.
Classification: LCC F495 .S48 2023 (print) | LCC F495 (ebook) | DDC 977.1/01—dc23/eng/20221207
LC record available at https://lccn.loc.gov/2022057353
LC ebook record available at https://lccn.loc.gov/2022057354

Dedicated to the diverse peoples

and communities of southeastern Ohio,

past and present, transplants and dispossessed

CONTENTS

ILLUSTRATIONS

Figures

FOREWORD

During my presidency at Ohio University, I was proud to support the conference "Settling Ohio: First Nations and Beyond," held on our campus in February of 2020. Prior to this conference, I read with interest the book by David McCullough titled *The Pioneers: The Heroic Story of the Settlers Who Brought the American Ideal West,* which gained considerable national attention but in many ways was limited in scope and focus and racialized the true dynamics of settlement of what is now southeast Ohio. I am now so pleased to see the evolution of this new book as an outcome of the conference and its important role in documenting more completely the role and voices of other overlooked groups.

I would like to thank Ohio University professors Brian Schoen and Tim Anderson for spurring the initiation of the conference and for serving as coeditors of this important book. I would also like to thank all those who supported the initial conference and the many who then contributed to this significant scholarly book. The Ohio University Departments of History and Geography, along with the Southeast Ohio History Center, the Central Regional Humanities Center, the Charles J. Ping Institute for the Teaching of Humanities, the OHIO Museum Complex, and Professor Nancy Stevens and Dr. Tanisha King-Taylor, along with student David Suman and Dr. Schoen, for all their work on the Black History mAppAthens tour, are just some of the entities and individuals who helped in this effort. In addition, I would like to recognize the Ohio University Press for publishing this important work and the crucial role they play in contributing to scholarly publications of key regional as well as national and international interest.

Ohio University's own history is a critical part of this dialogue. Established in 1804, Ohio University was one of the first public universities in the United States (and the oldest in the Northwest Territory) and helped to create a model and standards for higher education that were replicated elsewhere in the nineteenth century. It is also important to remember that Ohio became a state in 1803, and our university was an integral part of the growth of the state and the region.

This book provides a more comprehensive view of the multiple dimensions of "settlement," which began not with the first European Americans but perhaps as early as ten thousand years ago toward the end of continental glaciation. These true first settlers built this region's first dwellings and became what are the now state of Ohio's first farmers. This volume sheds important light on individuals and groups who have not received the attention they deserve. This includes insights into Indigenous populations, African Americans, and other immigrant groups who played a significant role in the settlement of what is now southeast Ohio.

I am honored that this critical scholarly dialogue was facilitated by scholars at Ohio University but also includes scholars from several other universities and organizations. Through this work, we understand more fully the complexity and diversity of groups who have called this region home well before our New England settlers, and we remember more completely the past and present, transplants and dispossessed peoples, of what is now southeast Ohio.

M. Duane Nellis
President Emeritus and Trustee Professor
Ohio University

ACKNOWLEDGMENTS

Writing books can sometimes be solitary pursuits. This one has not been. We are deeply appreciative of the efforts of many people who made this volume possible. The idea for the February 2020 conference from which this book was born emerged out of the Midwestern History Association annual meeting where the editors had the chance to hear Anna-Lisa Cox describe her then-new book. The idea received the generous support of Ohio University's Central Region Humanities Center and especially of its emeriti director, Judith Lee, and grant committee chair, Gary Holcombe, who were both enthusiastic about our effort. Ohio University president Duane Nellis generously marshaled some of his own office's funds and staff to bring our speakers to Athens. We are particularly thankful for the work of PR guru Carly Leatherwood; designer extraordinaire Stacey Stewart; and WOUB's Tom Hodson, who featured the conference and our keynote speakers on his national *Spectrum* podcast.

The College of Arts and Sciences leadership also gave generously of their time and talents. Lori Bauer pushed the word out and helped us attract a great crowd; Susan Downard gave us some useful suggestions for talking to alumni and donors; and Dean Florenz Plassmann attended nearly every session. History Department chair Katherine Jellison was supportive of this effort from the beginning and helped put us in touch with Chief Glenna Wallace. She also defrayed some extra expenses that arose, as did geography chair Dorothy Sack. The Ohio University events team of Nikki Ohms, Cimmeron O'Connor, and Dustin Kilgour made sure that everyone was comfortable and well fed. Jessica Cyders of the Southeast Ohio History Center arranged to bring *The Pioneers* exhibit to Athens and hosted a reception and roundtable that included discussions by Linda Showalter, Bill Reynolds, and Ray Swick. Jessica and intern

David Suman worked under a tight deadline to create a Black history of Athens walking tour that, with the heroic efforts of Tanisha King-Taylor and Nancy Stevens and her mAppAthens team, launched the day of the conference. If the event was as successful as presenters and audience members suggested it was, it was in no small measure because of the help of these individuals. We drew inspiration from the large audience turnout from Ohio University students, staff, and faculty and alumni, as well as many from the general public. It is likely that their enthusiasm, more than our charms, convinced the authors of this volume to convert papers into chapters. We thank each and every contributor for their efforts. They dazzled on stage, and they have done so here in print.

The Ohio University Press is a natural home for this collection, and we are thankful for the efforts of Ricky Huard and Beth Pratt, who supported its publication and ushered it into print with the help of Tyler Balli and our copyeditor, Theresa Winchell. We thank R. Douglas Hurt and an anonymous external reader whose enthusiasm for the manuscript paved the way for publication just as their suggestions helped improve the final product.

The ultimate inspiration for this book was, to a considerable degree, another book, *The Pioneers,* written by David McCullough and published in 2019. Had the Pulitzer Prize–winning historian not turned his considerable narrative skill to the story of New Englanders who settled Ohio, it is not certain we would have been motivated to expand upon that story. Sadly, Mr. McCullough passed away just a few weeks before this book headed into production. While there are interpretive differences that will be immediately apparent to readers, we wish to acknowledge the important contributions that David McCullough has made to American history and to public memory. Whether it be as the distinctive voice on countless documentaries or as the author of over twelve books, many of them best sellers, McCullough made history accessible to a wider audience, sparked the interests of millions of readers, and cared deeply about capturing and conveying the American experience. That we view *The Pioneers* as an incomplete account of the settling of Ohio does not mean that it is an inaccurate or unworthy one. Neither the study of the past nor the efforts to remedy its injustices are zero-sum games. There must remain ample room for many rich voices and perspectives. We dedicate this book to those of the diverse peoples who call or once called Ohio home.

Introduction

BRIAN SCHOEN

This book is the result of a collaboration launched in the summer of 2019. Its editors attended the annual Midwestern History Association conference in Grand Rapids, Michigan, where David McCullough's recently released book, *The Pioneers: The Heroic Story of the Settlers Who Brought the American Ideal West,* received a significant amount of attention, overwhelmingly negative, despite its ascent to the *New York Times* bestseller list. The book and its reception resonated particularly strongly with us because we came from Ohio University, a campus peppered with reminders of the "heroic" members of the Ohio Company of Associates and nestled south of a national forest named after their military protector, General Anthony Wayne. Indeed, as *The Pioneer's* acknowledgments suggests, its genesis came from the two-time Pulitzer Prize–winning historian's campus visit to deliver the commencement address in 2004, the year Ohio University celebrated its bicentennial.

Like many in our locale, we read and appreciated the book's humanizing of select individuals we knew only as names on buildings, and its description of early life in Marietta and smaller surrounding communities. Although we are both transplants, these are the places that many of our students call home, and we enjoyed learning more about the origins of our university and its claim to being the oldest public institution in the Old Northwest territory. I assigned the book in an Early American Republic class, and students from urban, suburban, and rural places alike devoured it with atypical resonance, several noting they had no idea "so much history happened here." Even longtime locals knew little about the Cutlers or that Blennerhassett Island was the center of a treason trial involving Thomas Jefferson and Aaron Burr, or that Gallipolis was settled by French refugees. It is understandable why, both off and on campus, the book inspired civic pride, and even a hoped-for increase in tourism. Told by one of the nation's master storytellers, *The Pioneers* brought welcome attention to a region that is at once part of both Appalachia and the Rust Belt, two areas with interesting histories and populations who have felt increasingly overlooked.

Yet, as midcareer scholars who study and teach this era, we share many of the frustrations on display at that conference in Michigan, criticisms subsequently reinforced in scorching academic reviews of the book's content and conclusions. Many of those can be found in the Summer 2021 issue of the *Journal of the Early Republic* and accompanying blogs available in *The Panorama*.[1] The central cast of *The Pioneers* was limited to a small group of White men, with a supporting cast of wives and daughters. Indian leaders such as Captain Pipe and a few escaped slaves briefly appear, but mostly as "others" seen only through the lens of the book's adventuring protagonists and not on their own terms. Unintentionally but problematically, the racialized assumptions of New England settlers substitute for a far more accurate, dynamic, fraught, and ultimately interesting understanding of how Ohio was "settled."

Accurate histories require a deep interrogation of sources, especially when they are scarce in number. In many key places—the Big Bottom Massacre and Ohio's 1802 debate over slavery, for example—the central characters' words are accepted as truth rather than as imperfect and possibly self-serving versions of events. The book's narrative arc, while offering compelling human stories of personal tragedy and triumph, ignored many of the new insights that rigorous research and debate has brought to light about this period, about westward settlement into this region, and especially about Indigenous peoples who inhabited it.

In the final analysis, we concluded that *The Pioneers* told a story that needed telling but did so in an oversimplified way that lacked context and unnecessarily silenced the voices of other overlooked groups whose stories also deserved to be told. The title, like the story, betrays a worldview, ultimately rooted in a nineteenth-century "Whiggish" understanding, whereby progress and civilization move from east to west and are "brought" forth almost exclusively by pale-skinned peoples. So, in the spirit of recovering a more holistic and accurate account, we designed a conference aimed at elaborating on important aspects of the book but also and especially on filling in the many gaps. For while the Ohio Company of Associates left an indelible, and even at times a positive, legacy, the story as told through their eyes was only a partial one. We sought to elevate the stories and voices of others and to offer a more complete assessment of the contributions of the many population groups who shaped the human and physical landscapes of the upper Ohio River valley. With the support of the Central Region Humanities Center and then university president Duane Nellis, we brought speakers to campus to share their expertise about both the topics covered in that book, but also those left out.

Our authors, all presenters at that conference, were asked to draw upon their deep research and pose questions and answers that are of interest to other scholars, but to avoid the jargon that sometimes bogs down academic writing. We believe they have succeeded, making this a volume of interest and utility to both scholars and a broader public curious to learn more about the diverse peoples and the dynamism and contestation that shaped the history of what became known as "Ohio." By adding new voices, offering broader context, and embracing and explaining the true complexity that defines the past, *Settling Ohio* offers us truer stories and ultimately deeper drama, stories perhaps more appropriate and relevant for our own complicated present. For one thing, it highlights that human settlement of the region was a continual process that began long before people of European ancestry arrived west of the Appalachian Mountains. First settlers likely came from the North and the West rather than the East. The settlement of the region by various Indigenous and European peoples that took place from the seventeenth through the nineteenth centuries was in truth a resettlement into terrain already shaped by the economic, social, and cultural activity of past peoples. Furthermore, the continual settling and resettling of the region ensured that geopolitical and social dynamics of the region remained constantly in flux, lending an admittedly ironic meaning to this volume's title.

The stories told in this volume draw from a rich vein of interdisciplinary work on the early American republic and on frontier and borderland studies that is too vast to fully summarize here. Rather than provide a complete encapsulation of the insights that geographers, anthropologists, educators, and historians have offered, this introduction provides a brief overview and frames new insights about the topics explored in this volume. As such, it seeks to highlight some of the themes that emerge from the chapters, appreciating that such collections necessarily prioritize the breadth and depth of knowledge of each individual author and topic at the expense of a clear or unified narrative.[2]

European settlers were of course not the first pioneers into the river valley that would become known as the Ohio, originally an Iroquois place-name. Archaeological evidence suggests the first pioneers to the region were the Adena, who may have arrived as early as 800 BCE, although the very first people arrived even earlier, perhaps eight thousand to ten thousand years prior. As Joseph Gingerich shows, they moved a lot of earth, creating the impressive conical mounds and effigy earthworks that remain a part of the state's landscapes even today. Judging from how they transformed the environment and the artifacts they left behind, they possessed the population density, economic prowess, and political ability to mobilize significant amounts of labor. Their efforts fascinated those of European ancestry who first encountered them and, as Chief Glenna Wallace's epilogue reminds us, leave an important legacy, the proper use and preservation of which demands attention.

We do not know precisely what brought early humans to this region, although presumably the area's river systems and the remarkable natural resources available in the Ohio River basin had something to do with it. Those assets ensured that the region we call Ohio attracted diverse Indigenous groups even before European contact, but especially as many were dispossessed of lands along the Eastern Seaboard and Great Lakes. Cameron Shriver shows us that displaced Indians created vibrant communities and trading posts, including Pickawillany (near present-day Piqua, Ohio), which in 1750 was possibly the most populous city in the Ohio River valley. Europeans and Indigenes engaged in trade that was generally mutually beneficial, and discerning Indian consumers negotiated the best deals they could.

During the colonial period, French and English traders traversed the region, and Virginia and Pennsylvania speculators covetously eyed it. Various Indian groups, though, including the Miami and Shawnee, dominated it, and contested one another for control of it. The Seven Years' War (as Europeans know it), or the French and Indian War (as White Americans called it), began to shift that story as access to trade and the lands west of the Appalachian Mountains emerged as a central motive for the conflict, one that Winston Churchill and subsequent historians have argued was the first "world war."[3] By several accounts, the restrictions that British imperial officials placed on access to the lands beyond the Appalachians contributed to colonists' dissatisfaction with British control, one of many complaints that precipitated a war for independence.[4]

The American Revolution brought British and American military outposts, and accelerated violence, including the horrific 1782 Gnadenhutten massacre, in which American militia murdered nearly one hundred innocent Lenape men, women, and children. No criminal action was ever taken against those who perpetuated that atrocity. Many Indian leaders, such as Captain Pipe, sought to remain neutral, but continued attacks eventually drew them into the conflict, often on the British side. The treaty ending the Revolutionary War furthered US aspirations for the wealth and opportunity that existed across the Ohio River. In an important and often underappreciated demonstration of national ambitions and a recognition that no individual state could exert sovereign power over their northwestern lands, Virginia (1784), Massachusetts (1785), and finally Connecticut (1800) ceded their western claims to the new national government.

Federal claims did not, as the subsequent chapters demonstrate, equal national control. The process of state-building was slow and messy work that included land ordinances, the Northwest Ordinance, and the often-muddled legal business of constitution making. Nor did settlers wait, as farmers and traders trickled across the mountains and the Ohio River, hoping to make better lives for themselves. Aspirations for wealth brought investment from White-controlled land companies and, as Anna-Lisa Cox reminds us, Black settlers. They were joined by French and especially German immigrants who, as Tim Anderson demonstrates, left an enduring mark on the state's cultural landscapes.

While the specific land that comprised the Ohio Company purchase proved to be rather unfertile, ample wildlife and more agriculturally productive lands were found farther west. The settlement's chief sources of revenue were, well, other immigrants. Trade continued to define the settlement, but eventually the arrival of new White settlers lessened the need to trade with Indian peoples. As Kim Gruenwald's chapter illustrates, individuals like Marietta's own Dudley Woodbridge Jr. tied together the growing number of White settlers via networks of credit that brought eastern and even European goods to "frontier farmers." The growth of the vast trading networks might lead one to conclude that White settlers were doing quite well for themselves. Many were, but as William Kerrigan's essay reminds us, most early US settlers were just scraping by. It was into this world that Johnny Chapman (a.k.a. Johnny Appleseed) arrived. By introducing an affordable supply of food at a crucial moment of increased settler mobility, Chapman furthered the ability of Ohioans to sustain themselves. Apples, eaten or distilled into cider, created a culture that transformed several aspects of Ohio life and even shaped the national political culture. Yet history is never static, and by the 1830s, new technologies and an emerging middle-class ethos recast apple culture, making Chapman into a folk hero of a bygone era.

A true account of the settling of Ohio must place the complicated story of Indian-White interactions in the upper Ohio River valley firmly at the center. Most new settlers of European descent did not come intending harm to Indian peoples. Indeed, the Ohio Company specifically made peace a goal and misinterpreted Captain Pipe's and others' initial greeting as a sign that they would be welcomed. Few investors or American settlers, however, developed the cultural awareness or empathy that would allow them to pursue peace, especially if it inconvenienced their material interests. In truth, their presence was quite unsettling to an already fragile geopolitical situation.[5] The political and social disorder experienced among Whites looking to settle Ohio pales in comparison to the long-term damage exacted upon Native peoples by the actions of Europeans and White Americans, and eventually the federal government. From start to finish, the acknowledgment of that loss (in some ways impossible to fully express) pervades this volume, even as several essays evidence just how resilient and adaptive Indian peoples were in the face of fast-changing realities.

Taken as a whole, this volume furthers the ongoing reimagining of what Americans still commonly refer to as "the frontier" but which many scholars call the "borderlands," a term that acknowledges there were people on both sides of a porous, largely imagined line. Scholarship on the Great Lakes and Ohio River valley has been at the forefront of such studies. For over half a century historians and geographers have considered White westward expansion less as a civilizing line whereby "pioneers" pushed westward, and more as a shared space of collaboration, negotiation, and contestation between different peoples who traded, shared cultures, and married one another in what one celebrated work from the 1990s referred to as a "middle ground."[6] Recent scholars, though, have pushed back against the idea of a fluid borderland in which multidirectional influences shaped White and non-White societies.[7] Borrowing from world history methods, some apply instead the term "settler colonialism" or what Bethal Saler describes, for the post-Revolutionary period, as a "settler nation" or "settler empire," terms suggestive of the asymmetrical power that European peoples brought with them.[8]

Settling Ohio both illustrates and somewhat problematizes this approach. Chapters herein acknowledge the fact that imperial and national armies supported White settlers' claims with devastating consequences for Indian peoples, including ultimately, for most, removal. Yet chapters also suggest the limits of reducing the story of eighteenth- and nineteenth-century Ohio to White conquerors versus conquered Indians. The competition for land, trade, and power took place not just between Indians and Whites but within those groups, with the presence of Black settlers further problematizing the story. Intra-Indian competition also shaped geopolitics. As Cameron Shriver notes, the region was not known as "Ohio Country" or as "Indian Country," but as "Miami Country, Shawnee Country, Wyandot Country, and Seneca-Cayuga Country." Furthermore, as John Bickers beautifully shows, internal group dynamics worked alongside the pressures exerted by US federal power to create fissures among the Miami, who, after the Treaty of Greenville, survived and found new ways to resist and preserve their shared identity. Nor was there a monolithic "White" opinion over what should happen in the West, which generated considerable political division within the United States. "Conquerors" came in many forms, including not just Black pioneers but also the multiple ethnic groups evidenced in Tim Anderson's cultural geography of the state, and within the competing companies that attempted to sell Indian lands. Taken as a whole, this book demonstrates the considerable value—and the necessary nuance required—in applying the methods of settler colonialism to Indian and borderland studies.

One benefit of applying such approaches comes from linking western expansion to another recent development in the historiography of the Early Republic: a new appreciation for the power of institutions, both governmental and nongovernmental. This approach, ascendant since the 1990s, sees politics less through the lens of parties or individuals and more as the product of policies carried out by an administrative state that used post offices, tax collection agencies, and, of special note here, land offices and armies to enact change.[9] Such methods are readily apparent within this volume, which suggests some of the ways that the region's political and cultural landscape was crucially shaped by the application of governmental power. By framing the "Northwest Ordinance" as a "Founding" constitutional document, contextualized by the formation of a more cohesive Indigenous confederation and the Ohio Company's planned settlement, Jessica Roney shows how the concept of western statehood was necessarily linked to national power and accelerated by four contemporaneous events. Born largely out of concerns of Indian war and a desire to pay off the national debt, the Northwest Ordinance offered a pathway to replicate Republican governance and, for citizens at least, eventual entrance into the union as equals. As important as that pathway toward stability proved, the trip down it remained bumpy. Indeed, Joseph Ross's chapter shows how the complexity of private-public partnerships, however designed, initially generated as much chaos as clarity, especially during the Federal era. It was not, he provocatively argues, until Jeffersonian Republicans controlled the federal land offices and brought about statehood that a modicum of political order emerged within the region.

Bill Hunter shows how the desire to nationalize Ohio led to Colonel Ebenezer Zane's congressionally funded postal road, a road that not only delivered the mail but transformed the physical space and economic lives of those leaving near it. Although small by twenty-first century standards, the federal government of the Early Republic, evidenced further in the repeated appearance of the US Army, left a lasting imprint on the peoples and geography of the Old Northwest.

While this book's focus is regional, the events that unfolded here are of global significance. The Hopewell mounds stand as some of the most impressive structures ever built in North America, evidence of a sophisticated and complex ancient civilization worthy of UNESCO status. The seventy-five-year period around which this book concentrates was one in which Indian groups and European empires battled for control over access to one of the more elaborate river systems in the world and to adjacent lands with a remarkable array of natural resources. As Cameron Shriver nicely shows, Ohio in the eighteenth century was not a coherent place but rather a constellation of men and women claiming and using different portions of land, and quite frequently fighting over it. Standing at the mouth of the Muskingum in 1763, one would have had little idea of what might become of lands that a recent royal decree announced were to be off-limits for British subjects and declared Indian possessions. There were multiple possible histories for the region. By 1816, however, control of the Upper Ohio was no longer in doubt. The French and Indian War, the Northwest Indian Wars of the 1790s, and those of the early 1800s that eventually became folded into the War of 1812 evidenced the near-constant tension and violence that accompanied that process. When something resembling peace was restored, American settlers expanded their economic and political activities, and Ohio's White and Black populations quickly expanded and diversified. Indian groups like the Miami and Shawnee, however, faced the possibility of cultural, or even actual, genocide or removal. That story, poignantly and tragically told by Chief Glenna Wallace, ended with the forced removal of groups like the Mixed Band of Seneca and Shawnee in the 1830s. For her people, false and broken promises forced unimaginable hardships and choices between bad and worse options.

A final thread woven through this book, then, is how we today might understand the cultural institutions and legacy of Ohio's earliest settlers of various ethnic backgrounds. One of the lasting legacies of the Ohio Company was the creation of Ohio University. Although it struggled financially in the early years, it has served, and continues to serve, students and the state for well over two centuries. New England settlers like Ephraim Cutler and Rufus Putnam carried with them a belief in public education and a faith in republican governance that endured and unquestionably shaped, in mostly positive ways, the civic life and cultural legacy of Ohio. Yet as Adam Nelson demonstrates in his chapter, well-intentioned ideals also clashed against hard political realities and racist assumptions. Who would foot the bill for educating people and how? What groups were deserving of a public education, a question that often left Black settlers and non-Anglo immigrants fending for themselves? Indeed, as Anna-Lisa Cox and Chief Glenna Wallace remind us, the battles to preserve those groups' heritage, although sometimes less immediately visible, are no less important. Ohio University rightfully stands proud as a site of knowledge creation, aimed at accomplishing just that. It serves as a beacon of hope not only for Ohioans but for diverse students across the country and around the world, including thousands of first-generation college students.

This volume, like the conference from which it emerged, challenges a misperception, common in academic circles and among the public alike, that there is an impossibly wide chasm between the type of work that academics do and the historical interest of the broader public. The public (or a certain subsection of the public), some professors are wont to lament, just do not want to be challenged by hearing the seedier or less celebratory parts of the American past. Humanists in particular fret about a public allegedly losing interest in our fields (a claim ironically similar to traditionalists' lamentation that people today do not care about the past). The conference organizers wondered that, too, as we built a program to be presented in a college town that, in the 2016 primary, went Bernie Sanders blue but is in a county that Trump handily won.

Our experience was a starkly different one. As we talked up the conference to civic groups and spread the word to alumni, it became clear that those who had read and enjoyed *The Pioneers,* and in several cases provided McCullough material, were eager to know more. They were excited to learn that Chief Glenna Wallace of the Eastern Shawnee nation would be joining us to tell her story. They wanted to know about the African American settlers who Anna-Lisa Cox shows fought discrimination and carved out communities. They were receptive to the idea, offered by Bill Kerrigan, that Johnny Appleseed's importance needed to be seen through the lens of class inequality. An audience of nearly three hundred people, about half of whom were from the general public, listened not just attentively but inquisitively and, best we could tell, empathetically, as John Bickers, a citizen of the Miami Tribe, welcomed them in Myaamiaataweenki (the Miami language) and explained how his ancestors coped with dispossession by creating a recognized sovereign nation. Although admittedly only one data point, and one taken from the generally generous and hospitable people of southeastern Ohio, the lesson we took from this is that people can handle the tough stuff and we do them and ourselves a disservice to assume otherwise. This book, then, is offered as testimony to the collective aim of not only remembering but also recovering and reclaiming the rich and diverse cultural heritage of this region.

Notes

1.   See special Critical Engagements symposium edited by Jessica Choppin Roney and Andrew Shankman, "Scholars, Scholarship, and David Mc-Cullough's *The Pioneers: The Heroic Story of the Settlers Who Brought the*

American Ideal West," Journal of the Early Republic 41, no. 2 (Summer 2021): 175–76. Also accompanying pieces in *The Panorama,* including Michael A. Blaakman, "How Should History Make Us Feel," *The Panorama: Expansive Views from the Journal of the Early Republic,* June 11, 2021, http://thepanorama.shear.org/2021/06/11/how-should-history-make-us-feel/.

2. See, for example, Andrew R. L. Cayton and Stuart D. Hobbs, *The Center of a Great Empire: The Ohio Country in the Early Republic* (Athens: Ohio University Press, 2005).

3. Quoted in H. V. Bowen, *War and British Society, 1688–1815* (Cambridge: Cambridge University Press, 1998), 7; Fred Anderson, *Crucible of War: The Seven Years' War and the Fate of Empire in British North America, 1764–1766* (New York: Vintage Books, 2001).

4. The role of the backcountry in shaping the coming of the American Revolution is explored in several recent works, including Patrick Spero, *Frontier Country: The Politics of War in Early Pennsylvania* (Philadelphia: University of Pennsylvania Press, 2016); Patrick Spero, *Frontier Rebels: The Fight for Independence in the American West, 1765–1776* (New York: W. W. Norton, 2018); Woody Holton, *Forced Founders: Indians, Debtors, Slaves, and the Making of the American Revolution in Virginia* (Chapel Hill: University of North Carolina Press, 2011); Patrick Griffin, *American Leviathan: Empire, Nation, and Revolutionary Frontier* (New York: Hill and Wang, 2008); Robert G. Parkinson, *The Common Cause: Creating Race and Nation in the American Revolution* (Chapel Hill: University of North Carolina Press, 2016); and Alan Taylor, *American Revolutions: A Continental History, 1750–1804* (New York: W. W. Norton, 2016).

5. Rob Harper, *Unsettling the West: Violence and State-Building in the Ohio Valley* (Philadelphia: University of Pennsylvania Press, 2018).

6. Richard White, *The Middle Ground: Indians, Empires, and Republics in the Great Lakes Region, 1650–1815* (New York: Cambridge University Press, 1991); Eric Hinderaker, *Elusive Empires: Constructing Colonialism in the Ohio Valley, 1673–1800* (New York: Cambridge University Press, 1997); and David Andrew Nichols, *Peoples of the Inland Sea: Native Americans and New Comers in the Great Lakes Region, 1600–1870* (Athens: Ohio University Press, 2018).

7. See, for example, Alan Taylor, *The Divided Ground: Indians, Settlers and the Northern Borderland of the American Revolution* (New York: Vintage Books, 2007).

8. Bethel Saler, *The Settlers' Empire: Colonialism and State Formation in America's Old Northwest* (Philadelphia: University of Pennsylvania Press, 2019). For a fuller discussion of this concept, see the special edition edited by Jeffrey Ostler and Nancy Shoemaker, "Settler Colonialism in Early American History," *William and Mary Quarterly* 76, no. 3 (July 2019).

9. Historians who lived through the New Deal and Great Society saw state power in the early period as practically insignificant. Yet scholars who

have lived through the political fights over deregulation and downsizing that started in the 1970s and took new form after the Cold War ended looked back to the early period and discovered there was sufficient power within federalism to shape outcomes. For good examples and summary views of this literature, see Richard John, "Government Institutions as Agents of Change: Rethinking American Political Development in the Early Republic, 1787–1835," *Studies in American Political Development* 11, no. 2 (Fall 1997): 347–80; Gautham Rao, "The New Historiography of the Early Federal Government: Institutions, Contexts, and the Imperial State," *William and Mary Quarterly* 77, no. 1 (2020): 97–128; William J. Novak, "The Myth of the 'Weak' American State," *American Historical Review* 113, no. 3 (June 2008): 752–72; and Max M. Edling, *A Revolution in Favor of Government: Origins of the U.S. Constitution and the Making of the American State* (Oxford: Oxford University Press, 2003).

1

The True Pioneers

A Brief Overview of Prehistoric
Native Americans in Ohio

JOSEPH A. M. GINGERICH

When Americans think of "pioneers," they think of people in historic contexts: settlers, inventors, and explorers who reached new frontiers in science or geographic exploration. They seldom think of the very first people in North America, those who were the first to explore, farm, establish settlements, and create monumental architecture. These first people were not the brave men and women that David McCullough talks about in his *New York Times* bestseller *The Pioneers: The Heroic Story of the Settlers Who Brought the American Ideal West.* The true pioneers were those American Indian populations that first saw and explored the North and South American continents. Their story begins more than 13,000 years ago.

The purpose of this chapter is to provide a very brief overview of the prehistory of what would become "Ohio" and to highlight the antiquity of human activity in that region. For context, the first people to navigate the landscape and extract resources in Ohio came long before the written record and more than 8,000 years before the building of the first pyramids in Egypt. Members of the public think about the first

American Indians as those who built the well-known earthen mounds, but the first people were here 8,000 to 10,000 years before many of the first mounds were constructed. These initial populations left evidence of their presence through artifacts and modification of the landscape, which would provide clues to pathways and key resources that would benefit later populations. Ohio is the home to some of the oldest known evidence of people in North America. It is also one of only nine independent domestication events in the world and the center of one of the largest feats of monumental architecture ever created. This chapter will summarize these extraordinary events and the true "pioneers" who are associated with them.

The Peopling of Ohio and North America

When Christopher Columbus arrived in the New World in 1492, the only thing he really discovered was that people were already here. There was immediate speculation about who these people were and from where they had come. In 1927, a discovery of a spear point in Folsom, New Mexico, with the remains of an extinct form of *Bison* established that people were here during the last ice age (22,000–12,000 years ago).[1] This find was followed by discoveries at Clovis, New Mexico, where an older spear point (named Clovis for the location) was found underneath the Folsom-style points also present at this site (fig. 1.1).[2] These Clovis points were associated with the remains of mammoth (*Mammuthus columbi*). Time and time again, Clovis-point finds have been associated with extinct ice age elephants, mammoths and mastodons, and sometimes bison throughout North America. These finds demonstrate that early people in North America were proficient hunters, capable of taking down the largest animals on the landscape. Based on these discoveries and the distinctiveness of Clovis points, which are found throughout North America, the manufacturers of Clovis points seem to have maintained similar lifeways and similar manufacture techniques across a large geographical area.[3]

Subsequent dating of Clovis sites across the continent shows that people of the Clovis culture existed within a very narrow time period, with some researchers suggesting that all sites date within 200 to 500 years of one another, mostly between 12,900 and 13,100 years ago, with the oldest

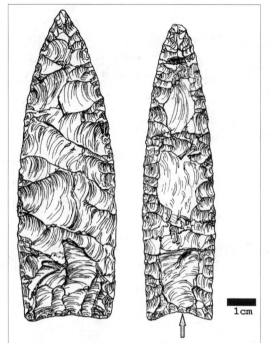

FIG. 1.1. Line drawing of Clovis points from the Clovis-type site. Arrow shows distinctive flute, a hallmark of Clovis technology. Source: Courtesy of Marica Barkley, Smithsonian Institution.

being 13,500 years ago.[4] Such consistency in material cultural within a tight time frame is consistent with a fast-moving and colonizing population, where hunter-gatherers moved camps often, maintained strong social networks, and eventually occupied regions throughout North America. In many instances, the long-distance movement of stone used to make tools (such as chert, flints, and obsidian) suggests that Clovis people operated in very large territories with large seasonal ranges, as well as direct straight-line movements of over several hundred kilometers.[5] In most parts of North America there is little of evidence of people prior to Clovis, suggesting that these "pioneers" found an abundance of plants and animals, with no competition. Under these conditions, large portions of the continent may have been explored within a few generations, and population size may have grown rapidly to match the signature that we see in the archaeological record. While we still debate the exact initial arrival and original routes taken by people into the Americas, most evidence points to northeast Asia as the starting point, with an arrival into the contiguous United States after 15,000 years ago (fig. 1.2).[6] Considering the speed of colonization, this is by far one of the more remarkable colonization stories in human history.

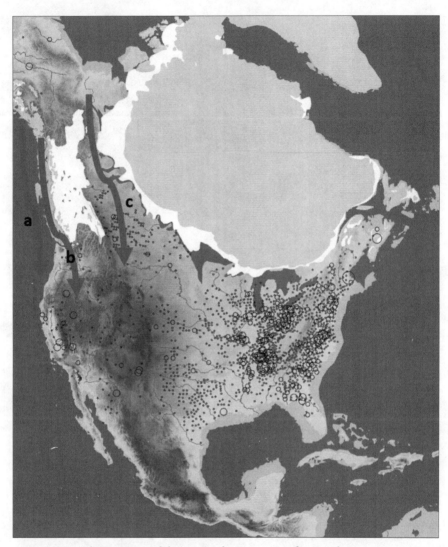

FIG. 1.2. Three most widely accepted entry routes for people enter-
ing North America after the last ice age: (a) a Pacific coast route passable
after 16,000 years ago, (b) an interior coastal route most passable after
15,000 years ago, and (c) the ice-free corridor probably open after 14,000–
14,500 years ago. Circles on map represent fluted point finds across North
America. Larger circles represent areas of greater concentrations. Sources: Modified from Open Access Paleoindian Database of the Americas
(https://pidba.utk.edu/maps.htm); and David G. Anderson et al., "Artifact
Distributions in the Southeast and Beyond" (paper presented at the Clovis in
the Southeast Conference and Exhibition, October 2005).

The First Ohioans

There is ample evidence of these early people in Ohio. The presence of Clovis (or fluted) points suggests that nearly every county in Ohio was populated between 12,300 and 13,000 years ago (fig. 1.3). Sites near and within Ohio also show probable exploitation of megafauna (animals over 100 kg) by these first people. The few intensely investigated sites in Ohio, dating to nearly 13,000 years ago, also show evidence of long-distance movements, which signals the use of large territories. They seem to have acquired great knowledge of the landscape, as evidenced by their use of nearly all adequate raw materials in the state to make tools and by their presence in almost every known environmental setting. Populations probably stayed in campsites for at the most a few months, and more commonly for days or weeks. Territories during these times were vast and fluid, and frequent social interactions would have been necessary for information, mating, and possibly resource exchange.[7] Subsistence practices were probably focused more heavily on hunting, but the collection of a wide variety of plant and animal species undoubtedly supplemented large game exploitation, with some plants and small game species playing a key role on a seasonal basis.[8]

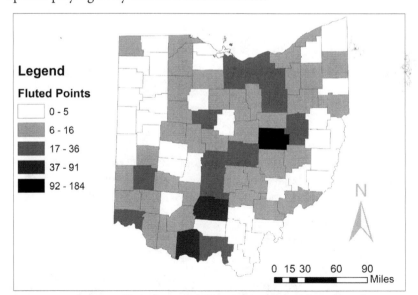

FIG. 1.3. Counts of fluted points (Clovis and variants) found in Ohio. Source: Author.

Possible Megafauna Interactions

When we study the subsistence practices of hunter-gatherers, we often use *optimal foraging theory*—what people should select or exploit if they intend to maximize their intake of calories for the amount of time or energy spent. This approach often explains why and what hunter-gatherers eat and pursue. When it does not explain dietary choices, we have to consider access to resources, environmental factors, processing limitations, and cultural taboos. On a continental scale, Paleoindians—the term given to the earliest populations in North America dating between approximately 11,000 and 13,500 years ago—tend to have followed an optimal foraging approach to their diet.[9] From this perspective, large game ranks the highest in caloric return rate, and this likely explains why they have been found more often in the archaeological record.[10] Over time, with increased human competition and the development of territories, diets become more diversified.

In Ohio, the Burning Tree Mastodon seems to show evidence of this lifeway. Located near Newark, Ohio, the discovery of this mastodon in 1990 suggests that early people in Ohio may have exploited this animal for food. This is evidenced by cutmarks on the bones and a unique arrangement of bones, which suggest that certain parts of the skeleton were removed and clustered together.[11] Similar practices have been documented in Wyoming, where mammoth bones were found piled up and interpreted to be meat caches where populations could have returned at later times to harvest uneaten portions.[12] Other finds in Michigan and Pennsylvania may provide additional examples of the exploitation of mammoths or mastodons over 12,500 years ago.[13] Sheriden Cave in Wyandot County, Ohio, shows Clovis artifacts in close proximity to peccary, caribou, and giant beaver.[14] In northern Ohio, many Paleoindian campsites may have been positioned at locations to exploit large herds of migratory caribou present near the Great Lakes.

Other Key Sites of the First Ohioans

Three of the largest known Paleoindian sites in Ohio are Paleo Crossing, Welling, and Nobles Pond. Paleo Crossing is considered one of the very few well-dated sites in eastern North America. Dating right at 13,000 years ago, this site exhibits Clovis artifacts and manufacturing techniques.[15] At this site, stone tools were found to have been made from materials that came from a source location in Indiana over 280 miles (450 km) away.[16] This demonstrates the extraordinary mobility of the people who occupied this site and speaks to the long-distance mobility that is one of the hallmarks of the Clovis culture and the first people in North America. In this case, it has been suggested that this movement may have been a part of a seasonal move to intercept caribou herds. Elsewhere in eastern North America, moves of equal or greater distances have been referred to as "pioneering" moves, representing the movement of people into a new area for the first time.[17] Because much of the toolstone from sites like these are from single sources and dominate the entire assemblages, it is unlikely that these materials were acquired through trade. Such moves by people on foot speak to both great knowledge of the landscape and excellent wayfinding skills, which likely allowed them to cover such a large territory in a matter of weeks.

The Welling Clovis site, located in Coshocton County, has long been considered a quarry-related base camp where populations came to extract stone for the refurbishment and manufacture of tools.[18] This appears to represent a major alternative site type to the one mentioned above where populations sought to camp near specific quarries or outcroppings of stone suitable for making tools.[19] Such locations may have played a key part in the colonization process, as they were likely not only a place to extract resources, but a possible location for the gathering of different groups of people as well.[20] These groups may have consisted of independent bands of three to five nuclear families that moved together. Early Paleoindian people likely mapped onto several very specific raw material sources across the country, using some on a cyclical basis and others more sporadically. Again, the extent to which certain stone sources were known seems to indicate considerable knowledge of large territories and the ability to quickly map onto resources. Some very distant sources of high-quality stone used during these first occupations were seldom or very rarely used by later groups.[21]

The Nobles Pond site, located in Stark County, is one of the largest known sites in the state, with large quantities of tools, projectile points, and debris of manufacture spread across a one-hundred-acre area, although most concentrations are confined to a twenty-acre area.[22] Many of these artifact concentrations likely represent single occupations, whereas the area as a whole was probably reoccupied. Such areas may represent favored locations of early occupations and key positions for extracting resources. Mark Seeman, who has intensively analyzed the site, considers the fluted-point technology at the site to be Gainey (a similar approach to spear point manufacture but a strategy that may postdate the foundational Clovis technology).[23] Such alterations in fluted-point technology may signal the experimentation or adjustment of strategies for functional or cultural purposes. In some cases, such changes may signal the beginning of territories, regionalization, and greater diversification among groups over time. In a few broader studies, which analyze points throughout the Paleoindian period, point styles seem to slowly depart from continental-wide Clovis technology and then rapidly shift around 12,300 years ago.[24] By this period and immediately after, we see many different technologies and material manifestations across North America. These changes seem to correspond with greater population growth and regionalization with people settling into particular geographic areas, broadening their diets, and reducing the size of their territories. Between 10,000 and 12,000 years ago, certain resource use and material culture become much easier to map to particular areas of the country.

The Archaic Period (~8,000 BCE to 500 BCE) and Increased Cultural Diversity

Over time, we see increased cultural diversity among populations across North America. With the onset of the Holocene Epoch (10,000 years ago), temperatures warmed and the ice sheets that blanketed Canada and parts of Ohio had been gone for at least 4,000 years. Temperatures also began to show less fluctuation, and sea levels stabilized to modern-day heights by around 5,000–6,000 years ago. By the Holocene, there were many indications that distinct territories among populations were developing. We see a number of different projectile point styles across the country and in Ohio. Land use patterns and territories began to shrink, and some of the first possible cemeteries started to appear as campsites were occupied for longer periods.[25] We also see the use of more local toolstone sources and the utilization of other landscape features, such as the uplands and rock shelters. Along with this change in land use, ground stone and plant processing tools appear in the archaeological record for the first time; these items are unknown or not clearly demonstrated from Paleoindian contexts.[26] The expansion of diets among foragers across the world is often correlated with environmental depletion, increased population size, and more sedentary populations. Simply put, once people can no longer move or choose not to move to where the most ideal resources exist, they must expand their diets to incorporate more types of food. This is also true as populations grow, which caused some groups to live outside of the carrying capacity of their original environment. As foraging theory suggests, the choice to expand diets often results in people taking lower-ranked resources, which can later be offset by a change in technology to improve the value (caloric return rate) of the food now being collected. In general, most moves to domestication around the world are thought to have been *push* events where populations were forced (or "pushed") into domestication and agriculture rather than *pulled* into it for some other benefit such as the accumulation of surpluses or wealth.[27]

While population size in North America remained very small throughout most of the Archaic period, populations in Ohio and neighboring regions seem to have dramatically increased during the Late Archaic period 3,000–4,000 years ago (ca. 800–2000 BCE). Sites became more common, and the length of stays at individual locations were typically longer when compared to any previous prehistoric period. As a general trend, we characterize much of the Archaic period as a time of intensified use of land and resources. Trade, watercraft building, and foraging for both fish and plants became more common. This may have also been the start of greater experimentation with plants that would eventually lead to the domestication of select species.

Sometime during this Late Archaic period, people began using plants more intensively, which eventually led to one of only nine independent domestication events ever documented in the world.[28] Here, in Ohio and nearby states, people domesticated plants that are known to be a part of the Eastern Agricultural Complex (EAC). EAC plants included forms of squash (*Cucurbita sp.*), sunflower (*Helianthus annus*), amaranth (*Amaranthus sp.*), sump weed/marsh elder (*Iva annua*), maygrass (*Phalaris caroliniana*), little barley (*Hordeum pusillum*), and erect knotweed (*Polygonum erectum*). These plants supplemented a diet of hunting and gathering that likely provided more stability, and perhaps periodic surpluses. Such surpluses may have supported the gathering of larger groups of people during certain times of the year or during communal gatherings such as mound building. The growth of these crops, which increased in use during the Early and Middle Woodland periods (~500 BCE–500 CE), were garden-size plots, smaller in scale than the larger fields that followed during the Mississippian or Fort Ancient periods.

During the transition from the Late Archaic to the Early Woodland Period there is increased evidence of differences in social status among individuals. Increased trade may have partially been fueled by this rise in inequality. Many burials in the Late Archaic and Early Woodland (800 BCE–10 CE) exhibit extreme differences in burial offerings and trade items, such as copper from around Lake Superior, seashells from the Gulf of Mexico, exotic toolstone, and exquisite figurines made from local stone. In the Late Archaic, large cemeteries and burials placed in glacial kames became a practice in parts of northern Ohio. Here, people buried their dead (perhaps only special individuals) in the gravel and dirt hills formed by glaciers. Many burials feature elegant artifacts, and some of these burials show evidence of cremation.[29] A famous example is the Ridgeway site in Hardin County, where roughly 380 glacial kame burials were discovered. The Ridgeway site likely represents a cemetery that was reused over an extended period. The Williams Site, also in northwestern Ohio, held the remains of at least five hundred people; radiocarbon dates from this site suggest that it was continually used for 500 years, between 850 and 350 BCE.[30]

It was at this time that the Adena Culture, which began sometime between 800 and 500 BCE and continued until 100 CE, emerged in southern Ohio, West Virginia, Kentucky, southeastern Indiana, and southwestern Pennsylvania.[31] This culture created the first earthworks in Ohio, marked most notably by conical mounds, but also circular enclosures (fig. 1.4). Like the aforementioned sites in northern Ohio, burial practices and ceremonialism among this group differed starkly from those of previous groups or cultures in Ohio. As discussed by Brad Lepper, burial practices, distinctive artifacts, and expressions of organization of labor such as mound building represent distinct social identities among groups.[32] These expressions in the archaeological record are also geographically distinct. The practice of creating cemeteries suggests increasing ties to particular places or territories. The creation of large mounds may have also conveyed a different sort of ownership or tie to the landscape. In their study of Middle Archaic groups in the central Mississippi basin, Douglas Charles and Jane Buikstra argue that

FIG. 1.4. Example of an Adena conical mound. Grave Creek Mound in West Virginia, one of the largest known Adena mounds (seventy feet high). Source: Author.

cemeteries developed when people began passing vital resources from one generation to the next.[33] In this scenario, the rights of kin groups to use land and control certain resources are partially cemented through increased religion and ritualism. They use this ritualism to justify their use of the land and resources to new generations. One form of ritualism might involve physically placing their ancestors in permanent locations or in highly visible locations on land once used by their ancestors. Charles and Buikstra also surmise that the highly visible placement of mounds atop ridgetops above valley floors might have been an ideal way to display such rights to the landscape. In Ohio, many burial mounds have been found on hills or ridgetop locations. Similarly, others suggest that mounds could serve as boundary markers between territories.[34]

The transition from the Late Archaic to Early Woodland period that began over 2,000 years ago offered some of the most visible manifestations of material culture, capturing the attention of later explorers and archaeologists. Some researchers have characterized the period from the Late Archaic to Early Woodland as a time of dramatic, if not revolutionary, change, as communities became more sedentary, ceramics came into use, ceremonialism increased, burial mounds and mound enclosures appeared, and groups began to domesticate plants.[35]

The later Middle Woodland Hopewell culture succeeded the Adena Culture and evidenced a flourishing material culture that is rare among hunter-gatherer groups. Increased ritualism, cooperation, and interaction led to some of the most impressive earthworks ever built. These, together with the earlier Adena mounds, left behind markers that continue to be marveled at over 2,000 years after they were constructed (fig. 1.5). At

GREAT MOUND AT MARIETTA, OHIO.

FIG. 1.5. The Great Mound at Marietta, based on an artist's rendering in 1848. Source: Squire and Davis, *Ancient Monuments of the Mississippi Valley*, Plate XLV, retrieved from Library of Congress. https://www.loc.gov/item/2003675053/.

this time, people who we refer to as the Hopewell lived in small hamlets primarily as hunter-gatherers, although some also practiced horticulture, maintaining small gardens of recently domesticated plants. Despite living (from what we can tell archaeologically) rather egalitarian lives, periodical gatherings of people occurred that led to massive mound building and the creation of a trans-American sphere of interaction.

When early White explorers arrived in Marietta, Ohio, the setting of much of McCullough's book, people noticed that large earthworks existed just beyond the confluence of the Muskingum and Ohio River (fig. 1.6).

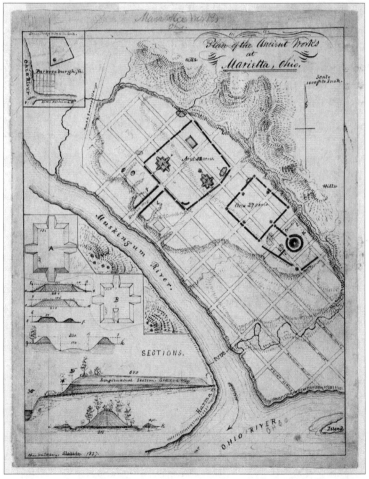

FIG. 1.6. The earthworks at Marietta, as discussed in McCullough's *The Pioneers*. Source: Charles Whittlesey, "Plan of the Ancient Works at Marietta, Ohio" (1837), Library of Congress.

As referenced in *The Pioneers,* when Manasseh Cutler asked Indian Chief Cornplanter who had built the great monuments in Marietta, he replied "he did not know who made them, nor for what purpose."[36] This statement was a testament to their antiquity. The Hopewell constructed a large number of earthworks across southern Ohio. Hopewell is derived from the name of a farmer outside of Chillicothe, Ohio, who owned the property where some of the first extensive excavations of Hopewell mounds took place in the early 1890s. When surveying the Marietta Earthworks, which covered several hundred acres, Ephraim Squire and Edwin Davis described the site as being "three-fourths of a mile long, by a half mile wide" with the two main enclosures encompassing fifty acres and twenty-seven acres in size.[37] Hopewell earthworks consisted of many shapes and forms, including circle mounds, enclosures, platform mounds, and linear mounds. When taken together, these constructed mounds form, or may be viewed as, a series of geometric shapes. The mounds may include burials or solely mounded earth that contribute to a larger complex.

One of the largest earthworks ever created by the Hopewell was the Newark Earthworks in Licking County, Ohio (fig. 1.7). The entire site extends over three thousand acres, with four prominent enclosures that include a square, two circles, and one large octagon. These enclosures seem to be linked by linear embankments that Squire and Davis referred to as parallel walls. As Squire and Davis were some of the earliest visitors to write extensively about their observations of the earthworks, their observations are important to include: "From the Octagon lead off three lines of Parallel walls: those extending south reach nearly two miles . . . the others reach upwards of a mile. . . . The walls composing singular lines are placed about two hundred feet apart." Parts of these linear features are "broad enough to enough to permit fifty persons to walk abreast."[38]

The terminology used by Squire and Davis, which included words like "pathways" and "causeways," leaves a clear impression that they thought many of these embankments or walls were designed as paths for people, or areas to be walked through. While we may never fully understand the exact meaning of the mounds or how they were used, it is hard not to conclude that they were deeply tied to ritualism, ceremonialism, or religious activities. The monumental scale of these mounds is unequaled by anything at the time in North America.

The small and egalitarian nature of Hopewell hamlets at this time suggests that several villages, and perhaps other groups from neighboring

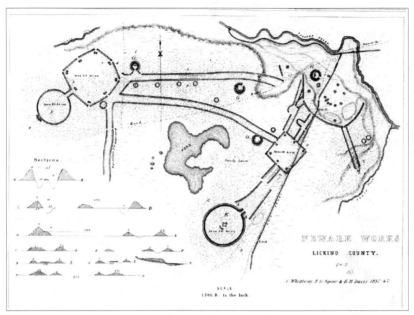

FIG. 1.7. Map of the Newark Earthworks, one of the largest ever created by the Hopewell. Source: Squire and Davis, Ancient Monuments of the Mississippi Valley, Plate XXV, retrieved from the Library of Congress. https://www.loc.gov/item/2021666743/.

regions, would have to had come together to create such extensive earthworks.[39] The nature of the ties that may have existed to other regions is unclear, but we know from the study of many Hopewell sites that a broad interaction sphere existed at this time. Ceremonial items, sometimes found in large quantities, within individual burials or Hopewell earthworks came from as far as the Rocky Mountains, the Gulf of Mexico, the Atlantic coast, the Great Lakes, and the southern Appalachians. Many researchers agree that the appearance of these items best fits the description of an "interaction sphere" rather than trade, as very few items coming from Ohio seem to have been found that would constitute the trade or exchange of goods.[40] Ancient DNA studies from Hopewell sites, which indicate genetic links to some of the geographic areas where items from the Hopewell Interaction Sphere originate, could suggest other social ties or mechanisms of exchange that are not as materially obvious to us.[41] Likewise, Lepper's assertion that people could have visited these Hopewell monuments or places like Chillicothe, Ohio (the center of much Hopewell activity), as a form of pilgrimage, like a modern-day

Mecca or Jerusalem is not, in my opinion, an exaggeration.[42] Chillicothe and the Scioto River valley offered residents and visitors breathtaking monuments that existed nowhere else in North America at this time. On a global scale, the effervescence of material culture, ceremonialism, and cooperative labor that flourished out of a seemingly egalitarian and smaller-scaled society is truly unique and holds few, if any, parallels in prehistory.

The Late Woodland (500–1200 CE) and Late Prehistoric Period (1000–1600 CE)

Immediately following the Hopewell, there is a radical change in the archaeological record. The evidence for any new earthworks is scant; the appearance of exotic, nonlocal items such as that represented by those in the "Hopewell Interaction Sphere" are nearly nonexistent; and the farming of domesticated crops seems to have waned. Some describe this time as a period where groups became more "inward looking," and others have used the term "collapse." Both Lepper and Abrams, however, reject the connotation of the term "collapse," arguing that life in Ohio continued and, in some areas, villages exhibited both population growth and longer occupations.[43] While the material signature of the Hopewell was so spectacular, it is easy to argue for a huge change in society, but such changes may have been more gradual than we can document with our current chronology. As summarized by Abrams, without evidence of major climatic change, deaths, disease, or economic failure, "the end of the Hopewell is far more benign, and comparable to any major transition measured through the archaeological record."[44] Regardless of how we describe this period, the end of the Hopewell did mark the end of a unique period in prehistory. The monumental architecture (earthworks) left by the Hopewell people are comparable in scale to the Great Pyramids of Egypt and the Roman Colosseum in Italy, making them worthy nominees for UNESCO World Heritage Site designation.

In the final millennia of Ohio prehistory, the archaeological record indicates an increase in population density, more permanent villages, and the continuation and eventual expansion of agriculture in some parts of the state. This period is capped by the impact of European expansion into Ohio. To begin with, it is important to emphasize that populations continued to rapidly expand over the roughly 1,000-year period before

European contact and that Ohio was home to many Native groups when Europeans first arrived in the region. Even shortly after the demise of the Hopewell, populations may have significantly increased in some areas. As outlined by Lepper, several sites in Ohio reveal a potential increase in the growth of crops within a few hundred years of the Hopewell. Increases in pollen (plant micro fossils that identify certain species) and other macrobotantical remains suggest the use of several domesticated plant species at some sites both during and after the Hopewell period. These data not only suggest an increase in the cultivation and harvesting of crops, but possibly the need to support larger populations. Villages such as the Childers site may have been home to upward of 120 people. This far exceeds any estimates for Hopewell hamlets. Some villages, such as the Water Plant site in Franklin County, show the presence of palisades and ditches that suggest some degree of competition and conflict among populations.[45] Such evidence is not uncommon in many areas of the world when populations grew rapidly and became more sedentary.[46]

By the very late Prehistoric period and the few centuries prior to European entry into the region, we see somewhat of a reemergence of inter- and intraregional connections, increased ceremonialism, an expansion of agricultural practices, and further increases in population size. Around 1100 CE, a new crop, maize, was introduced and adopted in parts of Ohio.[47] As documented by Anderson and Sassaman, much of the spread of maize into the Midwest and Southeast corresponds to the spread of Mississippian culture.[48] The Mississippian culture spanned parts of the Midwest and Southeast and represents some of the largest chiefdom-level societies anywhere in North America. The Mississippian site of Cahokia outside of St. Louis, Missouri, has been described as a central political-administrative complex exhibiting massive mound building, evidence of human sacrifices, and widespread trade or exchange of items. Anywhere from ten thousand to twenty thousand people may have been associated with this site, which was controlled by only one or a few leaders.[49]

In central and southern Ohio, there is evidence for attributes of Mississippian culture, such as the appearance of maize and artifacts. Perhaps Mississippian people themselves spread into the region.[50] Despite such evidence of direct or indirect interactions with Mississippian people, groups in Ohio seem to have maintained a separate cultural identity that has long been referred to as Fort Ancient. While Fort Ancient villages are nowhere near the size of centers like Cahokia or other large Mississippian sites in the Midwest or Southeast, the Fort Ancient culture indicates connections to outside groups and perhaps a difference in sociopolitical organization. While most researchers describe Fort Ancient societies as tribal, select sites and burials provide some evidence of hierarchies or special individuals in society.[51] The degree to which sites in Ohio at this time were connected to or influenced by Mississippian culture is debated, but places like the Sunwatch village site in Dayton may constitute one example of a large village where a more direct link to Mississippian culture or groups can be argued.[52] Fort Ancient villages were typically circular in shape, and some may have contained as many as two hundred people. Fort Ancient groups also revived some mound building, which occasionally included platform mounds (e.g., the Baum Site), effigy mounds (Serpent and Alligator Mounds), and burial mounds. These mounds, along with council houses, ceremonial plazas, and copper, brass, and shell trade items, speak to some of the ritualism and ceremonialism that was active during the Fort Ancient period.[53] In other areas of Ohio, some groups seem to have developed a similar degree of sedentism and a tendency to live in more permanent villages. These groups show less or even no affiliation with Mississippian culture and are referred to as Monongahela in the east, Whittlesey in the northeast, and Sandusky in the northwest.[54]

The villages in which Late Prehistoric groups lived were evident to European groups that first arrived in parts of Ohio in the late seventeenth century.[55] Archaeological evidence reveals that Native American groups traded with Europeans long before any permanent Euro-American groups were present in Ohio. Once Euro-American groups began the process of settling in Native American territory, the impact of these newcomers was immediately felt. Despite the highly visible presence and remnants of past groups such as the mounds at Marietta (which many people of European descent did not immediately attribute to Native Americans), the rights to land that had been used by Native Americans for thousands of years were severed. Euro-Americans possessed distinct technological advantages, which allowed them to rapidly build structures, palisades, and forts. These foundations would eventually support higher numbers of people, thus providing another key advantage.

A simple but easy way to understand and explain the increased conflicts between Native groups and later Anglo-American groups in the

Ohio River valley relies on the latter's use of the land.[56] During some of the initial explorations by the French and Spanish in parts of North America, their presence was often less impactful on Native people. While each of these groups eventually employed missionaries to try to convert Natives, some of these French and Spanish groups were small and moved quickly through the landscape in exploration, often using temporary camps as they extracted or searched for resources.[57] For Native Americans, the mentality of extracting resources, such as furs and minerals, was better understood, as they had lived for millennia extracting resources from large, if not boundless, territories. But the idea of permanent, exclusive small plots of land that could not be transgressed upon by others was likely just as foreign to Native people; as was the mere presence of these newcomers. Even in places where Native Americans conceded lands, Euro-Americans often pushed into new areas to form permanent settlements as populations grew or resources fluctuated. Increased interaction, such as trade, which often interrupted social or cultural norms, and increases in Euro-American population, which may have further promoted the spread of diseases, were crucial breaking points between Euro-Americans and Native Americans.[58]

As described in McCollough's book *The Pioneers,* the arrival of Euro-Americans in Marietta in the late eighteenth century was followed by a massive process of clearing land, building houses, controlling river access, and claiming land. Early European attribution of the impressive mounds around Marietta reveal their ethnocentrism and lack of cultural respect. Some early scholars thought the Spanish must have built them, and others like Squire and Davis credited them to the tribes of Mexico, Central America, or Peru.[59] By the 1800s, federal Indian policies resulted in the voluntary or forced removal of many Native Americans out of Ohio.[60]

Who Were the Real Pioneers?

I hope that readers will better understand the pioneering acts that were achieved by Native Americans long before White settlers began to arrive in places like Marietta in the late eighteenth century. The Native Americans whom settlers encountered were ancestors of the true first Americans who explored, adapted, and flourished on a brand-new landscape over 13,000 years ago. American Indians were the people that first created trails, mapped waterways, manipulated the landscape, and mapped onto resources. While there are always limitations based on technology and the focus of exploration, Native American groups left behind clues from thousands of years of exploration that undoubtedly paved the way for later settlers.[61] In many cases, the clustering of sites, artifacts, mounds, et cetera clued people in on where key resources were on the landscape. Even when such clues are minuscule, the evidence left behind rapidly increases the rate at which the landscape can be learned.[62] There are several documented cases where historic and modern-day roads follow well-known "Indian trails." Some archaeologists have even suggested, if not convincingly demonstrated, that scatters of some of the oldest artifacts in North America follow and correspond to historically documented Native American pathways.[63] Such data demonstrate how the first people, the true pioneers, influenced later groups, pathways, and settlement. The clues people follow on the landscape are often unconsciously acknowledged, but it often takes generations to learn the seasonal fluctuations of plants and animals, stream levels, and weather.[64] The advantages that later groups have, whether consciously or unconsciously acknowledged, make each subsequent exploration easier and more likely to succeed.

When we assess David McCullough's *The Pioneers,* we should be fascinated by the historic settlers who helped establish parts of the Northwest Territory that are now known as Ohio, but we cannot forget or include as a mere footnote the people who came before. We cannot begin the story with the first Native Americans who were encountered by White settlers nor even with the mounds alone, because the first people in the Americas date back thousands of years before. Their efforts, their knowledge of the landscape, and the artifacts they left behind led to the success of later groups. Ohio's prehistoric record exhibits some of the most fascinating events in human prehistory. Ohio is the center of one of only nine independent domestication events in the world, and is home to some of the oldest sites in North America and to some of the most impressive examples of human ingenuity and labor, chief among them the construction of the many geometric earthworks that have for so long fascinated visitors to this region. Their imminent listing as UNESCO World Heritage sites places them alongside the Egyptian pyramids, the Taj Mahal, and the Great Wall of China, which shows their importance on an international scale. When reflecting on the history of Ohio, we should be equally fascinated with those who lived here before our short historical record.

Notes

In writing this chapter, I greatly benefited from the work of Brad Lepper of the Ohio History Connection, who has summarized much of Ohio prehistory in a number of outlets (see notes). To those who enjoyed this brief summary chapter, I would recommend Bradley Lepper, *Ohio Archaeology: An Illustrated Chronicle of Ohio's Ancient American Indian Cultures* (Wilmington, OH: Orange Frazer, 2005); David Meltzer, *First Peoples in a New World: Populating Ice Age America* (Cambridge: Cambridge University Press, 2009); and David Anderson and Ken Sassaman, *Recent Developments in Southeastern Archaeology: From Colonization to Complexity* (Washington, DC: Society for American Archaeology, 2012). I am grateful to Tim Anderson and Brian Schoen for their invitation to speak at the Ohio Settlement Conference, as well as their patience in my completion of this chapter.

1.   David J. Meltzer, *Folsom: New Archaeological Investigations of a Classic Paleoindian Bison Kill* (Berkeley: University of California Press, 2006).
2.   John L. Cotter, "The Occurrence of Flints and Extinct Animals in Pluvial Deposits near Clovis, New Mexico; Part IV: Report on Excavation at the Gravel Pit, 1936," *Proceedings of the Academy of Natural Sciences of Philadelphia* 89 (1937): 1–16.
3.   Robert L. Kelly and Lawrence C. Todd, "Coming into the Country: Early Paleoindian Hunting and Mobility," *American Antiquity* 53, no. 2 (1988): 231–44; Gary Haynes, *The Early Settlement of North America: The Clovis Era* (Cambridge: Cambridge University Press, 2002); and Sabrina B. Sholts et al., "Tracing Social Interactions in Pleistocene North America via 3D Model Analysis of Stone Tool Asymmetry," *PLoS ONE* 12, no. 7 (2017): e0179933.
4.   See, for example, Michael R. Waters and Thomas W. Stafford, "Redefining the Age of Clovis: Implications for the Peopling of the Americas," *Science* 315, no. 5815 (2007): 1122–26; and Mary M. Prasciunas and Todd A. Surovell, "Reevaluating the Duration of Clovis: The Problem of Non-representative Radiocarbon," in *Clovis: On the Edge of a New Understanding,* ed. Ashley M. Smallwood and Thomas A. Jennings (College Station: Texas A&M University Press, 2015), 21–35.
5.   Kelly and Todd, "Coming into the Country"; and Christopher C. Ellis, "Measuring Paleoindian Range Mobility and Land-Use in the Great Lakes/Northeast," *Journal of Anthropological Archaeology* 30, no. 3 (2011): 385–401.
6.   Ben A. Potter et al., "Current Evidence Allows Multiple Models for the Peopling of the Americas," *Science Advances* 4, no. 8 (2018): eaat5473;

Michael R. Waters, "Late Pleistocene Exploration and Settlement of the Americas by Modern Humans," *Science* 365, no. 6449 (2019); and Meltzer, *First Peoples in a New World.*

7. Robert L. Kelly, "Colonization of New Land by Hunter-Gatherers," in *Colonization of Unfamiliar Landscapes: The Archaeology of Adaptation*, ed. Marcy Rockman and James Steele (London: Routledge, 2003), 44–58; David J. Meltzer, "Lessons in Landscape Learning," in Rockman and Steele, *Colonization*, 246–62; and Robert Whallon, "An Introduction to Information and Its Role in Hunger-Gatherer Bands," in *Information and Its Role in Hunter-Gatherer Bands*, ed. Robert Whallon, William A. Lovis, and Robert K. Hitchcock (Los Angeles: Cotsen Institute of Archeology, 2011), 1–28.

8. Joseph A. M. Gingerich and Nathaniel R. Kitchel, "Early Paleoindian Subsistence Strategies in Eastern North America: A Continuation of the Clovis Tradition? Or Evidence of Regional Adaptations?," in Smallwood and Jennings, *Clovis,* 297–318.

9. Nicole M. Waguespack and Todd A. Survell, "Clovis Hunting Strategies, or How to Make Out on Plentiful Resources," *American Antiquity* 68, no. 2 (2003): 333–52; and Gingerich and Kitchel, "Early Paleoindian Subsistence."

10. Waguespack and Survell, "Clovis Hunting Strategies."

11. Daniel C. Fisher, Bradley T. Lepper, and Paul E. Hooge, "Evidence for Butchery of the Burning Tree Mastodon," in *The First Discovery of America: Archaeological Evidence of the Early Inhabitants of the Ohio Area*, ed. William S. Dancey (Columbus: Ohio Archaeological Council, 1994), 43–57.

12. George C. Frison, "Cultural Activity Associated with Prehistoric Mammoth Butchering and Processing," *Science* 194, no. 4266 (1976): 728–30; and George C. Frison and Todd C. Lawrence, *The Colby Mammoth Site: Taphonomy and Archaeology* (Albuquerque: University of New Mexico Press, 1986).

13. Daniel C. Fisher, "Taphonomic Analysis of Late Pleistocene Mastodon Occurrences: Evidence of Butchery by North America Paleo-Indians," *Paleobiology* 10, no. 3 (1984): 338–57.

14. Brian G. Redmond and Kenneth B. Tankersley, "Evidence of Early Paleoindian Bone Modification and Use at the Sheriden Cave Site (33WY252), Wyandot County, Ohio," *American Antiquity* 70, no. 3 (2005): 503–26.

15. Metin I. Eren et al., "Paleo Crossing (33ME274): A Clovis Site in Northeastern Ohio," in *In the Eastern Fluted Point Tradition*, ed. Joseph A. M. Gingerich (Salt Lake City: University of Utah Press, 2018), 2:187–210.

16. Matthew T. Boulanger et al., "Neutron Activation Analysis of 12,900-Year-Old Stone Artifacts Confirms 450–510+ km Clovis Tool-Stone Acquisition at Paleo Crossing (33ME274), Northeast Ohio, USA," *Journal of Archaeological Science* 53 (2015): 550–58.

17. D. F. Dincauze, "Fluted Points in the Eastern Forests," in *From Kostenki to Clovis,* ed. Olga Soffer and N. D. Praslov (New York: Springer, 1993), 279–92.
18. Bradley T. Lepper, "Early Paleo-Indian Land-Use Patterns in the Central Muskingum River Basin, Coshocton County, Ohio" (PhD diss., Ohio State University, 1986).
19. William M. Gardner, "Stop Me If You've Heard This One Before: The Flint Run Paleoindian Complex Revisited," *Archaeology of Eastern North America* 11 (Fall 1983): 49–64.
20. David G. Anderson, "Paleoindian Interaction Networks in the Eastern Woodlands," in *Native American Interactions: Multiscalar Analyses and Interpretations in the Eastern Woodlands,* ed. Michael S. Nassaney and Kenneth E. Sassaman (Knoxville: University of Tennessee Press, 1995), 3–26; and Lepper, *Ohio Archaeology.*
21. Nathaniel R. Kitchel, "Questioning the Visibility of the Landscape Learning Process during the Paleoindian Colonization of Northeastern North America," *Journal of Archaeological Science* 17 (February 2018): 871–78.
22. Mark F. Seeman et al., "Paleoindian End Scraper Design and Use at Nobles Pond," *American Antiquity* 78, no. 3 (2013): 407–32.
23. Mark F. Seeman et al., "A Description of Fluted Points from Nobles Pond (33ST357), a Paleoindian Site in Northeastern Ohio," in Gingerich, *In the Fluted Point Tradition,* 379–405.
24. Sholts et al., "Tracing Social Interactions"; and Michael J. O'Brien et al., "Innovation and Cultural Transmission in the American Paleolithic: Phylogenetic Analysis of Eastern Paleoindian Projectile-Point Classes," *Journal of Anthropological Archaeology* 34 (2014): 100–119.
25. Glenn H. Doran, *Windover: Multidisciplinary Investigations of an Early Archaic Florida Cemetery* (Gainesville: University of Florida Press, 2002); and Christopher W. Schmidt et al., "Early Archaic Cremations from Southern Indiana," in *The Analysis of Burned Human Remains,* ed. Christopher W. Schmidt and Steven A. Symes (Amsterdam: Academic Press, 2008), 227–37.
26. Haynes, *The Early Settlement of North America;* and Gingerich and Kitchel, "Early Paleoindian Subsistence Strategies."
27. Jared J. Diamond, "Evolution, Consequences, and Future of Plant and Animal Domestication," *Nature* 418, no. 6898 (2002): 700–707.
28. Diamond.
29. Lepper, *Ohio Archaeology.*
30. Timothy J. Abel et al., "The Williams Mortuary Complex: A Transitional Archaic Regional Interaction Center in Northwestern Ohio," in *Archaic Transitions in Ohio and Kentucky Prehistory,* ed. Olaf H. Prufer, Sara E. Pedde, and Richard S. Meindl (Kent, OH: Kent State University Press, 2001), 290–327.

31. Lepper, *Ohio Archaeology.*
32. Bradley T. Lepper, "Ohio—the Heart of It All for Over 15,000 Years," *Journal of Ohio Archaeology* 1 (2011): 1–21.
33. Douglas K. Charles and Jane E. Buikstra, "Archaic Mortuary Sites in the Central Mississippi Drainage: Distribution, Structure, and Behavioral Implications," in *Archaic Hunters and Gatherers in the American Midwest,* ed. James L. Phillips and James A. Brown (New York: Academic Press, 1983), 117–45.
34. R. Berle Clay, "The Essential Features of Adena Ritual and Their Implications," *Southeastern Archaeology* 17 (1998): 1–21; Lepper, "Ohio."
35. Lepper, *Ohio Archaeology.*
36. David McCullough, *The Pioneers: The Heroic Story of the Settlers Who Brought the American Ideal West* (New York: Simon and Schuster, 2019), 62.
37. Ephraim G. Squire and Edwin H. Davis, *Ancient Monuments of the Mississippi Valley: Comprising the Results of Extensive Original Surveys and Explorations* (Washington, DC: Smithsonian Institution, 1848), 1:73.
38. Squire and Davis, 1:70.
39. Elliot M. Abrams, "Hopewell Archaeology: A View from the Northern Woodlands," *Journal of Archaeological Research* 17, no. 2 (2009): 169–204; Lepper, "Ohio"; Lepper, *Ohio Archaeology.*
40. Lepper, "Ohio."
41. Lisa A. Mills, "Mitochondrial DNA Analysis of the Ohio Hopewell of the Hopewell Mound Group" (PhD diss., Ohio State University, 2003); Lepper, "Ohio."
42. Lepper, "Ohio," 13.
43. Abrams, "Hopewell Archaeology"; Lepper, "Ohio"; and Lepper, *Ohio Archeology,* 172.
44. Abrams, "Hopewell Archaeology," 186.
45. Lepper, *Ohio Archeology,* 127; and Lepper, "Ohio," 10.
46. Robert L. Carneiro, "The Circumscription Theory: Challenge and Response," *American Behavioral Scientist* 31, no. 4 (1988): 497–511; Diamond, "Evolution"; and Rick J. Schulting and Linda Fibiger, eds., *Sticks, Stones, and Broken Bones: Neolithic Violence in a European Perspective* (Oxford: Oxford University Press, 2012).
47. Robert A. Cook and T. Douglas Price, "Maize, Mounds, and the Movement of People: Isotope Analysis of a Mississippian/Fort Ancient Region," *Journal of Archeological Science* 61 (2015): 112–28.
48. Anderson and Sassaman, *Recent Developments.*
49. Anderson and Sassaman; and George R. Milner, *The Moundbuilders: Ancient Peoples of Eastern North America,* 2nd ed. (London: Thames & Hudson, 2021).
50. Robert A. Cook, *SunWatch: Fort Ancient Development in the Mississippian World* (Tuscaloosa: University of Alabama Press, 2008); and Cook and Price, "Maize, Mounds, and the Movement of People."

51. James B. Griffin, *The Fort Ancient Aspect: Its Cultural and Chronological Position in Mississippi Valley Archaeology* (Ann Arbor: University of Michigan Press, 1943); and James B. Griffin, "Fort Ancient Has No Class: The Absence of an Elite Group in Mississippian Societies in the Central Ohio Valley," *Archaeological Papers of the American Anthropological Association* 3, no. 1 (1992): 53–59.

52. Cook, *SunWatch;* and Lepper, "Ohio."

53. Griffin, *The Fort Ancient Aspect;* Lepper, *Ohio Archeology;* and Lepper, "Ohio."

54. Robert A. Genheimer, ed., *The Late Prehistory of Ohio and Surrounding Regions* (Cincinnati: Cincinnati Museum Center, 2000); and Lepper, "Ohio."

55. Lepper, *Ohio Archaeology.*

56. Merwyn S. Garbarino and Robert F. Sasso, *Native American Heritage* (Prospect Heights, IL: Waveland Press, 1994).

57. This is of course a highly simplified explanation, and the French and Spanish also had major impacts on early Native groups. See broader discussions in Garbarino and Sasso, *Native American Heritage,* 427–30.

58. Anderson and Sassaman, *Recent Developments,* 178–88.

59. Lepper, *Ohio Archaeology,* 241.

60. David H. Thomas, *Skull Wars: Kennewick Man, Archeology, and the Battle for Native American Identity* (New York: Basic Books, 2001).

61. Marcy M. Rockman, "Knowledge and Learning in the Archaeology of Colonization," in *The Colonization of Unfamiliar Landscapes: The Archaeology of Adaptation,* ed. Marcy M. Rockman and James Steele (London: Routledge, 2003), 5.

62. Rockman and Steele, *Colonization.*

63. I. Randolph Daniel Jr. and Albert C. Goodyear, "Clovis Macrobands in the Carolinas," in Gingerich, *In the Fluted Point Tradition,* 240–47.

64. David J. Meltzer, "Modeling the Initial Colonization of the Americas: Issues of Scale, Demography, and Landscape Learning," in *The Settlement of the American Continents: A Multidisciplinary Approach to Human Biogeography,* ed. C. Michael Barton et al. (Tucson: University of Arizona Press, 2004), 123–37.

2

Situating Settlement in Ohio

The Eighteenth Century from Local and Atlantic Perspectives

CAMERON SHRIVER

For a century and a half of European exploration, trade, marriage, and missionizing, the "settlement" of Europeans was not a primary concern for people living in the Ohio Valley. Often, the state-building aspect of histories of the "Old Northwest" overshadow all previous histories and the various futures that might have taken hold in the region. It is difficult, but necessary, to look at the time and place as an open-ended story. For generations, historians have been wrestling with how to describe the place that became Ohio. Was it a frontier? Was it characterized by violence or cooperation? Was it the North, or the West, or part of the Atlantic World? Was it a marchland between peoples, or a place in which new societies were generated? Is Ohio best understood through its original *Ohi:yo'*, in the Seneca language meaning the Allegheny-Ohio River, or its other modern reference, the Seneca Nation's Allegany territory surrounded by the state of New York?[1] Must we see Ohio as a state-in-waiting, a land ripe for settlement by non-Native families? It—whatever it was—once had no established borders. The troubling fact is Ohio was not a coherent place in the eighteenth century.

Yet people in the eighteenth century certainly had ideas about the region and their role in its history. The possibilities were not closed to Ohio as we know it, but open to many prospects. Locals, and people far away, did not consider themselves on a continuum from "colonial" to "national," from "territorial" to "state." The watershed years 1795 or 1803 or 1812 meant nothing to them, of course. Likewise, settlement was not binary. Too often in US history, we think Europeans entered from the East, and Indians exited to the West. The reality was multidirectional. If we sit in the middle of the eighteenth century, somewhere between the river called by some "Ohio" and the lake called by some "Erie," without knowledge of the future, the view opens to a constellation of communities all vying to understand each other, to build and maintain relations, and to enrich their lives.

Paying attention to what Native American nations and European empires were doing in the eighteenth century decenters settlement as the only force acting on people's lives. In turn, the eighteenth century helps us reconsider the significance of the dispossessions, displacements, and deportations that attended the creation of the state of Ohio in the nineteenth century, a future that nobody foresaw in 1750 and few imagined in 1780. This chapter introduces just a few perspectives on the area that came to be the Ohio Country. From afar, merchants and imperial ministers considered their influence, profits, and competition with rival European monarchies. In the region that we now call Ohio, families dealt with issues such as commerce, control over information, diplomatic negotiations, and feeding their children.

Trade

Commerce was among the most significant drivers of European interest in the Ohio region. Among European powers of the Atlantic World, it was France who first claimed the Ohio River valley and Great Lakes. As early as the 1670s, French explorers had attempted to create friendly intercourse with its Native settlers. For a century, merchants carrying licenses and entrepreneurs acting illegally carried cloth, metal kettles, and other useful domestic items into Native communities. In return, most French merchant companies in the Ohio River valley operated to extract beaver pelts through Montreal and Quebec, and then to France. Beaver fur, their primary target, was there processed by hatters (using boiled fats and mercury) into beaver felt. In turn, milliners fashioned felt into hats. Absent umbrellas—a technology not yet widespread—rain-resistant beaver felt was valuable throughout rain-soaked Europe. Not only did beaver felt repel water, it was stiff enough to form durable wide brims. Great Lakes beaver fur adorned heads across France, Britain, the Low Countries, Germany, and Poland.[2]

The place that is now called Ohio included, in a typical year, perhaps a dozen French subjects throughout the "French" period in no permanent settlements. French settlers created hamlets along the Mississippi River, next to the Wabash River, and near Detroit, always surrounded by, and often including, more populous Native American communities. Supported by missionaries, traders, some small forts, and very little actual population, the French Empire claimed La Belle Rivière ("the beautiful river," now the Ohio River) and its environs. From a French perspective, the region sat between its colonies called Louisiana and New France. It remained controlled by Native communities, who had claimed it long before the French arrived. The place was Miami Country, Shawnee Country, Wyandot Country, and Seneca-Cayuga Country.[3]

British merchant companies from Philadelphia and Williamsburg began pursuing Ohio Country consumers in the 1730s, and in the late 1740s established a storehouse on the Great Miami River, at a city called Pickawillany, adjacent to the modern city of Piqua. In part, their trading partners pulled them there. Delawares and Shawnees, recently living nearer Philadelphia, had for generations bought and sold with Pennsylvania trading firms. These families moved west to avoid oversight and friction with Haudenosaunee Iroquois and Pennsylvania governments. Pickawillany was a boomtown—by 1750, the city was probably the largest in the Ohio Valley, as families from the region and even across the Mississippi decided to spend their summers there to shop and farm. The growing settlement drew Miami, Peoria, Piankeshaw, Wea, Kickapoo, Delaware, and Shawnee settlers.[4]

It was a good time to be an Ohio Valley consumer, and the trade at Pickawillany signaled a new kind of commerce. Rather than beaver, British companies wanted deerskins to transform into shoes, breeches, and gloves. The demand was incredible. One year, Miami and Illinois people traveled to Oswego in New York to sell 377 packs of skins there.[5] Kaskaskia and even French families from the Mississippi River journeyed east, hunting deer to trade to the English. La Mirande, Moreau, and party, for example, traded 360 "dressed skins" and 300 more undressed for an unnamed British buyer.[6] Two employees of one of the trading outfits reported that they had received "more Skins than they could carry with their Horses at one time." They had to make multiple trips to unload the packs of deerskins from Pickawillany to their warehouse on the Allegheny River.[7] Paul Pierce's outfit was caught on the Wabash River transporting four thousand pounds of skins.[8] A nervous French official learned that a British party had been to the Maumee River "several times with forty or fifty horse loads of goods."[9] Deerskins represented, during the height of this trade, between a quarter and half of all Pennsylvania exports to London.[10]

In return for deer leather, Philadelphia merchants offered new fashions. "Indian goods" included fabrics, guns, and a wide range of other merchandise. Trading firms focused on Native customers constantly negotiated with wholesalers who could deliver a mix of items matched to changing demands and tastes. Consider one shopping trip of a Delaware group hunting in Ohio and trading at Pittsburgh in 1759. The Delawares delivered skins of raccoon, fox, deer in both "dressed" and "parchment" preparations, bear, and "catt." The party received, in return, an equal value in brass kettles, black wampum (European-produced glass beads), cash, calico (a cotton fabric), stroud (an English wool produced for Native consumers), matchcoats (long outer coats), a ruffled shirt, gun flints, vermilion paint, twelve yards of "Taffity Ribbon" (taffeta silk used for appliqué), thirty yards of bedlace, four pairs of garters, knives, a razor, thread, combs, and a pair of scissors.[11]

Textiles made up the bulk of the trade in terms of volume and value in eighteenth-century Ohio transactions.[12] In fabric manufacturing in the 1740s and 1750s, British suppliers outpaced their French counterparts in terms of quality and quantity. British farmers produced immense quantities of wool—a tradition going back several centuries—at a pace French shepherds and wool makers could not match. French administrators in the New World experimented with directing bison breeding for wool manufacture, but this fizzled.[13] (Native women in Illinois could in fact make bison wool, "which they spin and make into rugs, braids, belts, and other things for their use.")[14] In addition to fabric, British dyes appealed to Native customers. Sources indicate that the Shawnee, Delaware, and Miami consumers wanted blankets of "deep blue or lively red," or, as another English trader wrote, wool "of the brightest and most flourishing collours."[15] Women wanted stockings in red, yellow, or green. A Frenchman at the mouth of the Ohio River on the Mississippi complained that all his customers had left for Pickawillany. Hoping to drum up sales, he sent samples of ribbons after the "façon d'Angleterre" to France to be copied, expecting to receive items then in demand. These included scarlet with black edges, and blue *limbourg* with a small white stripe. (Limbourg was a course wool cloth made for Native consumers, used as blankets or bedding.) And if consumers at Pickawillany matched the discernment to their south, then Native and Europeans could tell the difference between French and British textiles, primarily through fashions such as colors, as well as the weaves and fibers used.[16]

Guns also poured into the region from French and British merchants. Native Americans had over a century of experience with guns, and so the technology was neither new nor rare in eighteenth-century Native American hands. They bought guns not so much as implements of warfare, but rather as hunting tools. Pennsylvanians "brought a great quantity of arms," Natives reported to the French, and "brought goods in abundance which they gave at a low price."[17] Again, quality and quantity proved troublesome for French suppliers. Governor Vaudreuil blamed his colleagues in Rochefort, France, for not packing the required "trade guns and bullets" in 1752. It was bad timing, considering that Native families streamed to British warehouses in Ohio. Guns, he said, were "the most essential articles for presents to the Indians," without which the colony risked losing the alliances on which they depended.[18] Such "trade guns" were made specifically for Native consumers, who preferred shorter barrels than typical in Europe or the colonies. They also featured side plates embellished with a serpentine figure, as came to be expected by Native buyers.[19] When Shawnees and Wyandots visited a Delaware town in 1748, "there was a great firing on both sides; the Strangers first Saluted the Town at a quarter of a Mile distance, and at their Entry the Town's People return'd the fire, also the English traders, of whom there were above twenty."[20] Guns and munitions were plentiful in Native American communities.

Imagined through this brief overview of material trade, the land that would become the state of Ohio was an international and commercial place in the eighteenth century. Primarily settled by Native Americans of many ethnicities, nationalities, and religions, it was well connected to

Atlantic and indeed global networks. Traders operating through Philadelphia, Albany, or Williamsburg bridged markets stretching from the Rhine and Danube Rivers to the Mississippi and Ohio. The trade forces us to reconsider the Ohio landscape not as a wilderness filled by undifferentiated Indians, but as a set of communities peopled by discerning consumers and savvy suppliers.[21]

And we can be more specific. Women—who wanted specific colors of stockings, or particular types of fabric—certainly made many of the decisions. The volume of thimbles, needles, threads, ribbons, and fabrics makes their importance clear. Furthermore, communities of taste must have developed. The archaeological record, unfortunately, does not allow for ethnic identifications of trade goods in this period. But what should we make of a tantalizing clue offered by the Miami leader Mihšihkinaakwa in 1798? "Nation to nation, we recognize one another at first glance." His conversation partner, a French philosopher, was interested in racial differences, and Mihšihkinaakwa obliged by detailing how faces and bodies of the various Native nations differed. But could we interpret this as statement of national taste trends in fashion, personal adornment, or some other comment on ethnic differences?[22]

Maps

Hemispheric maps became popular in the age of European expansion. These ornate renderings flattened, by necessity, a dynamic and diverse multidimensional world. As they were used by European empires in the Age of Discovery, maps conveyed ownership over spaces and communities. As tools of empire, they transformed rivers, mountains, and seas into digestible charts. Although cartography was an art that patrons consumed, maps also helped Europeans imagine the known and the unknown world and make policy decisions. Maps, in the words of scholar Brian Harley, "redescribed the world, like any other document, in terms of relations of power and of cultural practices, preferences, and priorities."[23] This attitude toward mapmaking, and map consuming, stemmed from the European Middle Ages and its feudal realms. It continued with the splitting of the world into Portuguese and Spanish dominions, a precedent for European maritime empires set in papal bulls in the 1490s.[24] Throughout the Renaissance and into the Age of Enlightenment in the eighteenth century and even today, empires employed cartographers to collect and chart geographical knowledge. Cartography, the representation of space, was a tool of the early modern state.

Put simply, to map a space was to claim it. This was important because early European state-building was a jealous process. Portugal and Spain were the Atlantic World's earliest maritime empires, and their officials guarded precious geographic knowledge. France, Britain, Spain, and other outward-looking kingdoms mapped much of the world in this period. Ohio, if viewed on a map from Versailles or London, was part of a European story. As such, imperial ministers imagined Ohio's potential in the context of their ambitions in other places, such as Japan, China, Peru, Mexico, and Russia.[25]

Imperialists neither understood nor created Ohio as we know it. In Lewis Evans's important *A General Map of the Middle British Colonies* (1755), audiences saw the word "Ohio" twice: both north and south of the "Ohio R[iver]." Modern Ohio and Kentucky were equally Ohio. In Evans's design, those labels compete with another, in the same font, naming the region "Aquanishuonigy," a capitalized name stretching across what we would now recognize as modern Maine to Illinois. Consumer demand for Evans's map stemmed from the news that the French had built a new fort, called Duquesne, somewhere in the region in 1753.[26] (This was at modern-day Pittsburgh, a commanding spot on the upper Ohio River.) Likewise, John Mitchell's map (fig. 2.1) labeled the landscape by naming a group of people, "Ohio Indians," who (according to the map) lived in the upper Ohio River valley. Recruited by the president of Britain's Board of Trade to project dominion westward, Mitchell created a map that was part fantasy, part research.[27] In his cartography, modern Ohio encompassed Delawares, "Pickawillanees or Picts," and "Lower Shawnoes." These Indigenous locations are only upstaged by the giant VIRGINIA and SIX NATIONS (Haudenosaunee Iroquois) labels. A similar map, made the same year in France, labels the region through the Native American inhabitants: "Indiens de L'Ohio," as well as the "Twightwies" (Miamis) and "Illinois," alongside the colonial label "Louisiane," a French jurisdiction arching along the Mississippi and Ohio Rivers.[28] Seen together, these French and British 1755 maps illustrate a place with overlapping Indigenous and colonial occupants and claimants.

Given the global aspirations and realities of European empires in this period, it is worth noting that the Ohio Valley would be well down the list

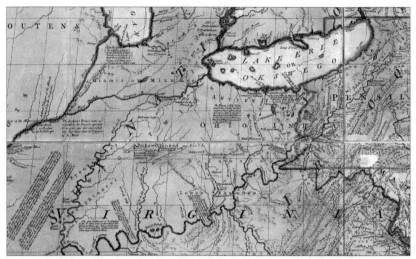

FIG. 2.1. From John Mitchell, *A map of the British and French dominions in North America, with the roads, distances, limits, and extent of the settlements . . .* (1755), detail showing the region that became modern-day Ohio. Source: Courtesy of Library of Congress, Geography and Map Division, Louisiana: European Explorations and the Louisiana Purchase.

of important colonies claimed by either Britain or France. To understand eighteenth-century Europe, it makes as much sense to study Macao or Manila as Pickawillany.[29] In the Atlantic basin, sugar, grown on small islands such as British Barbados or French Martinique, overwhelmed the value of any commodities exported from anywhere in North America.[30] Rather than buying and selling Native American goods, a well-connected British merchant would have chosen to invest in transporting enslaved Africans to the Caribbean, a much more profitable enterprise in the 1750s.[31]

Nonetheless, British subjects on both sides of the Atlantic saw Pickawillany as an opportunity, and in the eighteenth century, the area's residents found themselves at the epicenter of global geopolitics. For British ministers, Pickawillany's rise signaled increasing influence over the Ohio River valley. The place (or, more appropriately, the nations there) was important not only for the local merchants but relative to French claims of the same landscape and the near-constant wars between the two empires. For colonies to function, they needed security; they needed local allies. Pennsylvania's lieutenant governor James Hamilton, fresh from signing a treaty of amity with the Miamis, wrote that the trans-Appalachian networks into Ohio would "contribute greatly to the security of our Inhabitants in time of war, and tend considerably to enlarging of our Indian Trade, especially as we are assured by the Twightwee [Miami] Deputies that not less than twelve towns in their neighborhood are equally desirous with them to become our Allies, and to settle in Correspondence with us." Not to mention, he asserted, "the Intercourse between the French in Canada and the Mississippi would be greatly interrupted."[32] Armed with optimism after a few years of booming profits, the British Board of Trade in London gushed about the power of the Miamis and Shawnees to King George II: "Securing them to the British Interest will be of great Utility," they wrote, "on account of the security which, from Alliance with them, will be derived to your Majesty's Subjects."[33] Thinking globally, European monarchies constantly sought client nations—such as the Miamis or Wyandots, "secured to the British Interest"—to add to their composite empires. In this way, commercial and diplomatic influence connected relatively autonomous colonies to the imperial core.[34]

French colonial officials were playing the same game. To warn off these British upstarts—to keep the map of the Ohio Valley colored for France—in 1749, Pierre Joseph Céleron buried hunks of lead at various points along the river, stating it belonged to Louis XV (this included plates at the mouth of the Muskingum, Scioto, and Great Miami Rivers). The upper Ohio Valley was a valuable piece of real estate in the 1750s, either as a southeasterly outpost of the French Empire or as a far westerly point of the British American holdings. Native Ohioans who actually lived and controlled it enjoyed the imperial rivalry. The chief's house at Pickawillany flew the British flag, but when French allies arrived bearing gifts, he raised the French colors too.

The idea that both Bourbon French and Hanoverian British flags could fly at Pickawillany made no sense in the language of European imperialism. These monarchies and their administrations viewed territory as exclusive, a zero-sum game in which the earth was split among Christian kingdoms. French or British travelers and traders allowed their empires to imagine Ohio as a French or British colony. For the French in the 1750s, the Ohio River valley and the Great Lakes were part of New France, one of the many royal colonies in its global empire. For the British in the same period, the Ohio River valley and Great Lakes were western portions of the colonies of Virginia, Pennsylvania, and Connecticut, respectively. Because the charters that established these colonies came from the British monarch, and because those charters did not specify a western boundary, British colonists claimed the region as a matter of imperial law.[35] British imperialists were particularly inventive. Veering from French and Spanish philosophies, British maps began, unevenly, to illustrate empty space where Native Americans lived.[36] This version of territory—in which a monarch asserted exclusive rights to land and trade—pitted those monarchs against each other. Céleron, upon finding traders from Pennsylvania in New France (in the Ohio Country), wrote to Pennsylvania's governor: "I hope, Sir, that you will be so good as to prohibit that trade in the future."[37] The proprietors of Pennsylvania were incensed at the "Party of French" who had "laid claim to that Country and the Tribes of Indians" there. Perhaps building a fort would "protect the trade, and be a mark of Possession."[38]

To see Ohio only from Versailles and London is to miss the view from Philadelphia and Williamsburg. Landed gentry and elite entrepreneurs there also gazed at Ohio, seeing profits not only in trade but in the land itself. They included the Washingtons, Lees, Jeffersons, the governor of Virginia Robert Dinwiddie, and others who formed land companies. The best known is the Ohio Company of Virginia, a group of prosperous men who amassed capital and political influence to stake claims on the region. They hoped not to settle themselves, but to resell the land at a profit. After several attempts, they finally pushed their petition to British king George II in early 1749. The Earl of Halifax, the monarch's top adviser, approved their plan to sell Indian land because it "would be a proper step towards disappointing the views and checking the incroachments of the French."[39] They employed one Christopher Gist to travel through the Indian Country and report on likely locations for Virginians to settle.[40] Acquiring land speculatively would become a significant revenue source for Virginia's elite. And when the Crown restricted, or appeared to restrict, access to land from the colonists, they rebelled, leading to independence.[41]

The view from Philadelphia and London was informed by traders—Native and non-Native—going back and forth across the Appalachians. Thus, the *material* trade at Pickawillany fostered an *information* trade between colonists and Indians. This exchange of information made its way into the hands of cartographers and influenced decision-making up and down the chain of authority, in both Native American and European nations.

The constant effort on the part of empires to acquire useful information about the places and peoples they claimed demonstrates a less sure-footed, more fumbling version of European colonialism in the region. Indeed, eighteenth-century imperial maps themselves are artifacts of a modernizing impulse in Europe to geometrically organize and represent geographic and social reconnaissance.[42] Many British traders were ordered to report intelligence, including geographic and political information, back to Williamsburg or Philadelphia, and were paid for these services. John Patten sketched a map of his route through Native settlements all the way to Detroit; his pack train earned him 950 pounds sterling, plus a 50 pound reward from Pennsylvania, for the route information.[43] The Philadelphia leadership asked Chegeree, a Seneca man, to fill out a questionnaire on his travels down the Ohio River, including answers to questions such as "How far is it from Twightwee Town . . . to the Forks of Missisippi[?] . . . What Land is in Between the two places[?]" and "Is Wauabash navigable all the way[?]"[44] When the Miamis themselves went to Lancaster, Pennsylvania, Pennsylvanians offered them friendship and gifts. The same day, the Miami delegate, who claimed to represent twenty towns, chalked a map of the Ohio, Wabash, and Mississippi Rivers for them.

There was no clear Native-Newcomer dichotomy. Diplomatic agreements help us understand the centrality of information in this world. Pennsylvania and Miami leaders agreed to peace in 1752, including that each party would report "evil-minded Persons, or Sowers of Sedition" and would not "give Credit to the said Reports."[45] A conference in western Pennsylvania in 1753, attended by various Ohioans, produced sentiments such as "Last Spring when you heard of the March of the French[,] You were so good as to send us word that we might be on our guard. We thank you for this friendly Notice."[46] The Indigenous speaker, an Oneida, instructed the Pennsylvanians to keep settlers in the East, but he proposed that a trader, George Croghan, should live in the mountains and that Pennsylvania might appoint its own messenger, "to keep up our Correspondence." (Croghan had married a Mohawk woman, perhaps bolstering his credentials or access to intelligence networks.)[47] At this conference and another in northern Virginia, the Ohioans asked their colonial allies to report proceedings to the Iroquois in New York to keep them apprised of their decisions and sentiments.

Native American Settlement

Because Ohio—or, the place that became Ohio—was controlled by Native Americans, it requires us to think about Native conceptions in addition to European ones. Native social and political formations differed (and continue to remain distinct) from European ones, of course, and were no less diverse. Because Ohio was not a meaningful unit, it requires us to think through the myriad towns and nations of the region.

Pickawillany was a new settlement in construction between 1747 and 1752, when it was destroyed by Ojibwe and Ottawa men from the north. In constructing a new settlement at Pickawillany, Native American settlers sought independence from both British and French imperial controls. At Pickawillany (in the Miami language, *Pinkwaawilenionki,* "Place of the Ash People"), the primary *akima* (male leader) was a Piankeshaw man, *Meemeehšhkia,* also known as Old Briton by his English-speaking contacts. Piankeshaws, Weas, and Miamis all spoke the Miami-Illinois language, and came from towns along the Wabash and upper Maumee Rivers. These communities formed the bulk of the settlers at Pickawillany, a town that quickly grew from a few dozen families in the late 1740s to about three thousand in the early 1750s.[48]

As George Ironstrack has argued, creating a new political unit at Pinkwaawilenionki should be seen as an attempt to build a beneficial relationship with allies in the East without severing ties with Illinois and Wabash towns in the West.[49] At least in the short term, the location proved wise. Joining in a coalition that included Pennsylvania, New York, Virginia, the Haudenosaunee Confederacy, Delawares, Shawnees, and others, these western Algonquians found new diplomatic and economic freedom. As Miamis moved east and Shawnees and Delawares moved west, Indians could reasonably choose their trading partners on a case-by-case, evolving basis. French and British merchants were thus forced to cater their services to Ohio Natives' needs. (Notably, this included colonists traveling to Native communities for trade, more often than the other way around.) "To preserve the Ballance between us & the French is the great ruling Principle of the Modern Indian Politics," a British commentator observed in 1754.[50] With imperial counterbalances, Miami, Wyandot, Delaware, and Shawnee people could effectively play off these Europeans and stoke the competition, even between Virginia and Pennsylvania interests. At times, Native leaders asked for storehouses and garrisons to facilitate local trade. They even offered land grants to separate groups of French and British subjects to increase the rivalry and investment in their homelands.[51] Competition, carefully managed by Native diplomats, drove down the price of European goods, while Native leaders demanded more gifts.

Pickawillany was not the only dynamic town in what would come to be called Ohio. And, its residents were not the only ones interested in forging prosperity in the region. Others immigrated from the East. Many Iroquois-speaking families, citizens of the Six Nations of the Haudenosaunee Confederacy, moved to the region. Pennsylvania's governor wrote that "numbers of the Six Nations have late left their old Habitations" on the western reaches of New York and Pennsylvania, and moved to the Ohio Country, and they were "more numerous there than in the countries they left."[52] Sometimes called Mingos, hundreds of Senecas and Cayugas moved to the upper Ohio River valley and Cuyahoga River valley in the middle of the eighteenth century.[53]

Delaware and Shawnee families likewise pioneered the foothills and plains as they made new lives in the Ohio Country. These communities, both Algonquian speakers, had most recently lived in proximity and alliance in the Susquehanna River and Delaware River valleys, a place with Seneca and other Iroquois-speaking families. In the 1730s, the avaricious proprietors of Pennsylvania under James Logan had expected to monopolize the Indian trade in the Susquehanna River valley, where Shawnees and Delawares lived. And, in 1737, a dubious land purchase in eastern Pennsylvania convinced people that their futures lay further from Philadelphia. They increasingly migrated to the Ohio River valley "in search of autonomy."[54] Ohio offered plentiful game for food and trade and fertile soils for agriculture on which all residents depended.

Shawnees were both old settlers of the Ohio River valley and recent transplants. In the 1640s, most Shawnee families moved from the central Ohio Valley, where they had lived in large farming settlements since beyond memory. Some traveled north and west, joining Illinois, Miami, and Kickapoo communities on the upper Mississippi River and the Illinois River. More traveled south and east, building towns on the borders of British colonies. For example, one Shawnee community established a new trading base on the fall line of the James River, where it could more easily access the markets of coastal Virginia. Others participated in the material and human trade in the orbit of Charleston in Carolina, sometimes with their neighbors, the Westos, who had also migrated from the shores of Lake Erie.[55]

With Shawnees came their tribal siblings. Primarily, they spoke Lenape and Munsee, eastern versions of the Algonquian language family unintelligible to the Algonquian-speaking Miamis, Shawnees, and Ottawas in Ohio. These easterners came to be known as Delawares, and they established towns along the Muskingum, Hocking, Monongahela, and Scioto Rivers.[56] Creating distance between themselves and Pennsylvania's government also had the advantage of loosening the oversight of Haudenosaunee Iroquois who, in conjunction with Pennsylvania officials, sought to control aspects of Delaware politics, trade, and movement. As Alumapees proclaimed, "each of them," the Delawares and Iroquois, "are to manage their own affairs."[57]

Wyandots, too, built new settlements south of Lake Erie in this period. The band following a Wyandot leader named Orontondi (also called Nicolas) was particularly noteworthy, paralleling many of the same dynamics as Pickawillany. Descendants of the Huron-Wendat Confederacy and speaking an Iroquoian language, these Wyandots left their compatriots living on the Detroit River, and settled most thickly near Lake Erie, on Sandusky Bay. Trade and alliances pulled them farther south and east, as well. Orontondi was an alliance-builder. Like other Native people, he keenly felt the near complete cessation of French goods when the British successfully blockaded shipping during King George's War (1739–48). He argued that Great Lakes Native peoples could free themselves of French trading monopoly, and he was right. Wyandot leaders in 1748 presented a wampum belt "very Curiously wrought" featuring the image of seven human figures "holding one another by the hand," beginning with the Wyandots on one end, through nations of the Haudenosaunee Confederacy, to the governor of New York on the other end. Orontondi's message circulated throughout the Lake Erie watershed and beyond.[58]

Ohio was a settled and cosmopolitan place. The journey of Thomas Hutchins (fig. 2.2), while limited, illustrates an interconnected world of towns linked by roads. The journal of Virginian Christopher Gist helps us to imagine it from ground level. Picking up his journey from the upper Ohio River near modern Pittsburgh, on November 24, 1751, he and his party left Shannopin's Town, a Delaware community. The next day, they

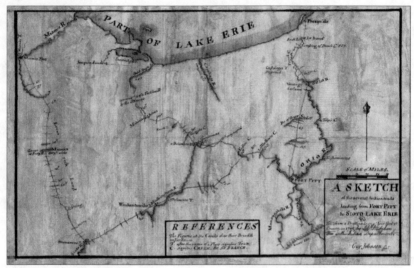

FIG. 2.2. Guy Johnson's copy of Thomas Hutchins, *A sketch of the several Indian roads leading from Fort Pitt to Sioto, Lake Erie &c . . .* (1762). Source: Thomas Gage Papers, courtesy of William L. Clements Library, University of Michigan.

arrived at Logstown, a trade depot. Reaching the Beaver River, he set out overland toward Pickawillany, a well-known road arcing across hilly terrain toward the southwest. After several days, he reached the upper Muskingum and an Ottawa town on December 7. After some travel and rainy days, he arrived at "Muskingum a Town of the Wyendotts," one hundred families in all. Here, he spent Christmas, and then a couple of weeks gathering news to gauge the safety of traveling on. By mid-January, he left the Wyandot town and went five miles to another town and, several days later, to Hockhocking, a small Delaware town. The next day he was on to Maguck, another Delaware town, where he stayed a few days. Setting out again, he traveled fifteen miles "to a small Town called Harrickintoms," finally on the Scioto River. Two more days brought him to a Delaware town of twenty families and "a Negro Man." After a day of council, he went another several miles to the mouth of the Scioto River, a place settled by about one thousand Shawnees and including homes on both sides of the Ohio River and a ninety-foot-long council house. Joined by Croghan and his partner, Gist then made the last leg of the route to Pickawillany, "one of the strongest Indian Towns upon this Part of the Continent."[59]

Indigenous Ohio presents a dizzying array of ethnic, religious, and political arrangements. They lived at places like Mahoning, Conachek, Hockhocking, Kiskimentas, Wandachales, Whitewoman's Town, Wakatomica, Cuyahoga, and Mahican John's Town. They lived at Lower Shawnee town and Le Baril's village. There were Moravian Delawares, Catholic Wyandots, Shawnee ceremonial religions, and Miami medicine lodges. Alliances stretched to Europe, confederacies sometimes formed, and usually, local villages charted independent courses.

Warring for Ohio

The Seven Years' War (often dubbed in America the French and Indian War) was a global conflict caused, in part, over what Ohio might become—far from the first, or last, time people would battle over what the region should be, and who should belong there. In 1752, when French-allied Ojibwe and Ottawa men ransacked British-allied Pickawillany, they sparked an ever-widening conflagration. It was exacerbated in 1754, as small French and British forces attempted to warn each other out of the upper Ohio River valley, and then mobilized into imperial warfare. It combusted with Britain's ally, Prussia, advancing toward France's ally, Austria, plunging much of Europe into war.

The violence of the Seven Years' War can be explained through an imperial lens as a war of maps. Which color would Ohio be, the French color or the British color? These territorial arguments were important to rulers and their egos and their mercantile subjects, as well as the forward-thinking provincial elites who hoped, one day, to be able to make their own property claims on their empire's territory. Which families would profit, entrepreneurs in Montreal or gentry near Williamsburg? After initial French successes in the early 1750s, the British military asserted itself in Canada and Pennsylvania. British soldiers took command of the French posts by 1760, when the war ended in North America. The British victory in the Seven Years' War, solidified in the 1763 Treaty of Paris, transferred French claims to Ohio to the British Crown.

British victory in the Seven Years' War presented a problem: Britain now claimed a vast swath of territory from the French without a plan for managing it. It is one thing for an empire to claim territory, but quite another for it to meaningfully influence the people living in that territory.

The trans-Appalachian West, Florida, and Canada ("an immense waste of savage country," as one English pamphleteer put it) was filled with perhaps two hundred thousand Native people.[60] For the Indigenous residents, according to the historian Daniel Richter, "the structural framework upon which the modern Indian politics had depended for two generations imploded with a few strokes of European pens. . . . Thus the ring of competing imperial powers that had provided an odd security to the Indian country it surrounded suddenly collapsed, replaced by a novel advancing frontier line."[61] At the head of the Ohio River, the recently built French fort, called Duquesne, was destroyed in 1758; a new fort, called Pitt, was constructed by British engineers in 1760. Along with Detroit and eventually Fort Chartres on the Mississippi River, Fort Pitt formed the vertex of a triangle encompassing the Ohio Valley. These three were essential nodes for a small British presence in a vast and dynamic region. The forts allowed them to recolor their maps. But the British—like the French—would never control the territory we call Ohio.

Visions of Ohio's future diverged between colonists in America and officials in London. On one hand, colonists had expected to exercise control over this "conquered" territory. Land speculators would acquire title to swaths of land and sell them to settlers. Imperial ministers, on the other hand, restricted colonial settlement from reaching west of the Appalachian Mountains. Native subjects would maintain their sovereignty there as allies of the Crown, and the colonies would slowly re-create a commercial relationship with Ohio's Native nations. The end of the Seven Years' War thus sparked disagreements over the future of Ohio that would eventually lead to rebellion in the 1770s.[62]

For residents in the Ohio region, the conflict and its aftermath centered on what the region was already. The violence endured and committed by those living there was about which merchants would be allowed to trade, and in which towns, and whose fashions would be available next year, and at what prices. Many Ohio Valley nations vacillated between empires over the course of the war. With its outcome assured in the late 1750s, they forged an alliance with the British. In the process, Native leaders negotiated the protection of their land in Ohio and an express prohibition against British settlement, as well as a promise that the British would withdraw their garrisons once the war was officially over. Shawnees, Delawares, and Miamis must have believed that peace would usher in a new wave of commerce. They expected Pickawillany 2.0.

The economic boom never arrived. Bankrupt from the expensive Seven Years' War, British policymakers began restricting gifts to Native families. The absence of guns, gunsmiths, and powder made Native consumers "extremely uneasy," as a British soldier reported in 1762. The same year, British Fort Miamis' commander was able to provide "but meer trifles" to the local Miami community. Given Britain's inability or unwillingness to meet consumer demand, many Native communities chastised British officials. And given the obvious lack of French counterbalance, they began planning to pull the French Empire back into the Great Lakes and reinvigorate competition among merchants.[63]

In addition to restricting merchandise, Britain limited government employment, implementing a kind of hiring freeze. Britain placed its colonial ambitions in a tiny diplomatic staff. Just after the British takeover of New France in 1760, the list of those working in the "Department of Indian Affairs to the Westward" (Fort Pitt and Detroit) included twelve men: three men at Fort Detroit, a gunsmith and his assistant at an unidentified location, two interpreters at an unknown location, four at Fort Pitt, and at Fort Miamis, "a French Man Interpreter."[64] Ministers considered a dozen to be too many salaries to support.[65]

In the meantime, the British effort focused on a small team in Indian affairs stationed at Fort Pitt. George Croghan led Indian affairs there. Croghan had emigrated from Ireland and been a trader at Pickawillany, called by a rival the "King of the Traders." He had three subordinates. One was his half brother; another was a thirty-year-old veteran named Thomas Hutchins, who would become a cartographer of the Ohio Valley. His third subordinate alternated between Thomas McKee and his son Alexander, both of whom had deep familial ties with the Shawnees.[66] The avaricious Irishman was bold and colorful, and tended to inflate his own ability to understand and influence Native American politics.

In reality, George Croghan's reports to his superior during and immediately after the Seven Years' War helps us understand that his ill-fated attempts at managing Indian affairs in Ohio for the empire were largely dependent on Indians who, suspicious of the new restrictions on trade, kept Croghan and his colleagues at arm's length. Croghan created a job description for his assistants: "one of them by Turns to Travel throu ye Indian Settlements where Traders go amongst ye Dallaways Shawnes & to ye Miamies & Sandusky and to Return to Fort Pitt, then ye other to take his Turn."[67] This description of his assistants making "tours" through

Indian Country suggests not an expansion of British power, settlement, or knowledge, but rather a restriction to Ohio's edges.[68] Croghan's daily journal further reveals that his job consisted mainly of guesswork, parsing rumors from visitors to Fort Pitt and dispatching informants and spies he hoped would allow the British Empire to maintain its tenuous claims on the region.

With nothing to offer Native nations, Croghan's ability to collect information faltered even before the Seven Years' War officially ended. For example: in 1762, he received a report of a large, secret Native conference near Detroit. "They were Meditateing something against us," Croghan heard from his Native spy, who "flatly refused telling [him] any further." Department bureaucrats at Detroit similarly began hearing menacing rumors. In 1763, several years into Croghan's tenure, Native communities revolted against British colonialism. This conflict, dubbed Pontiac's War after one of its leaders, the Ottawa called Pontiac, brazenly manifested—as it revealed—the related problems of commerce and information. For starters, Indian Affairs' personnel remained few. The department was meant to handle diplomacy with perhaps a hundred thousand diverse people with a bureaucracy of *twelve*. Britain claimed the Ohio region by conquest, then all but cut it loose.

It became increasingly clear to Croghan and others under his leadership that many Native families were angry over the price and quantity of trade after the Seven Years' War. Some demanded blood, but many were not so anti-British. Most expressed anger at the trifles they received, and consistently demanded an increased supply of gunpowder and lead. Given their precarious situation in Indian Country, Indian Affairs' officials never revealed that austerity was policy. Native communities filled the information void with their own theories. Thus, many believed that the British were withholding munitions to allow Cherokees to invade from the South. Croghan himself reported this rumor, "that the English would take their Country from them & bring the Cherokees there to settle & to enslave them."[69] Simultaneous with the Treaty of Paris in 1763, Indigenous communities throughout the central Great Lakes united to force British evacuation of their homelands. Although Pitt and Detroit survived, places like forts at Sandusky, Miamis, and Michilimackinac did not. Some of those assaults were bloody affairs, while others looked more like ordered evacuations.

Thus, at the end of the French and Indian War and Pontiac's War, European forts stood at the beginning and end of the Ohio River—at Pitt and Chartres—with none in between. Ironically, the end of war fought for territorial ambitions left the Ohio Valley in firm Native control. Britain claimed a landscape it never coordinated. In 1763, British officials acknowledged this reality issuing a royal proclamation that deemed the territory west of the Appalachians off-limits to British settlers. This proclamation and the higher taxes Americans were expected to pay came as a shock to colonial Americans, who had interpreted victory as opening these western lands for them and their progeny.[70] Within a decade, many of these Americans, having declared their own independence from Britain, less discriminately carried arms across the Ohio River, determined to create a landed empire. But even then, it would be many years after the creation of the new nation that non-Native communities would attain any level of control over the region. The United States was the first to consider the land itself as the primary commodity of Ohio.

The Seven Years' War, then, was among the most significant events in the eighteenth century. The fact that the first global war started in Ohio—that it was initially *about* control of the Ohio River valley—was significant, albeit complicated. The focus on European mapping, on fashions and trade, and on Native American diversity and decisions in the middle of the eighteenth century helps us to see Ohio from multiple perspectives. Those points of view are necessary because Ohio was not a coherent place in the North American continent. It was Shawnee Country, Delaware Country, or Miami Country. It was Ohi:yo', the Ohio and Allegheny River. It was the backcountry of Pennsylvania, or the upper country of New France. Its people were tied to Atlantic-wide trade networks. And they were intertwined intimately with the landscape and ecologies of the place. Most were *from* there; some had *arrived* there.

These perspectives, in turn, require us to shift our own. The process of state-building during and after the American Revolution, a project wholly intertwined with Euro-American settlement and Native American dispossession, would have to be invented. Simply put, nobody in the eighteenth century foresaw the state-sponsored deportation of Native nations from their homelands. That creation of the state of Ohio was not the inevitable outcome for the region. What it was, and indeed who belonged there, was far from settled.

Notes

1. I take inspiration on these questions from, among others, Catherine Cangany, *Frontier Seaport: Detroit's Transformation into an Atlantic Entrepôt* (Chicago: Chicago University Press, 2014); François Furstenberg, "The Significance of the Trans-Appalachian Frontier in Atlantic History," *American Historical Review* 113, no. 3 (2008): 647–77; Andrew R. L. Cayton, "Writing North American History," *Journal of the Early Republic* 22, no. 1 (2002): 105–11; Michael Witgen, "The Indian Menace in David McCullough's *The Pioneers*," *Journal of the Early Republic* 41, no. 2 (2021): 225–32; Susan Sleeper-Smith, *Indigenous Prosperity and American Conquest: Indian Women of the Ohio River Valley, 1690–1792* (Chapel Hill: University of North Carolina Press, 2018); Richard White, *The Middle Ground: Indians, Empires, and Republics in the Great Lakes Region, 1650–1815* (New York: Cambridge University Press, 1991), esp. ix; and Michael N. McConnell, *A Country Between: The Upper Ohio Valley and Its Peoples, 1724–1774* (Lincoln: University of Nebraska Press, 1992), esp. 1–4.
2. Thomas Wien, "Exchange Patterns in the European Market for North American Furs and Skins, 1720–1760," in *The Fur Trade Revisited: Selected Papers of the Sixth North American Fur Trade Conference*, ed. Jennifer S. H. Brown, W. J. Eccles, and Donald P. Heldman (East Lansing: Michigan State University Press, 1994), 25; and J. F. Crean, "Hats and the Fur Trade," *Canadian Journal of Economics and Political Science* 28, no. 3 (1962): 373–86.
3. Richard White, *The Middle Ground*.
4. Eric Hinderaker, *Elusive Empires: Constructing Colonialism in the Ohio Valley, 1673–1800* (New York: Cambridge University Press, 1997), 29–32, 42.
5. "Return of Western Tribes Who Traded at Oswego," August 20, 1749, in *Documents Relative to the Colonial History of the State of New-York* (Albany: Weed, Parsons, 1855), 6:538 (hereafter *New York Colonial Documents*).
6. Macarty to Vaudreuil, March 18, 1752, in *Collections of the Illinois State Historical Library* (Springfield: Illinois State Historical Library, 1940), 29:515–17 (hereafter *CISHL*). On Illinois interest in Pickawillany, see Robert Morrissey, *Empire by Collaboration: Indians, Colonists, and Governments in Colonial Illinois Country* (Philadelphia: University of Pennsylvania Press, 2015), 178.
7. Examinations of Morris Turner and Ralph Kilgore, *Minutes of the Provincial Council of Pennsylvania* (Harrisburg, PA: State of Pennsylvania, 1851), 5:482 (hereafter *MPCP*).
8. Albert T. Volwiler, *George Croghan and the Western Movement* (Cleveland: Arthur H. Clark, 1926), 21.

9. "Report of Le Porc Epic, March 15, 1750," in *CISHL* 29:168.

10. Total value in 1742–47: £13,467. Total value in 1748–53: £44,469. The figures come from Stephen H. Cutcliffe, "Colonial Indian Policy as a Measure of Rising Imperialism: New York and Pennsylvania, 1700–1755," *Western Pennsylvania Historical Magazine* 64 (1981): tables 1 and 2.

11. "Pittsburgh, June the 19th, 1759," in Pittsburgh Waste Book, Pittsburgh Waste Book and Fort Pitt Trading Post Papers, Darlington Digital Library, University of Pittsburg, https://digital.library.pitt.edu/islandora /object/pitt%3A31735061278424/viewer#page/4/mode/2up.

12. Dean L. Anderson, "The Flow of European Trade Goods into the Western Great Lakes Region, 1715–1760," in *The Fur Trade Revisited: Selected Papers of the Sixth North American Fur Trade Conference*, ed. Jennifer S. H. Brown, W. J. Eccles, and Donald P. Heldman (East Lansing: Michigan State University Press, 1994), 93–115.

13. Maurepas to Hocquart, April 1, 1748, in *CISHL* 29:57–59; and Michel to Rouillé, August 6, 1749, in *CISHL* 29:101.

14. Quoted in Sophie White, *Wild Frenchmen and Frenchified Indians: Material Culture and Race in Colonial Louisiana* (Philadelphia: University of Pennsylvania Press, 2012), 75.

15. Macarty to Vaudreuil, January 15, 1752, LO 327, Vaudreuil Papers, Huntington Library; Volwiler, *George Croghan,* 30; and Theodore Calvin Pease, "Introduction," in *CISHL* 29:xviii.

16. Quoted in Balvay, *L'Épee et La Plume, Amerindians et Soldats des Troupes de la Marine en Louisiana et Au Pays D'en Haut (1683–1763)* (Stint-Nicolas, Quebec: Les Presses de L'Université Laval, 2006), 213; White, *Wild Frenchmen,* 73, 204–5; see also Harold A. Innis, *The Fur Trade in Canada: An Introduction to Canadian Economic History,* rev. ed. (1930; repr., Toronto: University of Toronto Press, 2001), 79–80.

17. Raymond to Jonquiere, January 5, 1750, in *CISHL* 29:155.

18. Vaudreuil to Rouillé, April 8, 1752, in *CISHL* 29:483.

19. David J. Silverman, *Thundersticks: Firearms and the Violent Transformation of Native America* (Cambridge, MA: Belknap Press, 2016), 12–13, 131–32.

20. "Journal of Conrad Weiser Esqr.," in *MPCP* 5:350.

21. For more on Native consumerism in the fur trade, see Shephard Krech, ed., *The Subarctic Fur Trade: Native Social and Economic Adaptations* (Vancouver: University of British Columbia Press, 1984).

22. Constantin François de Chassebœuf, comte de Volney, *Tableau du climat et du sol des États-Unis d'Amérique* (Paris, 1803), 2:441.

23. J. B. Harley, *The New Nature of Maps: Essays in the History of Cartography* (Baltimore: Johns Hopkins University Press, 2001), 35; also David Buisseret, *Monarchs, Ministers and Maps: The Emergence of Cartography as a Tool of Government in Early Modern Europe* (Chicago: University of Chicago Press, 1992).

24. Max Savelle, *The Origins of American Diplomacy: The International History of Angloamerica, 1492–1763* (New York: Macmillan, 1967); and Anthony Pagden, *Lords of All the World: Ideologies of Empire in Spain, Britain and France, ca. 1500–1800* (New Haven, CT: Yale University Press, 1995).

25. Barbara E. Mundy, *The Mapping of New Spain: Indigenous Cartography and the Maps of the Relaciones Geográficas* (Chicago: University of Chicago Press, 1996), 1–9; and Paul Mapp, *The Elusive West and the Contest for Empire, 1713–1763* (Chapel Hill: University of North Carolina Press, 2011), 170–93.

26. Lewis Evans, *A General Map of the Middle Colonies* (Philadelphia, 1755), copy at Geography and Map Division, Library of Congress. The history of this map is explored in Martin Brückner, *The Social Life of Maps in America, 1750–1860* (Chapel Hill: University of North Carolina Press, 2017), 25–41.

27. S. Max Edelson, *A New Map of Empire: How Britain Imagined America before Independence* (Cambridge, MA: Harvard University Press, 2017), 36–38.

28. Robert de Vaugondy, *Partie de l'Amerique Septentrionale, qui comprend le Cours de l'Ohio, la Nlle: Angleterre, la Nlle. York, le New Jersey, la Pensylvanie, le Maryland, la Virginie, la Caroline* (Paris, 1755), David Rumsey Map Collection.

29. On European Pacific Ocean interests during the eighteenth century, see Mapp, *Elusive West,* 261–329.

30. For an overview of British American economies, see John J. McCusker and Russell R. Menard, *The Economy of British America, 1607–1789* (Chapel Hill: University of North Carolina Press, 1985); see also Nuala Zahedia, "Economy," in *The British Atlantic World, 1500–1800,* ed. David Armitage and Michael J. Braddick (New York: Palgrave MacMillan, 2002), 51–68; and Laurent Dubois, "The French Atlantic," in *Atlantic History: A Critical Appraisal,* ed. Jack P. Greene and Philip D. Morgan (New York: Oxford University Press, 2009), 137–61.

31. For example, David Hancock, *Citizens of the World: London Merchants and the Integration of the British Atlantic Community, 1735–1785* (New York: Cambridge University Press, 1995), 172–219.

32. "At the Court House at Lancaster, Wednesday, July 20th, 1748," in *MPCP* 5:308–310.

33. Representation of the Board of Trade to the King, March 16, 1753, C.O. 5/1367, pp. 24–26, Colonial Office documents, Public Record Office, Kew, London.

34. H. G. Koenigsberger, "Composite States, Representative Institutions and the American Revolution," in *Historical Research* 62 (1989): 135–53; and J. H. Elliot, "A Europe of Composite Monarchies," *Past and Present* 137 (1992): 48–71.

35. Daniel K. Richter, *Before the Revolution: America's Ancient Pasts* (Cambridge, MA: Harvard University Press, 2011), 373.

36. Juliana Barr and Edward Countryman, "Introduction," in *Contested Spaces of Early America,* ed. Juliana Barr and Edward Countryman (Philadelphia: University of Pennsylvania Press, 2014), 18–20.

37. Quoted in William R. Nester, *The French and Indian War and the Conquest of New France* (Norman: University of Oklahoma Press, 2014), 133.

38. "An Extract from the Proprietarie's Letter," February 9, 1751, in *MPCP* 5:515.

39. Quoted in Francis Jennings, *Empire of Fortune: Crowns, Colonies and Tribes in the Seven Years War in America* (New York: Norton, 1988), 12–13.

40. Jennings, 18–19; and Hinderaker, *Elusive Empires,* 136–39.

41. Woody Holton, "The Ohio Indians and the Coming of the American Revolution in Virginia," *Journal of Southern History* 60 (August 1994): 456.

42. Brückner, *The Social Life of Maps in America,* 3.

43. Patten's Journal in Howard N. Eavenson, "Who Made the 'Trader's Map'?," *Pennsylvania Magazine of History and Biography* 65, no. 4 (October 1941): 420–38.

44. *Map of the Country about the Mississippi,* ca. 1755, Library of Congress Geography and Map Division.

45. Instructions to George Croghan, April 25, 1751, *MPCP* 5:522–23.

46. "At a Meeting of the Commissioners and Indians the Third Day of October, 1753," in *MPCP* 5:674.

47. William J. Campbell, "An Adverse Patron: Land, Trade, and George Croghan," *Pennsylvania History* 76, no. 2 (2009): 119.

48. George Ironstrack, "From the Ashes: One Story of the Village of Pinkwi Mihtohseeniaki" (master's thesis, Miami University, 2006).

49. Ironstrack, "From the Ashes," 25–30.

50. Peter Wraxall, *An Abridgment of the Indian Affairs; Contained in Four Folio Volumes, Transacted in the Colony of New York, from the Year 1678 to the Year 1751,* ed. Charles Howard McIlwain (Cambridge, MA: Harvard University Press, 1915), 1.

51. Campbell, "An Adverse Patron," 123.

52. Hamilton to Clinton, September 20, 1750, in *MPCP* 5:463.

53. Jon W. Parmenter, "The Iroquois and the Native American Struggle for the Ohio Valley, 1754–1794," in *The Sixty Years' War for the Great Lakes, 1754–1814,* ed. David Curtis Skaggs and Larry L. Nelson (East Lansing: Michigan State University Press, 2001), 107.

54. Stephen Warren, *The Worlds the Shawnees Made: Migration and Violence in Early America* (Chapel Hill: University of North Carolina Press, 2014), 194.

55. Sami Lakomäki, *Gathering Together: The Shawnee People through Diaspora and Nationhood, 1600–1870* (New Haven, CT: Yale University Press, 2014), 24–70.

56. Amy C. Schutt, *People of the River Valleys: The Odyssey of the Delaware Indians* (Philadelphia: University of Pennsylvania Press, 2013), 104–8; McConnell, *A Country Between*, 54–60.

57. Quoted in McConnell, 59.

58. Hinderaker, *Elusive Empires*, 41; White, *The Middle Ground*, 193–96; and "Journal of Conrad Weiser Esqr.," in *MPCP* 5:351.

59. William M. Darlington, ed., *Christopher Gist's Journals* (Pittsburgh: J. R. Weldin, 1893), 34–48.

60. Quoted in Colin Calloway, *The Scratch of a Pen: 1763 and the Transformation of North America* (New York: Oxford University Press, 2006), 8.

61. Daniel K. Richter, *Facing East from Indian Country: A Native History of Early America* (Cambridge, MA: Harvard University Press, 2001), 187.

62. Patrick Spero, *Frontier Country: The Politics of War in Early Pennsylvania,* (Philadelphia: University of Pennsylvania Press, 2016), 172; Fred Anderson, *Crucible of War: The Seven Years' War and the Fate of Empire in British North America, 1754–1766* (New York: Alfred A. Knopf, 2000), esp. 524–28, 745–46; and Woody Holton, *Forced Founders: Indians, Debtors, Slaves, and the Making of the American Revolution in Virginia* (Chapel Hill: University of North Carolina Press, 1999), 3–38.

63. "Journal of Thomas Hutchins," September 1762, *The Papers of Sir William Johnson,* ed. James Sullivan et al. (Albany: University of the State of New York, 1921–65), 10:528; Holmes to Bouquet, March 17, 1762, in Sylvester K. Stevens and Donald H. Kent, eds., *The Papers of Henry Bouquet* (Harrisburg: Pennsylvania Historical Commission, 1940–43), 9:52; Gregory Evans Dowd, *War under Heaven: Pontiac, the Indian Nations, and the British Empire* (Baltimore: Johns Hopkins University Press, 2002); and Michael A. McDonnell, *Masters of Empire: Great Lakes Indians and the Making of America* (New York: Hill and Wang, 2015), 216–17.

64. "George Croghan's Return," January 12, 1761, in *The Papers of Sir William Johnson* 3:300. This is probably either Pierre Chene dit Labutte or Elleopole Chene dit Meni, both employed later. See also 5:264, 289, 382, 675.

65. Robert Monckton to Croghan, April 6, 1761, in Nicholas B. Wainwright, ed., "George Croghan's Journal: April 3, 1759 to April 30, 1763," *Pennsylvania Magazine of History and Biography* 71, no. 4 (1947): 404n177.

66. Quoted in Larry L. Nelson, *A Man of Distinction among Them: Alexander McKee and British Indian Affairs along the Ohio Country Frontier, 1754–1799* (Kent, OH: Kent State University Press, 1999), 63.

67. Croghan to Johnson, October 12, 1761, *The Papers of Sir William Johnson* 3:551.

68. "Return of Fort Pitt Department," *The Papers of Sir William Johnson* 3:860–61.

69. Croghan to William Johnson, November 1765, in *Early Western Travels*, ed. Reuben Gold Thwaites (Cleveland: Arthur H. Clark, 1904), 1:171.

70. Calloway, *The Scratch of a Pen*.

3

Who Speaks in the Name of the Miami Nation?

JOHN BICKERS

In the winter of 1824, Meehcikilita (Le Gros) and Pinšiwa (Jean Baptiste Richardville) held a series of meetings with Charles Trowbridge at Fort Wayne, Indiana. For the last several years, Michigan territorial governor Lewis Cass had sent Trowbridge to Indigenous communities across the Great Lakes to acquire linguistic, historical, and cultural information. The two elderly leaders had worked closely together with other Myaamia (Miami Indian) leaders for decades to reshape the Myaamia political landscape, to adapt to the internal and external pressure that threatened the fabric of their society. Their interviews with Trowbridge allowed them to reflect on their lives and how they had permanently changed Myaamia political institutions under their leadership. In their conversations, they emphasized that since their origins as a people, Myaamiaki had been politically divided into independent villages across their homeland, which they called Myaamionki (the Miami Country). Although connected through a shared language, culture, and ancestry, they lived in a decentralized society with politically autonomous villages, which provided each community the flexibility to make their own decisions.

Each village operated around separate gendered political organizations, in which men and women organized their own councils headed by *akimaki* (male civil leaders), *akimaahkwiaki* (female civil leaders), and *neenawihtoowaki* (war leaders), maintaining a complementary balance between both men and women and war and peace.[1] Akimaahkwiaki oversaw the village's agricultural practices and the production of material goods, while akimaki were charged with regulating their village's interactions with foreign nations, including going to war and leading peace delegations. Civil leaders lacked any coercive authority and were bound by the servant-oriented ethos of *eekimaawinki* (Myaamia civil leadership) to mediate disputes within their communities, often in coordination with male and female village councils. Although they could influence or persuade, civil leaders could not command. Akimaki and akimaahkwiaki, through training and experience, strived to achieve consensus to maintain the health of their community. In other words, Myaamia civil leaders needed to act in ways that would serve not their own self-interest but, rather, that of their villages and lineages. In contrast, neenawihtoowaki were afforded more authoritative power. A male neenawihtoowaki's ability to go to war was dependent on his ability to persuade both the young men and their female counterparts of the necessity to do so; however, once war was declared, it was reported that "all authority is vested in" him. They were entrusted to "decide all questions relating to the march and places of encampment as well as the time and place of attack upon the enemy."[2]

By the time Meehcikilita and Pinšiwa met with Trowbridge, they and their Myaamia allies had unified their people under a centralized nation. For the previous twenty years, the two had been members of "a united council," called the Miami National Council, composed of all Myaamia "war and village chiefs."[3] This "united council" was imagined by its founders as a middle path of moving toward a centralized form of government while maintaining the core cultural aspects of Myaamia society and gendered politics. The original members of the National Council specifically sought to protect the sovereignty of individual villages by consciously limiting its authority to male-specific tasks, such as international diplomacy with the United States and other tribal communities. This new model allowed villages to retain most of their autonomy to self-regulate. Rather than relying on militant resistance or political acculturation, Myaamia leaders, on a foundational level, based their resistance to American expansion through the National Council in traditional Myaamia political culture.

This chapter examines the context in which the Miami National Council was formed, and the debates and conflicts within Myaamia society over who should head the Miami Nation. Rather than being divided between assimilationist and traditionalist factions as some other Native communities were, Myaamia leaders understood that the expansion of the United States and the incursions made by its citizens required Myaamia adaptation. Consequently, the questions that emerged before them were the degree to which they believed Myaamia society needed to change in the face of American imperialism and, equally important, who should make that determination. The success of the National Council came not because it sought nationalization but because it was a reaction to the radical changes proposed by a minority of Myaamia leaders who believed that their people's survival depended upon swift assimilation into American society. By uniting under a single political body, the members of the National Council strengthened their ability to negotiate with a young United States, which was lustful for their lands. Rather than reject the move toward nationalization, the majority of Myaamia leaders sought to harness it as a tool to protect their cultural and political autonomy.

The earliest sparks of Myaamia nationalism began with Mihšihkinaahkwa (Little Turtle), a prominent neenawihtoowa from Le Gris's Town (Fort Wayne, Indiana). He had been a critical leader in the Northwest Indian Wars, playing a significant role in Harmar's Defeat (1790), St. Clair's Defeat (1791), and the Battle of Fallen Timbers (1794), before seeking peace at the Treaty of Greenville in 1795. During the Greenville conference, Mihšihkinaahkwa, who served as the principal Myaamia speaker, informed General Anthony Wayne, who led the American delegation, of "the boundaries of the Miami Nation," which encompassed all of present-day Indiana and parts of Illinois and Ohio.[4] His territorial claims included certain lands that General Wayne and the United States claimed to have purchased through what Myaamia leaders saw as "three fraudulent treaties," Fort Harmar (1798), Fort McIntosh (1785), and Fort Stanwix (1784), to which they had not assented. By ascribing definitive national borders to Myaamionki (the Miami Country), Mihšihkinaahkwa appropriated "American ideas of land ownership and boundaries" to rebuke the legitimacy of those treaties by claiming the lands, previously sold by other tribal communities, as the "[Myaamia] country."[5]

The decentralized nature of Myaamia society meant that while Mihši-hkinaahkwa could speak for the other Myaamia leaders present and their constituents, he could not legitimately speak for all Myaamia people. While they were negotiating the Treaty of Greenville, they were not the only Myaamia delegation engaging with a foreign power. Since the 1780s, Pakaana, an akima (male civil leader) from Kiihkayonki (Fort Wayne) and Pinšiwa's (Jean Baptiste Richardville) uncle, headed a delegation in the Missouri Country hoping to build a new relationship with the Spanish Empire. They distrusted the idea of peace with the Americans and sought new alliances in the West that might provide safer spaces for their people. Their journey was part of a broader migration pattern of Great Lakes tribal communities who wished to separate themselves from the Americans. Shawnee, Delaware, and Peeyankihšia (Pianke-shaw) communities, among others, sought to form settlements near Ste. Genevieve and Cape Girardeau to escape the American violence.[6] In his absence, however, Mihšihkinaahkwa and his delegation had sold not only Pakaana's village of Kiihkayonki but also a segment of the portage between the Wabash and St. Mary's Rivers that had been managed by Pakaana and his sister Tahkamwa (Mary Louise Richardville Beaubien) and which connected the Great Lakes to the Mississippi River.[7] Whoever controlled the portage theoretically controlled the flow of trade across eastern North America, making it a desirable piece of property.[8] Although a young Pinšiwa was present for the negotiations, serving as an acting akima in his uncle's stead, he was a relatively inexperienced leader and was not given an opportunity to speak during the treaty conference.

In exchange for land cessions, the United States agreed to annual payments of $1,000 in goods and merchandise to Myaamiaki, leaving the open question of who was to receive said goods and distribute them.[9] Throughout the colonial period, gift giving had been a staple in Great Lakes alliance-making practices between Indigenous communities and European imperial powers. In their earliest interactions with French colonial leadership, Myaamiaki and other Great Lakes communities entered into a system of alliance chiefs. These chiefs, who were usually already recognized leaders in Indigenous communities, received increased influence by acting as "conduits of the presents" given by European government officials. By receiving and distributing gifts within their communities, tribal leaders could increase their personal power and demonstrate their fitness for leadership roles by providing for their communities, a pattern that dated back to the colonial period. While these earlier forms of gift giving were relatively unstructured, the new system proposed by the Treaty of Greenville not only regulated the amount and frequency of gift giving, but it also created official channels from the American state to federal Indian agents who passed on the gifts to the leaders they recognized. This new promise of annual gifts from the United States opened the door for an ambitious Myaamia leader to transform himself into an "American alliance chief" and increase his power by controlling the distribution of goods into their community.[10] Remaining on the Greenville treaty grounds for over a week after the signing, Mihšihkinaahkwa (Little Turtle) met with General Wayne and requested that the United States hire his son-in-law Eepiihkaanita (William Wells) as the official Myaamia interpreter. Wayne agreed.[11]

Born into an Anglo-American family and raised in Kentucky, Eepiihkaanita, at the age of thirteen, was captured by a militia of Myaamia warriors in 1783 and adopted into a Myaamia family. As an adult, he married multiple Myaamia women, one of whom was Mihšihkinaahkwa's daughter. During the Northwest Indian Wars, he initially fought with his Myaamia relatives but later defected to the United States to serve as spy under General Wayne. Nevertheless, he maintained a good relationship with his father-in-law, serving as his interpreter during the treaty proceedings.[12] By arranging for his kin to be the official interpreter for all Myaamia people, the vast majority of whom did not speak English, Mihšihkinaahkwa ensured that when the Americans heard a Myaamia voice, it would be his own. Although not pleased with the amount of land he was required to sell in order to make peace, he thought he could use the new status quo created at Greenville to increase his power in ways that would benefit his community, as well as himself. And when the United States made the first annual payment of goods in September of 1796 through Eepiihkaanita, he handed them directly to Mihšihkinaahkwa, who signed for them and distributed them as he saw fit.[13] Their political rivals accused the two of redirecting "the greater part of the annuities & provisions" intended for the entire Myaamia community toward Mihšihkinaahkwa's own village, called Turtletown.[14] At Greenville, Mihšihkinaahkwa had established the national borders of the Miami Nation, and in its aftermath, he presented himself as the leader of the Miami Nation, with he and his allies asserting that they spoke "for the whole of the Miamis."[15]

As he began his transition from a neenawihtoowa to an akima, a process that typically took years, Mihšihkinaahkwa understood that a critical aspect of his legitimacy as an American alliance chief was to maintain the United States' support. As a result, he made repeated visits to the United States to meet with federal officials. Witnessing the burgeoning American Empire during those visits, he marveled that it had only been a short time "since the whites first set foot among us, yet already they swarm like flies; while we, who have been here nobody knows how long, are still as thin as deer." He knew that as the United States' population increased, so would the number who would travel west into Myaamionki. Moreover, he noted, "When I walk the streets, I see every body busy about something; one makes shoes, another hats, a third cloth, and all live by their work. I say to myself, which of these things can I do? Not one. I can make a bow, catch fish, kill deer, and go to war, but none of these things are done here." Through his travels, Mihšihkinaahkwa came to believe that "if things do not greatly change, the red men will disappear very shortly" and "melt like the snow before the sun."[16]

He concluded that if Myaamia people were going to survive American expansion, they needed to change. While in Baltimore, he and Eepiihkaanita met with a Quaker organization that sought to proselytize Indian Country as part of their "civilizing" mission to assimilate Native peoples into American culture. Like many other Protestant missionary organizations, they emphasized American gender roles as a crucial mechanism toward constructing a civilized society.[17] They were aghast to discover that Myaamia and other Native women controlled agricultural practices, viewing it as an abuse of power by lazy men who forced their wives to farm. They argued that Myaamia society needed to reform itself around American gender norms, requiring that men take up their responsibility in the fields as farmers.

With their help, Mihšihkinaahkwa and Eepiihkaanita began to promote an Americanization program in which Myaamia men would be taught how to farm, and as a result, Myaamia women would be stripped of their authority over agricultural practices. At Mihšihkinaahkwa's invitation, a delegation of Quakers made repeated visits to Fort Wayne in an attempt to convince Myaamia people to begin the process of assimilating into American society. They started by fencing small parcels of land where they could teach male-controlled agriculture.[18] Through his actions, Mihšihkinaahkwa threatened to destabilize the traditional gender norms central to Myaamia life. He likely saw American expansion already as a threat to that balance and perhaps thought that if Myaamia people could control the instability, they could minimize the chaos.

By 1798, Pakaana and his delegation had returned from the Mississippi River, presumably shocked to find that their homes and Pakaana's ancestral claim to the portage had been sold to the United States. In response, they, along with other Myaamia leaders, repudiated Mihšihkinaahkwa's leadership. As individuals who had been trained from early adolescence to become akimaki, they recognized that Mihšihkinaahkwa's behavior was not demonstrative of civil leadership, which required "the consent and support" of their community.[19] They saw that he instead maintained the mentality of a neenawihtoowa, who relied upon his own ability and knowledge. While in Philadelphia that same year, meeting with French historian Constantin Volney, Eepiihkaanita explained that "already it requires great management for [Mihšihkinaahkwa] to preserve" his status, and that he faced threats of violence from tribal members.[20]

Traditionally, the political autonomy of Myaamia villages meant that Mihšihkinaahkwa's new role as an akima would have affected only his own village. The Treaty of Greenville, however, had altered that. By providing an annual payment of a thousand dollars' worth of goods in exchange for selling communal land, it theoretically placed control of those goods in the hands of a centralized leader, a position which Mihšihkinaahkwa had already claimed for himself. To avoid this kind of centralization, in December of 1798, Pakaana and his coalition contacted the secretary of war requesting they "be furnished with their portion of the Goods, under the Greenville Treaty separately" from Mihšihkinaahkwa. To this unusual request, the secretary responded that he would allow it, but only "if the whole Nation will consent."[21] For Pakaana's party to accomplish their goal, Mihšihkinaahkwa would have to surrender his newfound authority. Despite Pakaana and his allies' petition, the annuities remained a single payment, indicating that Mihšihkinaahkwa was unwilling to acquiesce to the request of his fellow leaders.

Opponents to Mihšihkinaahkwa's leadership were able to find some success through their interactions with Indiana territorial governor William H. Harrison, who openly reported to federal officials that the vast majority of the Myaamia people (he claims nine-tenths) followed Pakaana and Pinšiwa (Jean Baptiste Richardville) and "utterly abhor both Wells and Turtle." He went on to further state that when "Wells speaks of the Miami Nation being of this or that opinion . . . he must be understood as meaning no more than the Turtle and himself."[22] Startled by this development, Mihšihkinaahkwa and Eepiihkaanita contacted General James Wilkinson, whom Eepiihkaanita had served under during the Northwest Indian Wars, to aid them in their cause. They accused Harrison of doing "us more harm than any man that ever came into our Country." Specifically, they claimed that Harrison had "made new Chiefs among us," likely in reference to Mihšihkinaahkwa's political opponents. As an American alliance chief, Mihšihkinaahkwa's claim to legitimacy as a national leader came from the United States, and losing the support of Harrison put his political career in jeopardy. His only hope was that the federal government would rebuke Harrison. To add a sense of urgency, he warned Wilkinson that Harrison's "conduct will finally set us at war with each other."[23] For the sake of the peace created at the Treaty of Greenville, they argued that the federal government needed to remove Harrison from office.

Desperate to maintain their position, Mihšihkinaahkwa and Eepiih- kaanita had, in reality, only further threatened their relationship with the federal government. General Wilkinson had forwarded the letter to Secretary of War Henry Dearborn, who was livid after reading it. In his response to Eepiihkaanita, the secretary berated him, ordering that he "ought to confine [his] official correspondence to this Office & Govr Harrison," including any complaints he might have. Furthermore, Dearborn warned that in the future, they should not "substantiate it by such threats of war as the Little Turtle has thought proper to make."[24] The message was clear, the federal government did not operate upon Mihšihkinaahkwa's whims, and by presuming such, he had placed his position as an American alliance chief in greater jeopardy. It is highly probable that Dearborn also forwarded the message to Governor Har- rison, increasing Mihšihkinaahkwa's precarious political position with the United States.

At the same time, Myaamia akimaki had begun to alter traditional political structures to challenge Mihšihkinaahkwa's claims to national leadership. By the spring of 1805, nine village leaders, including Pakaana, Meehcikilita (Le Gros), Osage, Waapeehsaya (White Skin), and others, came together, as the "elders of the Nation of the Miami," to create a single national political body, called the Miami National Council, and to nominate Pinšiwa to become *maawikima* (principal chief) of the Miami

Nation.[25] Up to this time, in moments requiring intervillage action, a coalition of leaders could select a specific person to speak for the interests of the whole. However, the office of maawikima was different; it was a new and permanent position designed to mediate the needs of different villages and village leaders to form a unified consensus.[26] Although the position eventually became synonymous with the nation's spokesman, it originally functioned more like a strategist, working with akimaki (and neenawihtoowaki) to design cohesive national policies. This can be seen through their selection of Pinšiwa, who was praised for his intelligence and tactical abilities but noted for his reserved personality and hesitancy to speak in council.[27]

A minimalist form of government, the Miami National Council functioned under the principle of subsidiarity, which posited that the "central government authority should act, and only act, when a government function cannot be performed competently at a more local level."[28] Such a political structure would ensure the protection of village autonomy. This national body only held sessions for "important occasions touching the sale of lands, war, or the international administration," at which time "the war and [civil] chiefs form a united council, at which the matter is debated and decided upon." This description, which Pinšiwa and Meehcikilita provided for Trowbridge, suggests that the Miami National Council was a confederation of male village councils, designated to address international issues.[29] In contrast to Mihšihkinaahkwa's attempts to diminish the power of Myaamia women, this new nationalist system maintained the power of akimaahkwiaki and female village councils, while male councils would select their representatives on the National Council.

Representing all but a few villages, the Miami National Council could speak with authority for most Myaamia communities, but they still lacked the legitimacy from the United States that Mihšihkinaahkwa continued to hold by a thread. While leaders of the Miami National Council had convinced Governor Harrison that Mihšihkinaahkwa "has little or no influence with his own Tribe," they needed to convince Harrison and the federal government that they were the appropriate leaders with whom to negotiate.[30] Their chance came a few months later, in June 1805, when General John Gibson and Francis Vigo were sent to Fort Wayne to organize a treaty conference to negotiate the sale of the White River region. In response, Mihšihkinaahkwa requested a recess, stating, "The Miamies wish for time to consider on the subject of [the] speech, we hope you will not think hard at our not making up our minds immediately." Seeing this, Pakaana used the opportunity to inform them that "he wanted to go on to Vincennes now and would go at any time. [Mihšihkinaahkwa] had no right to say the Indians wanted time to think on it, that was not the case."[31] As significant a threat as the United States must have appeared to many Myaamia leaders, the internal threat that Mihšihkinaahkwa and Eepiihkaanita represented was far more concerning at the time. National leaders were willing to enter into new negotiations with the United States and, if necessary, cede more territory to them, as long as it demonstrated that Mihšihkinaahkwa did not speak for Myaamia people.

The Myaamia delegation that arrived at Vincennes that fall was composed of National Council members Pakaana (who signed using his nickname Keekaanwikania), Pinšiwa, Owl, and Waapahsaya, in addition to Mihšihkinaahkwa. Their primary purpose for attending the negotiations, which took place at Harrison's Grouseland mansion, was to correct what they perceived to be the Delaware Tribe's illegal sale of Myaamia lands the previous year.[32] Delaware communities had been living in the White River region, in contemporary central Indiana, since the late eighteenth century with permission from the Peeyankihšiaki (Piankeshaws), a Myaamia-related community. Following the Treaty of Greenville (1795), in which the Delaware Tribe ceded most of its territory in Ohio, the region became their principal population center.[33] In 1803, when Delaware and Myaamia leaders met in Fort Wayne to discuss the ownership of the White River valley, the Delaware left the meeting believing they had obtained full title to the region. While Myaamia leadership argued that they "meant nothing more than an assurance to the Delawares that they should occupy the country as long as they pleased, but they had no intention to convey an exclusive right."[34] Their misunderstanding quickly became a contentious issue between them, and the National Council used the opportunity to argue that the United States needed to repurchase the land from them for the sale to be legitimate, a proposal that would increase their annuity payments.[35]

When the negotiations began in August 1805, Eepiihkaanita and Mihšihkinaahkwa knew they needed to use the opportunity to repair their damaged relationship with Harrison if they hoped to maintain their political position. Before the conference started, they met privately with the governor, assuring him, as Harrison phrased it, of their "friendly disposition as well towards the Government and myself individually." After he promised Eepiihkaanita a "general indemnity & act oblivion for the past," he was convinced that they would "exert themselves to bring the present conference to a happy issue," a prediction that appeared to come true. Rejecting the Miami Nation's claims, Harrison successfully argued that Delaware's land sale was legal, the Myaamiaki had given the land to the Delaware, and the Peeyankihšiaki had already ceded their claims to the territory. He refused to discuss the National Council's claims to the region any further. If they wanted to increase their annuity payments, then they needed to sell more land. In addition to acknowledging the Delaware's claim to the ceded territory, Myaamia leadership, in the resulting treaty, sold roughly two million acres in southern Indiana. Despite his success, Harrison left the treaty conference concerned for future land cessions as "a knowledge of the value of land is fast gaining ground" among the tribes, noting that one akima stated "he knew that a great part of the land was worth six dollars per acre," far less than Harrison had paid for it.[36] In short, if the United States wanted to continue to expand the Indiana Territory, they were going to have to pay a fair price for it.

The treaty also included a provision that as Myaamiaki, Waayaahtanooki (Weas) and Kineepikomeekwaki (Eel River Miamies) "were formerly and still consider themselves as one nation," they confederated into a single political body which required that "the United States do hereby engage to consider them as joint owners of all the country on the Wabash and its waters."[37] The three communities shared a common ancestry, language, culture, and, most importantly, a shared claim to Myaamionki. The provision also mandated that neither community could sell any portion of Myaamionki without the consent of the others. Although the Myaamia decision to centralize certainly diminished Harrison's ability to manipulate Myaamia leaders into further sales, they were not the only communities that resided within the bounds of Myaamionki. The land continued to function as a shared territory, where different tribal communities maintained their distinct interests. By confederating into a single political body, Myaamia Waayaahtanwa and Kineepikomeekwa leaders could hinder Harrison's ability to purchase more territory. Subsequently, Waayaahtanwa and Kineepikomeekwa akimaki gained seats in the Miami National Council, sending representatives to all future Myaamia treaty conferences. To further protect Myaamionki, the Myaamia delegation also wanted to include the Peeyankihšiaki (Piankeshaws), another related community, in their confederation. Harrison, however, refused to agree because he believed that it would interfere with the United States' plan to purchase the last of the Peeyankihšiaki claims to Myaamionki (the Miami Country).[38]

In the ensuing years, Myaamia leaders, and their Waayaahtanooki and Kineepikomeekwa allies, sought to convince the War Department to remove Eepiihkaanita (William Wells) from his position. They recognized that as long as Eepiihkaanita continued to operate as their agent and distributor of annuities, Mihšihkinaahkwa (Little Turtle) would continue to have a voice in Myaamia-American foreign relations. By exploiting their concerns over his "connection with & partiality for the Myamy Nation," they strove to convince his superiors that Eepiihkaanita was more dedicated to serving Myaamia interests than American ones.[39] Meeting with federal agents, Pinšiwa (Jean Baptiste Richardville) claimed that Eepiihkaanita had encouraged Myaamia leaders to refuse to sell any more territory to the United States, violating his status as an Indian agent. He told them that he was "much surprised to hear an officer who had taken an oath in the manner Wells had done to support the Government of the United States express himself in the manner Wells had done."[40] Concurrently, John Johnston, who managed the trading factory at Fort Wayne, sought Eepiihkaanita's position for himself, reporting to his superiors that Eepiihkaanita and Mihšihkinaahkwa were disruptive elements who threatened American interests.[41]

Viewed with distrust by both Myaamia and American political operatives, Eepiihkaanita had found himself in a very tenuous position. Since 1806 he had been facing increasing pressure from within the War Department after Secretary Dearborn called an investigation into "some incorrectnesses [which] are mingled with Mr Wells' Agency Accounts."[42] Pressure from his superiors forced Eepiihkaanita to act more as a federal agent if he wanted to maintain his position. He promised Governor Harrison that "I will exert myself to the utmost to forward the views of the President among the Indians of this agency," and he recommended to Secretary Dearborn that the United States should move "to extinguish the Indian title to the [Myaamia] land on the Wabash."[43] The damage, however, had already been done. In August of 1807, Dearborn admonished Eepiihkaanita's conduct as a federal agent, stating "either that you possess no kind of useful influence with the chiefs in your agency or that you make an improper use of what you possess. In either case you cannot be considered as well qualified for the place you hold."[44]

Eepiihkaanita's (William Wells's) talents as an Indian Agent came, in part, through his relationship with Mihšihkinaahkwa (Little Turtle), but it was precisely that same relationship that threatened to destroy his career. He was too attached to his father-in-law for either Myaamiaki or federal officials to trust him. And in 1809, after Secretary Dearborn investigated him on several charges, including illegally selling whiskey, and after Beaver of the Delaware and Blackhoof of the Shawnee both accused him of "cheating the Delawares of their annuities," Eepiihkaanita was finally removed from office and replaced with his political rival, John Johnston.[45] If Mihšihkinaahkwa was to retain what little authority he had left, without Eepiihkaanita's assistance, he needed the support of the American state, and particularly that of Governor Harrison. Johnston, however, did not have a vested interest in bolstering support for Mihšihkinaahkwa, choosing to recognize that National Council leaders represented the nation, while Mihšihkinaahkwa and his allies were "far inferior in consequence to any of the Chiefs."[46]

As Myaamia, Delaware, Potawatomi, and American delegations came together at Fort Wayne in the fall of 1809 to discuss another land cession, Mihšihkinaahkwa needed to present himself to Governor Harrison as a viable alternative to the National Council leaders, especially now that Eepiihkaanita was removed from his post. After the second day of negotiations, he met in private with Harrison "to know whether the dismission of Mr. Wells from his employment as Agent would effect [sic] his standing with the Government." Without Eepiihkaanita's help, Mihšihkinaahkwa was unsure about the future of his relationship with the United States and Indiana Territorial leaders. Harrison responded that as long as he conducted himself in the negotiations in a manner that was expected of him, he would maintain his position. To this, Mihšihkinaahkwa assured him "unequivocally that he would exert himself to the utmost of his power to effect the proposed Treaty."[47] As long as he could ensure further land cessions to the United States, he could maintain his position as an American alliance chief.

Throughout the conference, tensions flared as the Potawatomi and Delaware delegations exhibited full support for the land cession, demanding that Myaamia leadership consent to it. As Harrison attempted to keep the peace between the two groups, Mihšihkinaahkwa, true to his assigned role, apologized to the Potawatomi and Delaware leaders for causing "so much difficulty," asking that they might break for the day to discuss the matter further among themselves. However, when negotiations resumed, the National Council continued to refuse the sale, even threatening war against the Potawatomis, a threat which was seconded by the shouts of the young Myaamia men present. Besides Mihšihkinaahkwa, only Eempahwita (Silver Heels), an akima from the Mississinewa River, publicly spoke in favor of the treaty.[48] As the days passed and the meetings continued, the National Council's determination diminished as the Potawatomi, Delaware, and American delegations, along with Mihšihkinaahkwa and his few allies, relentlessly pushed for a further land cession.

Sensing weakness, Harrison deployed a new tactic, presenting himself in a private meeting with Myaamia leaders "not as the Representative of the President but as an old friend," seeking to alleviate "everything that oppressed their Hearts." In their conversations, National Council leaders questioned the rationale behind the Potawatomi and Delaware presence at the negotiating, claiming they were the sole owners of the territory in question. They could not understand why those communities should be included in the negotiations. In an act of quick thinking, Harrison assured them the Potawatomi and Delaware were present only "as allies of the Miamies not as having any right to the land," without mentioning that if the treaty were ratified, they would still be paid the same amount as the Miami Nation. Furthermore, the Myaamia and Kineepikomeekwa (Eel River Miami) leaders were uncomfortable about additional land cessions without the Waayaahtanooki (Weas), who were absent. If they were to agree to the sale, the treaty needed to include a clause that it could be ratified only with Waayaahtanooki approval afterward. As members of their confederation, they would not agree to sell any portion of Myaamionki without their consent. Finally, before they would agree to anything, they demanded Harrison acknowledge the National Council as "the real Representatives of the Miami Nation and that he should always consider them as such." He could no longer consider, or engage with, Mihšihkinaahkwa as a national leader in the future.[49] Surely seeing this as a victory, Harrison agreed to their demands. The following day he presented a draft of the proposed treaty, which included a clause that Waayaahtanooki approval was necessary before the treaty could be ratified.[50]

While nine Waayaahtanwa akimaki ratified the treaty the following month, by the fall of 1810, Myaamia, Kineepikomeekwa, and

Waayaahtanwa leaders began expressing their dissatisfaction with the land cession. Rumors spread that President James Madison had not authorized Harrison to make the treaty in the first place and that the Potawatomi had forced the Myaamia and Kineepikomeekwa delegations to sign their treaty under threats of violence. When Pakaana reported those complaints to their new agent, John Johnston, he dismissed their concerns as mere rumors created to undermine the relationship between Myaamiaki and the United States. He knew that Pakaana had attended the negotiations and had signed the treaty. Johnston threatened Pakaana that if Myaamia leadership continued to speak of such ill-founded rumors, he "would build a bridge of warriors with rifles in their hands" against them, adding that while they "had lost Genl. Wayne," their "country furnished many Genl. Waynes." It is unclear why Johnston believed that threatening Myaamia leaders with war would deescalate tensions; and in fact, his poor behavior served only to increase them. Perhaps in an attempt to sidestep his own diplomatic blunders, Johnston claimed that the discontent was not the fault of the United States, nor of himself, but instead was indicative of outside agitators.[51] Given his acceptance of the National Council's demands to disregard Mihšihkinaahkwa's leadership and only confirm the treaty with the Waayaahtanooki's permission, Harrison was shocked by the reversal, writing to the secretary of war that he had received reports as recently as July 1810 that Myaamia leadership had no complaints regarding the treaty.[52]

Their change of heart was more likely a response to a religious movement headed by an emerging spiritual leader among the Shawnee named Tenskwatawa. After experiencing a series of visions, Tenskwatawa, also known as the Shawnee Prophet, preached a nativist message of revitalization and reform, which he planned to extend to all Native peoples. In his short time as a religious leader, Tenskwatawa had spread chaos across the southern Great Lakes, quickly gaining a following of fervent believers. Attacking what he perceived to be the "decline of traditional moral values among the Shawnees and neighboring tribes," he blamed traditional spiritual leaders, claiming that their medicines were evil and their bundles, which they believed to contain spiritual power, needed to be destroyed. By immediately challenging rival medicine men, Tenskwatawa undercut those who would have the authority to oppose his leadership. Labeling their spiritual practices, as well as Christianity, as witchcraft, he traveled from village to village to root out rival religious practices. When he arrived among the Delaware along the Aankwaahsakwa Siipiiwi (White River), his followers seized accused Christians, witches, and those "possessed by the Evil Spirit." The prisoners were tortured, interrogated, and if found guilty, burned alive. As his message spread, he found new disciples among the Wyandot, Potawatomi, Kickapoo, Ottawa, Ojibwe, and other communities.[53] Presumably thanks to the efforts of the Miami Nation Council to maintain peace in the region, American officials, like William Henry Harrison, noted that most Myaamia people did not ally themselves with Tenskwatawa.

Part of the Myaamia opposition to Tenskwatawa and his brother Tecumseh stemmed from their challenge to traditional political leaders who had sought to maintain the peace established at the Treaty of Greenville. Chief among Tenskwatawa and Tecumseh's grievances against the new status quo was the ongoing cessions of land to the United States, for which they primarily blamed the Indigenous leaders, like the Miami National Council, who had signed the previous treaties. They argued that Americans were children of an evil spirit and, therefore, any leaders who sought peace with the United States were traitors. The Treaty of Fort Wayne in 1809 served only to incense them further, as they argued that "the ceded territories belonged to all Indians" and threatened to kill any leaders who had signed the treaty. Many of Tenskwatawa's followers acted upon his orders, and within the year, Leather Lips, a Wyandot leader who had signed the Treaty of Greenville and opposed Tenskwatawa, was murdered by his own people.[54] Although Harrison had received reports that some Myaamia people and their leaders had found some merit in Tenskwatawa's message, he remained optimistic.[55] He blamed any hostile actions on the Potawatomi, Kickapoo, and Shawnee, whom he believed were sent by Tenskwatawa. Myaamia people, he argued, "have been so much frightened by the threats of the Prophet and his party." While it is not clear how receptive the majority of Myaamia people were to Tenskwatawa's message, many Myaamia leaders, viewing the chaos around them, were undoubtedly frightened that their people might violently turn on them. The Myaamia fears of Tenskwatawa and his followers were amplified after the "Prophet" and his brother had relocated to the mouth of Kiteepihkwana Siipiiwi (Tippecanoe River) the year before. Their new village, Prophetstown, was in the center of Myaamionki, where the Miami Nation claimed "exclusive pretentions to the lands."[56] Using his argument that the land belonged to all Native peoples, Tenskwatawa intentionally violated the Miami Nation's sovereignty by relocating to their country without their permission.[57]

Harrison did, however, begin to put more explicit pressure on Myaamia leaders to give an "absolute disavowal of all connection with the Prophet and as they are the owners of the land he occupies," they needed to "express to [Tenskwatawa] their disapprobation of his remaining there."[58] In the face of increasing tensions between the Shawnee brothers and the United States, Harrison held Myaamia people and their leaders responsible for finding a solution; any problems in Myaamionki were Myaamia problems. In response to Harrison's pressure, on September 5, 1811, Myaamiaki, Waayaahtanooki, and Kineepikomeekwaki leaders held a conference with him to address their concerns. Speaking for the confederation, LaPoussiere, a Waayaahtanwa akima, promised the governor that "the hearts of the Miamies is good," and assured him that "we have not let you go, we yet hold you by the hand, neither do we hold the hand of the Prophet with a desire to injure you." They stressed their neutrality and reminded Harrison of the ninth article of the Treaty of Greenville, which required them to notify the United States of any impending threat by another tribe. They further assured him "that no information from any quarter has reached our ears to injure any of your people or ours, except from yourself."[59]

Mihšihkinaahkwa (Little Turtle) and his allies, however, rejected any notion of neutrality, pledging their loyalty to Governor Harrison and the United States. Although he lost his national standing, he continued to serve as an akima for his village, Turtletown, and maintained a few close allies. As he told Harrison, he had demanded that Myaamiaki "have nothing to do with the Prophet; that the Prophet was an enemy of Governor Harrison's and Governor Harrison's of his; that if they formed any kind of connection with the Prophet it would make the Governor enemies of theirs." Mihšihkinaahkwa appears to have been attempting to regain Harrison's favor, hoping to regain his status as a national leader through his patronage.[60] The National Council's continued protest against the Treaty of 1809 ultimately had the unwanted effect of reviving Harrison's opinion of Mihšihkinaahkwa, who continued to fully support his agenda in opposition to Tenskwatawa and Tecumseh. In his correspondence with the secretary of war, Harrison indicated that Mihšihkinaahkwa was "unequivocally on our side," and recommended supporting him.[61]

Despite his efforts, Mihšihkinaahkwa could not capitalize on Harrison's resurgence of faith in him. For months, he had been suffering from gout, and on July 14, 1812, he died from it in Eepiihkaanita's home in Fort Wayne.[62] A complicated figure, both his friends and enemies could not deny that Mihšihkinaahkwa had played an influential role in shaping, for better or for worse, Myaamia society in the late eighteenth and early nineteenth centuries. A month after his death, a Potawatomi militia besieged Fort Dearborn at Chicago, commanded by Nathan Heald, whose wife Rebecca Wells Heald was Eepiihkaanita's niece. Upon hearing the news, Eepiihkaanita gathered a group of Myaamia men, all likely from Turtletown, to defend the fort and escort his White relatives to safety. Although he succeeded in rescuing his niece and her husband from the fort, he did not survive the battle. Several Potawatomi killed him during the attack and ate his heart out of respect for his bravery as a fighter.[63] Following both men's deaths, none of their remaining allies had the influence to challenge the National Council and were instead forced to operate within its system or abdicate their leadership roles.

Although they had achieved a decisive victory against their most powerful political opponent, time had not softened the opinion of Pinšiwa (Jean Baptiste Richardville) or Meehcikilita (Le Gros) regarding Mihšihkinaahkwa (Little Turtle) and Eepiihkaanita (William Wells). The two men continued to hold a grudge, informing Trowbridge during their conversations in 1824 that Mihšihkinaahkwa was "not considered a Miami." Instead, they said that he descended from a "frenchman, who traded from the Mississippi to the Lakes, purchased in the west an Iowau girl and adopted her as his daughter. In one of his subsequent visits from Montreal he employed a Mohiccan Indian, partly civilized to accompany him in capacity of a servant." After some time, the Iowa woman and Mohican man married and settled in a Myaamia village, where they had several children, the eldest of whom was Mihšihkinaahkwa.[64] Although he had been dead for over a decade, and there is no evidence for their claims, the two men wanted to continue to damage the reputation of their former rival by stripping him of even his Myaamia identity. Unbeknownst to Trowbridge, the National Council had several years earlier also removed Eepiihkaanita's children from tribal rolls, asserting that they were not "recognized as Indians."[65] Perhaps in an attempt to demonstrate how Myaamiaki (Myaamia people) might assimilate into American society, Eepiihkaanita (William Wells) had chosen to send his children to

Kentucky to be educated by his brother Samuel Wells and other White relatives. As adults, they had primarily chosen to live in American society.[66] Without Eepiihkaanita's or Mihšihkinaahkwa's influence to protect them, Myaamia leadership, in a decision that was likely both personal and political, chose to identify them as American and not Myaamia.

The Treaty of Greenville and the expansion of the United States into Myaamionki (the Miami Country) in the early nineteenth century brought Myaamia society to a crossroads. Unsure of their future, some leaders, like Mihšihkinaahkwa, after being defeated by the United States in battle and witnessing the growth of its civilian population, believed that the Myaamia people could not withstand American expansion unless they engaged, to some degree, with federal civilization policies. Others, like Pakaana and Pinšiwa, believed they could continue to defend their people against the United States by building political unity, heretofore unknown among their people, through the National Council forming a collective front against the United States. Unfortunately, before they could address the external threat of the United States, they first needed to deal with the internal threat that Mihšihkinaahkwa and his policies represented. They could not protect Myaamia society in their negotiations with the United States if Mihšihkinaahkwa undercut them by supporting American assimilationist programs.

They understood that a degree of collective change was necessary; however, the founders of the Miami National Council believed that they needed to modify their existing political system using Myaamia political values. Their embrace of the idea of "nation" was not an imitation of the American model, but rather a reformulation of how traditional structures might better work together toward common ends. Only by doing so could they present a defense strong enough against the United States so that they did not "melt like the snow before the sun," as Mihšihkinaahkwa feared.[67] The most important difference between them was their approaches. Pakaana, Pinšiwa, and their allies strove to reshape Myaamia political organization on a national level but under the principle of subsidiarity. They worked in concert with other village leaders, thus maintaining village autonomy as much as possible even as they strove to collaborate toward unified decision-making. Meanwhile, Mihšihkinaahkwa, using his relationships with Eepiihkaanita and other American officials, sought to unilaterally reconfigure Myaamia society from the top without his people's consent.

As the War of 1812 covered the Great Lakes region in violence, the National Council now had to balance itself between three factions: Pinšiwa (Jean Baptiste Richardville) and the original National Council members who argued for neutrality in the conflict between the United States, Great Britain, and Tecumseh and Tenskwatawa; Mihšihkinaahkwa's former allies, who sought an alliance with the United States; and finally a third faction populated by many young Myaamia men who, tired of land cessions to the United States, clamored for war. The remainder of the War of 1812 only strengthened the influence of Pinšiwa and his allies on the National Council and across Myaamia society. In September of 1812, a few months after Mihšihkinaahkwa and Eepiihkaanita's deaths, many young Myaamia men participated in the unsuccessful sieges of Fort Wayne and Fort Harrison, in the hopes of removing the United States from traditional Myaamia lands. In the aftermath, William Henry Harrison ordered the destruction of almost every significant Myaamia village, with care taken to destroy their food supplies whenever possible.

After the dust settled, it became clear to any dissenters of Pinšiwa and Pakaana's policy of neutrality that military resistance to the United States was no longer viable nor would ingratiating themselves with state or federal officials protect their community from American imperialism.[68] Over the next several years, the National Council turned its gaze away from the United States, boycotting the subsequent land cession Treaty of Fort Meigs in 1817 and instead focusing on community improvements by investing their annuities in the construction of blacksmithing shops, mills, and tribal housing, among other infrastructure projects. They also regulated who had access to these funds by developing tribal citizenship laws. Through their conflicts with Mihšihkinaahkwa, Eepiihkaanita, and the United States, the Miami National Council had organized a series of autonomous villages into a new nation. They had changed Myaamia political society forever, from peoplehood to nationhood.

Notes

1.   For examples of these positions in other Great Lakes communities, see Rebecca Kugel, "Leadership within the Women's Community: Susan Bonga Wright of the Leech Lake Ojibwe," in *Native Women's History in Eastern North America before 1900: A Guide to Research and Writing,* ed. Rebecca Kugal and Lucy Eldersveld Murphy (Lincoln: University of

Nebraska Press, 2007), 169–70; and Cary Miller, *Ogimaag: Anishinaabeg Leadership, 1760–1845* (Lincoln: University of Nebraska Press, 2011).

2. Charles Trowbridge, *Meearmeear Traditions* (Ann Arbor: University of Michigan Press, 1938), 16–21. For other accounts of Indigenous leadership in the Great Lakes, see Miller, *Ogimaag*; Rebecca Kugel, *To Be the Main Leaders of Our People: A History of Minnesota Ojibwe Politics, 1825–1898* (East Lansing: Michigan State University Press, 1998); and Edmund Jefferson Danziger, *Great Lakes Indian Accommodation and Resistance during the Early Reservation Years, 1850–1900* (Ann Arbor: University of Michigan Press, 2009), 4–8.

3. Trowbridge, *Meearmeear Traditions*, 16.

4. "Minutes of a Treaty with the tribes of Indians called the Wyandots, Delawares, Shawanese, Ottawas, Chippewas, Pattawatamies, Miamies, Eel River, Kickapoos, Piankeshaws, and Kaskaskias, began at Greenville, on the 16th day of June, and ended on the 10th day of August, 1795," in *American State Papers, Documents, Legislative and Executive, of the Congress of the United States, Class II, Indian Affairs,* ed. Matthew St. Clair Clarke and Walter Lowrie (Washington, DC: Gales and Seaton, 1832), 1:570–71 (hereafter *ASPIA*); Harvey Carter, *The Life and Times of Little Turtle: First Sagamore of the Wabash* (Champaign: University of Illinois Press, 1987), 145–55; and Andrew Cayton, "'Noble Actors' upon 'the Theatre of Honour,'" in *Contact Points: American Frontiers from the Mohawk Valley to the Mississippi, 1750–1830,* ed. Andrew Cayton and Fredrika J. Teute (Chapel Hill: University of North Carolina Press, 2012).

5. Cameron Shriver, "Four Versions of a Little Turtle Speech at Greenville, 1795, and a Conversation about Them," *Aacimotaatiiyankwi* (Myaamia community blog), April 13, 2021, https://aacimotaatiiyankwi.org/2021/04/13/four-versions-of-a-little-turtle-speech-at-greenville-1795.

6. John Sugden, *Tecumseh: A Life* (New York: Henry Holt, 1998), 53–54; Stephen Warren, *The Shawnees and Their Neighbors, 1795–1870* (Champaign: University of Illinois Press, 2008), 74–75; and John F. McDermott, ed., *The Spanish in the Mississippi Valley, 1762–1804* (Champaign: University of Illinois Press, 1974), 2:60.

7. "Treaty with the Wyandot, Etc," in *Indian Affairs, Laws and Treaties,* ed. Charles J. Kappler (Washington, DC: Government Printing Office, 1904), 2:39–45.

8. Karen Marrero, "'She Is Capable of Doing a Good Deal of Mischief': A Miami Woman's Threat to Empire in the Eighteenth-Century Ohio Valley," *Journal of Colonialism and Colonial History* 6, no. 3 (Winter 2005): 1–20.

9. "Treaty with the Wyandot, Etc," 2:39–45.

10. Richard White, *The Middle Ground: Indians, Empires, and Republics in the Great Lakes Region, 1650–1815* (Cambridge: Cambridge University Press, 1991), 178–80, 510.

11. "At a private conference, on the 12th August, with the Miamies, Eel river, and Kickapoo Indians," *ASPIA*, 1:583; and Anthony Wayne to William Wells, November 20, 1795, Miami File, Great Lake-Ohio Valley Indian Archives, Glenn A. Black Laboratory of Archaeology, Indiana University, Bloomington (hereafter GBLA).

12. Carter, *Little Turtle*, 113; and William Heath, *William Wells and the Struggle for the Old Northwest* (Norman: University of Oklahoma Press, 2015), 97.

13. Major Strelle to Colonel England, August 20, 1795, *Michigan Historical Collections,* (Lansing: Michigan Historical Commission, 1989), 15:4–5; John Hamtramck to Anthony Wayne, October 4, 1795, Miami File, GBLA; and "Receipt by 2 Miami Chiefs for annuity goods for the Miamies due from Treaty of Greenville," September 7, 1796, Miami File, GBLA.

14. William Henry Harrison to Henry Dearborn, July 10, 1805, *Manuscripts from the Burton Historical Collection* (Detroit: University of Michigan Library, 1916), 1:90.

15. "Conference with the Several Indian Chiefs Assembled, & Washington's Reply," November 29, 1796, John Adams Papers, Papers of the War Department, https://wardepartmentpapers.org/s/home/item/55727.

16. C. F. Volney and Charles Brockden Brown, *A View of the Soil and Climate of the United States of America: With Supplementary Remarks upon Florida; on the French Colonies on the Mississippi and Ohio, and in Canada; and on the Aboriginal Tribes of America* (Philadelphia: J. Conrad, 1804), 375–76, 384–85.

17. Bernard W. Sheehan, *Seeds of Extinction: Jeffersonian Philanthropy and the American Indian* (Chapel Hill: University of North Carolina, 1974), 119–47.

18. George Ellicott and Gerard T. Hopkins, "Report of the Committee on a Visit to the Miami of the Pottowattomi Nations in 1802," pp. 2–14, Typescript 1929, Baltimore Yearly Meeting of the Religious Society of Friends, Committee Appointed for Indian Affairs, Edward E. Ayer Digital Collection, Newberry Library, Chicago.

19. Miller, *Ogimaag,* 66.

20. Volney and Brown, *A View of the Soil,* 426.

21. "Speech of the Secretary of War to the Chiefs and Warriors of the Putawatimee, Ottawa, and Chippewa Nations," December 24, 1798, James McHenry Papers, Papers of the War Department, 1784–1800, https://wardepartmentpapers.org/s/home/item/65841.

22. William H. Harrison to Henry Dearborn, March 3, 1803, *Messages and Letters of William Henry Harrison* (Indianapolis: Indiana Historical Commission, 1922), 1:76–77

23. William Wells to James Wilkinson, October 6, 1804, Letters Received by the Secretary of War: Main Series, 1801–1870, Roll 2, National Archives and Records Service, Washington, DC.

24. Henry Dearborn to William Wells, December 24, 1804, Letters Sent by the Secretary of War, Roll B, Miami File, Great Lakes-Ohio Valley Indian Archives, GBLA.

25. "Grant Made to Jean Baptiste Richardville by All of Us Elders of the Nation of the Miami," May 25, 1805, RG75, M234, Reel 355, Letters Received by the Office of Indian Affairs, National Archives, Washington DC.

26. The term "maawikima" can also loosely translated as "head chief."

27. Milo M. Quaife, ed., "A Narrative of Life on the Old Frontier: Henry Hay's Journal from Detroit to the Miami River," *Proceedings of the State Historical Society of Wisconsin* 63 (1915): 223; and Abel Pepper to William Crawford, November 6, 1838, Ratified Treaty 234, Documents Relating to the Negotiation of the Treaty of October 23, 1834, with the Miami Indians, National Archives, Washington, DC.

28. Philip C. Kissam, "Alexis De Tocqueville and American Constitutional Law: On Democracy, the Majority Will, Individual Rights, Federalism, Religion, Civic Associations, and Originalist Constitutional Theory," *Maine Law Review* 59, no. 1 (2007): 60.

29. Trowbridge, *Meearmeear Traditions,* 16.

30. Clarence Edwin Carter and John Porter Bloom, *Territorial Papers of the United States* (Washington DC: National Archives and Records Service, 1939), 7:293–95.

31. Indian Council, June 21, 1805, *Messages and Letters of William Henry Harrison,* 1:137–40.

32. "Treaty with the Delawares, Etc., 1805," *Indian Affairs, Laws and Treaties,* 2:80–82; and D. P. Milligan to the Commissioner of Indian Affairs, 1855, RG75, M234, Roll 645, Letters Received by the Office of Indian Affairs, National Archives, Washington DC.

33. Roger Ferguson, "The White River Indiana Delawares: An Ethnohistoric Synthesis, 1795–1867" (PhD diss., Ball State University, 1972), 47–51.

34. Ferguson, 162–64.

35. William Harrison to Henry Dearborn, August 26, 1805, *Messages and Letters of William Henry Harrison,* 162; and "Treaty with the Delaware, 1804," *Indian Affairs, Laws and Treaties,* 2:71.

36. William Henry Harrison to Henry Dearborn, August 10, 1805, *Manuscripts from the Burton Historical Collection,* 1:98; William Harrison to Henry Dearborn, August 26, 1805, *Messages and Letters of William Henry Harrison,* 162; and Stewart Rafert, *Miami Indians of Indiana: A Persistent People, 1654–1994* (Indianapolis: Indiana Historical Society, 1994), 69–70.

37. "Treaty with the Delawares, Etc., 1805," 2:80–82.

38. William Harrison to Henry Dearborn, August 26, 1805, *Messages and Letters of William Henry Harrison,* 162–64.

39. William Kirk to Henry Dearborn, July 20, 1807, Miami File, GBLA.

40. John Gibson and Francis Vigo to William Harrison, July 6, 1805, *Messages and Letters of William Henry Harrison*, 1:141–46. For the animosity between Eepiihkaanita and Pakaana/Pinšiwa, see Patrick Bottiger, *The Borderland of Fear: Vincennes, Prophetstown, and the Invasion of the Miami Homeland* (Lincoln: University of Nebraska Press, 2016), 89–90.

41. John Gibson and Francis Vigo to William Harrison, July 6, 1805, *Messages and Letters of William Henry Harrison*, 1:141–46; and Leonard U. Hill, *John Johnston and the Indians: In the Land of the Three Miamis* (Piqua, OH, 1957), 58–59.

42. Henry Dearborn to John Johnston and James Whipple, May 7, 1806, Miami File, GBLA.

43. William Wells to William Harrison, June 1807, *Messages and Letters of William Henry Harrison*, 218; and William Wells to Henry Dearborn, March 31, 1807, Miami File, GBLA.

44. Henry Dearborn to William Wells, August 5, 1807, Miami File, GBLA.

45. Henry Dearborn to John Johnston, January 27, 1809, John Johnston Papers, 1801–1860, Roll 1, Ohio History Connection; Henry Dearborn to John Johnston and James Whipple, May 7, 1806, Miami File, GBLA; Bottiger, *The Borderland of Fear*, 98; and Heath, *William Wells*, 331.

46. John Johnston to the Committee of Friends, May 26, 1808, Miami File, GBLA.

47. "Journal of the Proceedings at the Indian Treaty at Fort Wayne and Vincennes September 1 to October 27, 1809," *Messages and Letters of William Henry Harrison*, 1:366.

48. *Messages and Letters of William Henry Harrison*, 1:367–69.

49. *Messages and Letters of William Henry Harrison*, 1:370–74, 388.

50. Robert Owens, *Mr. Jefferson's Hammer: William Henry Harrison and the Origins of the American Indian Policy* (Norman: University of Oklahoma Press, 2007), 203–6; and R. David Edmunds, *The Potawatomis: Keepers of the Fire* (Norman: University of Oklahoma Press, 1978), 169–70.

51. John Johnston to William Harrison, October 14, 1810, *Messages and Letters of William Henry Harrison*, 1:476–80.

52. William Harrison to William Eustis, November 7, 1810, *Messages and Letters of William Henry Harrison*, 1:483.

53. R. David Edmunds, *The Shawnee Prophet* (Lincoln: University of Nebraska Press, 1985), 34–53.

54. Warren, *The Shawnees and Their Neighbors*, 36–37; and Edmunds, *The Shawnee Prophet*, 81–82.

55. William Harrison to William Eustis, June 15, 1810, *Messages and Letters of William Henry Harrison*, 1:427–28.

56. William Harrison to William Eustis, December 24, 1810, *Messages and Letters of William Henry Harrison*, 1:497.

57. Bottiger, *The Borderland of Fear*, 91.

58. William Harrison to William Eustis, August 7, 1811, *Messages and Letters of William Henry Harrison,* 1:549–50.
59. William Harrison to the Miami, Eel River, and Wea Tribe of Indians, September 4, 1811, *Messages and Letters of William Henry Harrison,* 1:576–80.
60. *Messages and Letters of William Henry Harrison,* 1:580–82.
61. William Harrison to William Eustis, April 14, 1812, *Messages and Letters of William Henry Harrison,* 2:33–34.
62. Gayle Thornbrough, *Letter Book of the Indian Agency at Fort Wayne, 1809–1815* (Indianapolis: Indiana Historical Society, 1961), 21:161.
63. Heath, *William Wells,* 379–85; and Richard C. Knopf, ed., *Document Transcriptions of the War of 1812 in the Northwest* (Columbus: Ohio State Museum, 1957), 2:28.
64. Trowbridge, *Meearmeear Traditions,* 87.
65. Benjamin Parke to John Calhoun, December 7, 1818, Benjamin Parke Papers, 1816–1818, folder 2, Indiana Historical Society.
66. Carter, *Little Turtle,* 200, 247–252; and Heath, *William Wells,* 396–97.
67. Volney and Brown, *A View of the Soil,* 385.
68. William Harrison to William Eustis, October 13, 1812, *Messages and Letters of William Henry Harrison,* 2:174–78; and Zachary Taylor to William H. Harrison, September 10, 1812, in Richard C. Knopf, ed., *Document Transcriptions of the War of 1812 in the Northwest* (Columbus: Ohio Historical Society, 1958), 4:236–38.

4

Ohio, the Northwest Ordinance, and the Constitutional Foundations of the United States

JESSICA CHOPPIN RONEY

Pity the predicament of Ensign John Armstrong. A New Jersey–born veteran of the American Revolution, he spent two weeks in the spring of 1785 deep in the rough and dangerous Ohio Valley attempting to roust Anglo-American settlers from their recently—and illegally—established homesteads west of the Ohio River on the ancestral lands of Wyandot, Miami, and Shawnee peoples. Representatives of the United States government had negotiated the Treaty of Fort McIntosh in January 1785 with a handful of members of the Wyandot, Delaware, Ojibwe (Chippewa), and Ottawa nations. In return for land cessions in what is currently southern and eastern Ohio, the US commissioners promised to respect Indian land rights farther west, to distribute goods, and that any "person not being an Indian" who settled on their land "shall forfeit the protection of the United States, and the Indians may punish him as they please." It was this treaty Ensign Armstrong was attempting with fruitless determination to enforce.[1]

The men, women, and children Armstrong and his soldiers evicted were recognizably his countrymen, many of them born, like his own parents, in Ireland. From their own perspective, the illegal settlers were attempting to do just as generations of Euro-Americans had done before them: build prosperity and civilization on land they believed was otherwise going to waste. They did not take kindly to Armstrong's show of force. In Mercer's Town, he had to arrest one man named Ross "who seemed to be obstreperous" and send him back to Wheeling, Virginia (today West Virginia) in irons. In another instance, he was threatened by an armed posse, but they backed down before his authority (and possibly the soldiers he commanded). Nonetheless, Armstrong continued to lead his men from settlement to settlement, down more than seventy miles of the Ohio River, burning out homesteads and turning families off their recently stolen land. Every river bottom, he asserted, had "one or more families living thereon." Meanwhile, east of the river, in an attempt to staunch the flood of settlers, he distributed copies of his instructions and the Fort McIntosh Treaty and "had them posted up at most public places . . . in the neighborhood through which these people pass." It did no good. "Notwithstanding they have seen and read these instructions, they are moving to the unsettled countries by forties and fifties," he lamented. And as soon as he passed on, squatters promptly returned—sometimes the very ones he had just removed, including even that obstreperous man, Ross. Armstrong's commander explained to Congress that the US military had limited reach in these sorts of expeditions—at most 150 miles—and even then only sporadically. He warned, moreover, that the moment he marched his men away from their fort, "Emigrators to Kentucky" would demolish the structure, a sign of their lack of respect for the US military and their hunger for the fort's valuable timber, nails, and other supplies.[2]

Settlers of European descent defied the Treaty of Fort McIntosh openly—with their bodies by being where they were not supposed to be, but even more worryingly (from the standpoint of national authorities) by adopting a stance of brazen political defiance. John Emerson circulated an "Advertisement" in March 1785, just months after the Treaty of Fort McIntosh, calling on White, male settlers west of the Ohio to elect representatives for a convention to frame their own constitutional government. They had every right to do so, Emerson asserted. "All mankind, agreeable to every constitution formed in America," he exhorted, "have an undoubted right to pass into every vacant country, and there to form their constitution. . . . Congress is not empowered to forbid them, neither is Congress empowered . . . to make any sale of the uninhabited lands." Emerson did not explicitly address the recently signed Treaty of Fort McIntosh, but perhaps the timing of his call for a constitutional convention reflected a concern that with Indian title legally "extinguished," US authorities would take it upon themselves to divvy up and sell the land—which was, indeed, precisely what they intended to do. Many men like Emerson ("squatters," East Coast policymakers called them) thought they had the best claim to the land of the Ohio Valley because they were the ones risking life and limb and putting in the back-breaking work to clear and farm the land. They were prepared to defend their claims against the interference of Congress and the likes of the unenviable John Armstrong.[3]

Of course, the lands in question were not in fact "uninhabited" or "vacant" as Emerson suggested. The Ohio Valley was home to the Shawnee, Lenape, Ohio Iroquois (Mingo), and Miami nations. The vast majority of these people did not recognize the validity of the Treaty of Fort McIntosh any more than did the illegal White settlers. Indigenous polities operated through egalitarianism and persuasion, so for any treaty to enjoy legitimacy, it needed broad and collective assent. The negotiations of Fort McIntosh were far from meeting this standard. Few nations were represented, and the men who had signed were not representatives of their nations, had been coerced at gunpoint, and claimed that the terms they agreed to were not those in the final written treaty. Most Ohio Valley villagers rejected it outright. "You are drawing close to us," remarked Shawnee leader, Kekewepelethy, "so near our bedsides that we can almost hear the Music of your Axes felling our Trees, and settling our Country." Kekewepelethy warned, however, that his homeland had been "given to us by the Great Spirit." "Keep your people on that side [south of] this River," he admonished, or "you will find all the People of our Colour in this Island Strong, unanimous, and determin to act as One Man in Defence of it . . . [and] we shall take up a Rod and whip [you] back to your side of the Ohio." His challenge that "all the People of our Colour" were united was no idle threat. Beyond the Ohio Valley, the more distant Ottawas, Potawatomies, and Ojibwes of the Great Lakes had a direct interest in preventing further incursions from White American settlers. Kin, trade, and military relationships bound the Indigenous peoples of the Ohio Valley as well with the Haudenosaunee (Iroquois), Cherokee, and Muscogee (Creek) nations. Throughout the 1780s, leaders across national lines worked to foster a strong confederacy to repel the twin threats of violent attacks and permanent White settlements. Secretary of War Henry Knox briefed Congress in 1787 that if the United States attempted to attack "the Wabash [River] Indians it will be very difficult if not impracticable to prevent the other tribes from joining them."[4]

The US government, under heavy burden of post–Revolutionary War debt, needed to find a way at once to conciliate and awe fractious White settlers and Indigenous peoples alike if it were ever to impose its will on the region. "The whole western territory is liable to be wrested out of the hands of the Union, by lawless adventurers, or by the savages," Knox warned Congress in the pivotal summer of 1787.[5] However, the debt was spiraling so badly out of control that Congress could not finance military intervention. Even after White farmers in western Massachusetts rose up in the short-lived Shays' Rebellion, Congress failed to raise more funds for the army. The estimated national debt to domestic creditors was nearly $39 million, and another $9.5 million to foreigners. Congress had no money. By 1787, it had failed to make interest payments to Spain and defaulted on a loan from France; it could only make its interest payments to the Dutch by obtaining new loans. The republic stood on the brink of financial ruin.[6]

From the beginning of the confederation of states, Congress had looked hungrily to the West as the answer to its almost fantastical war debt. Beginning in the summer of 1776 with promises to pay soldiers in land bounties, the United States had mortgaged its future on the sale of western land. The rich agricultural lands of the trans-Appalachian West had been legally closed to White speculators and settlers alike under British rule but were now theoretically opened to them by American independence. "Theoretically," because in reality, sovereign Indigenous polities had control over land that had been for uncounted generations their homelands. Entirely disregarding those claims, the states bickered among themselves about how they would divvy up the land. Did the West belong to individual states like Virginia or to all the states in common? Slowly, tediously, and acrimoniously, the question resolved itself, mainly in favor of common, national ownership. With the Treaty of Fort McIntosh in 1785 allegedly extinguishing the claims of Indigenous peoples (although, as we have seen, it really had not), Congress looked forward eagerly to selling the ceded land. "I presume Congress will soon try whether they can agree on the best mode of sinking Part of their Debt by this Land," one congressman eagerly wrote George Washington in the same letter in which he passed on the news of the just-signed treaty. However, it was easier to project than to realize such land sales. Congress noted in 1787 that little of the land of the Ohio Valley had been surveyed because of the threat from Indigenous defenders and "some discontented and adventrous" White settlers, and yet, under the present exigencies, "the Troops in the service of the United States, are more likely to be reduced than encreased in number." Congress worried that "from these circumstances your Committee think that the loss of the lands is seriously to be apprehended." Delay "would very probably be attended with the entire loss of that fund." If the United States could not find a way to monetize the West, its finances might never recover and the fragile union would collapse.[7]

Meanwhile, questions remained about how to survey and sell the land and how it would be organized politically. The two considerations were tightly bound. Some thought the land should be sold as quickly as possible, but to do that meant selling to people with cash, and many of these people wanted (a) the best land they could get and (b) lots of it. The problem with everybody getting the best land they could was that such land was not necessarily contiguous. How could the United States govern or defend scattered pockets of settlement? George Washington, by contrast, advocated "compact and progressive seating" as the mechanism to "give strength to the Union [and] admit law & good government." But that meant somehow convincing some settlers to accept less-desirable plots when better land was still available a short distance farther on, and that in turn necessitated strong social and political organization, which, at the moment, did not exist. The problem with selling multiple plots of land at once was that this strategy privileged wealthy buyers who usually did not intend to settle on it themselves but instead intended to sell that land in smaller parcels at much higher prices to actual settlers, a practice known as "speculating." Washington, who since the 1760s had been a speculator in western lands himself, had no good words for this type of speculation. He warned "speculators, who are prouling about like Wolves in every shape, will injure the real occupants & useful citizens; & consequently, the public interest." By jacking up the price of land, speculators might impede the rapid settlement of small-farm holders, the precise people policymakers wanted to settle in Ohio. But Congress needed funds desperately and immediately. What to do? One potential speculator in Massachusetts perked up his ears as soon as he heard of the Treaty of Fort McIntosh. He wanted at once to know how Congress would allocate lands. Did "they mean to permit adventurers to make a scramble for them (as has been the case in this State and Virginia)," he wondered, or would they "fall on a more regular plan"? Either way, he began making plans to profit off the land allegedly made available by the Treaty of Fort McIntosh.[8]

Then the political status of these new colonial outposts needed to be ironed out. During the Revolution, Americans had asserted the centrality of popular sovereignty and self-determination. Now, that same rhetoric in the mouths of men like White Ohio settler John Emerson, with his calls for a local constitutional convention and his assertion that Congress had no power over the White people or land west of the Ohio River, was deeply worrying to proponents of a strong national government. The pretensions of "squatters" like Emerson—men who had not paid for their land but claimed it by right of occupancy—interfered with US interests as badly as speculators: it led to dispersed settlement, put no money in the bankrupt national treasury, stole land from and provoked violence with Indigenous Americans, and asserted a dangerous independence from national authorities' oversight. The stirrings of Ohio independence, moreover, were not isolated. White settlers in Vermont, Kentucky, the Tennessee Valley, and the Cumberland Valley were likewise writing constitutions and compacts, advocating for statehood, and in some cases even exploring independence or alliance with British Canada or Spain. US power on both a domestic and international stage depended on imposing order and authority on its own peripheries. It needed a mechanism for conciliating White settlers' demands for self-determination. In a confederation of states, that meant admitting distant polities (eventually) as new states, but by what process? Would they have equal status with the original states? How could political self-determination in a republican system pair with the desperate need of the national government to profit directly and as quickly as possible off the land?[9]

Ensign John Armstrong, hopelessly but doggedly attempting to control White settlement northwest of the Ohio River in 1785, thus represented the fulcrum of many pressure points. His mission was to enforce a treaty that both White and Indigenous people resented and disregarded;

represent a government neither group necessarily recognized; prevent (if at all possible) the outbreak of a war the United States government could not afford to fight, but still less could afford to lose; and help facilitate conditions in which the national government could profitably sell the land without encumbrance from those same Indigenous people, White squatters, or elite White speculators. He was to do this with so few resources that when he and his troops marched away from a fort, they could not be sure whether when they returned it would remain standing or be stripped for parts. Armstrong understood the stakes. He wrote urgently "that if the honorable Congress do not fall on some speedy method to prevent people from settling on the lands of the United States west of the Ohio," it would soon be entirely out of their control, "inhabited by a banditti whose actions are a disgrace to human nature."[10]

By 1787, as one Boston newspaper put it, "the joys of the American Independence are mingled with anxiety." The writer argued that they were in "a political phrenzy," and (with extreme exaggeration) that "the western community" could field a militia of twenty thousand men demanding "EQUAL LIBERTY with the thirteen states, or *a breach of peace,* and *a new alliance!*" meaning potentially civil war, secession, and alliance with Spain or Britain. The American union needed to create a strong union out of the thirteen existing states and figure out what to do about the rash of self-declared (or threatening to do so) states, and it needed to find some way to profit off that western land or face national bankruptcy with a host of domestic and international consequences.[11]

Four interconnected events in the summer of 1787 changed everything. First, the federal Constitution was drafted and sent to the states for adoption. Simultaneously, the Northwest Ordinance was passed by Congress. Hanging over both of these events, the imminent threat of a "general war" with a newly formed confederation of Indigenous nations lent a particular urgency to settling the Ohio Valley. And finally, the dramatic Ohio Company and Scioto Company purchase of vast tracts of land in what later became the state of Ohio transformed that urgent need into a reality.

The federal Constitution set up a much stronger union. A robust national government with more powerful legislative, executive, and judicial branches gained the power to make war, regulate commerce, coin money, and raise taxes. Not all powers went to the national government, however. The Constitution set up a federal government, one in which some powers pertained at the national level and others remained with the states. The radical innovation of the Constitution, however, was to explain that this divided government caused no paradox of governance—no conundrum of which entity, state or national, was most powerful or sovereign over the other. The Constitution asserts that the split government it sets up can be contained in one system because ultimately power is not divided at all: it resides in the people. They are sovereign—not the states, not the national government—and they can allocate power however they want between state and federal entities without, however, splitting sovereignty, because sovereignty forever lies with the people. The new constitution answered some of the most pressing problems the young republic faced, making it possible for federal authorities to begin to forge a stronger union, repay the national and state debts, negotiate international treaties, and build (i.e., fund) military power.

The Constitution, however, had precisely nothing to say about the organization of the western lands or the process by which new states would be admitted into the union. Article IV, Section 3 of the federal Constitution gives Congress the power to "make all needful Rules and Regulations" for federal territories and admit new states, and it mandates that no new state could be carved out of an existing state without its permission. The next section provides that "the United States shall guarantee to every State in this Union a Republican Form of Government." It does not spell out by what process new states may be admitted, what their status will be, or how a republican form of government will be implemented. On the expansion of the union of states, one of the most urgent issues in 1787 when more than half the nation's putative territory was "unorganized" as states, the Constitution is silent.[12]

The reason for this absence is that the question was being decided elsewhere. The Constitution may seem like the most important thing that happened that summer, but it had not yet supplanted the existing government, and Congress was still at work. On July 10, in the midst of the debates over the new constitution, several men serving double duty as both congressmen and convention delegates hurriedly left Philadelphia for New York, where Congress was in session. Two of them wrote the governor of their state, explaining that their decision was "absolutely Necessary for the great purpose of the Union" and essential to "the protection of our Western Citizens." They went to ensure the passage of the second major event of the summer: the adoption of the Land Ordinance of 1787—more commonly known as the Northwest Ordinance.[13]

The Northwest Ordinance organized the territory north of the Ohio River so that it might be sold to prospective settler-landowners and organized into state governments that would be brought into the United States through an orderly, clearly delineated process. The ordinance mandated that the territory would be divided into at least three and no more than five states. Under territorial government, it would be governed by an appointed governor and other officials. When it had five thousand freemen, the territorial voters could elect a legislature that could pass local laws but only subject to the absolute veto of the governor. When the population had reached sixty thousand free people, they could write a republican constitution and apply for admission to the union. Moreover, the ordinance prohibited slavery in the entire Northwest Territory, although it provided no mechanism to enforce the prohibition.[14]

The Northwest Ordinance, then, was the second transformative event that summer. From the beginning, it acted as a constitutional document. It was not the federal Constitution that dealt with the future growth of the American union; that was the work of the Northwest Ordinance. It answered two pressing sets of questions. First, who could set up new polities in the new American union and upon what basis? And, second, what kind of a union would these new United States be? The framers of the Northwest Ordinance, paying attention to the unruly and worrisome experiments in settler-sovereignty in the Tennessee Valley, Kentucky, Vermont, and Ohio, determined who has the right to set up new polities, and that is Congress. Self-determination proved too chaotic, too antithetical to entrenched economic interests, too contrary to the good of the United States as a whole. The governments established under the terms of the Ordinance of 1787 were explicitly *not* self-initiated, *not* sovereign, and *not* participatory. Even once the first population threshold had been passed to form a legislature, the governor retained an indefinite absolute veto, empowering him, if anything, still more. Pause a moment and imagine how Samuel Adams would have responded had King George III tried that in Massachusetts! Or Patrick Henry in Virginia! Think about this too: in 1803, the year Ohio became a state and passed out of territorial status, a full 40 percent of the United States was governed under territorial government. Nonparticipatory government extended over a wide geography, and in some places over a long chronology. This form of colonial governance could extend significantly in time too. Wisconsin remained under territorial government for sixty-one years, becoming a state only in 1848.[15] Moreover, the reach of the Northwest Ordinance extended beyond the Northwest Territory for which it was originally written. As Congress organized new territories—the Southwest (1790), Mississippi (1798), and Indiana (1800) Territories—it did not write new laws, or even copy and paste the bulk of the 1787 law into the new ones: it merely stipulated in each new territory that the inhabitants "shall enjoy all the privileges, benefits, and advantages set forth in the ordinance . . . for the government of the territory . . . northwest of the river Ohio" with the exception of the prohibition of slavery, which remained legal in the Southwest and Mississippi.[16]

The third phenomenon transforming the course of events in the summer of 1787 was the appearance of an ever-more cohesive confederation of Indigenous nations advocating for their own right to collective self-determination. This confederation, which had been coalescing since the end of the Revolutionary War, included nations in a great arc stretching from what is today upstate New York, through the Great Lakes region and the Ohio Valley, and south through what is now Kentucky, Tennessee, Mississippi, Alabama, and Georgia. Indigenous soldiers from Canada to the Gulf of Mexico threatened to coordinate and close the trans-Appalachian West to White settlement. In the past, an important strategic advantage enjoyed by Euro-Americans had been the ability to play different Indigenous nations off one another. No major conflict against Indigenous nations had yet been won by Europeans without other Indigenous allies. If the nations formed a united front and worked together, the threat to the fragile young nation was very real indeed, and particularly to its desperate aspirations to profit from western land. The hasty, underhanded, and unjust treaties negotiated at Fort Stanwix (New York, 1784) and Fort McIntosh (Ohio, 1785) and the flagrant disregard for Cherokee land protections in the Treaty of Hopewell (North Carolina, 1785) had enraged Indigenous nations and given them common cause. They began exploring the possibility of broad unity against the external threat of White invasion, and in so doing, articulated a very different vision for the future of the Ohio Valley and the greater trans-Appalachian West.[17]

Letters among Euro-Americans in the spring and summer of 1787 bristled with fear of an approaching all-out war, encompassing literally the entire western frontier of the United States. "The intelligence from the western country plainly indicates the hostile disposition of a number of Indian Nations," Congress reported in March. "From the motions of the Indians to the southward as well as the northward, and the exertions made in different quarters to stimulate the various nations against the Americans, there is the strongest reason to believe that . . . the war will become general, and will be attended with the most dangerous and lasting Consequences." Meanwhile, the governor of North Carolina urged settlers west of the Appalachian Mountains to put aside their differences and instead bend "each man's mind [to] be employed in considering your common defence against a savage enemy." "We have great reason to apprehend a general Indian war," he warned, involving "northern and southern Indians." "If you should be so unhappy as to be divided among yourselves, what may you not then apprehend and dread." On July 10, three days before Congress passed the Northwest Ordinance and while the Constitutional Convention worked in Philadelphia, Secretary of War Henry Knox broke the news to Congress that "in the present embarassed state of public affairs and entire deficiency of funds an indian war of any considerable extent and duration would most exceedingly distress the United States," and that "the expences [would be] intolerable." Then, just eight days later, with the ink still drying on the Northwest Ordinance, Secretary Knox was back to alert Congress that he had just received a speech from something new, the "United Indian Nations," which included representatives from the Haudenosaunees, Hurons, Delawares, Shawnees, Ottawas, Ojibwes, Potowatomis, Miamis, and Wabash Confederacy. The United Indian Nations demanded that henceforth Congress must treat with the "general voice of the whole Confederacy" as a single entity unless a "fresh rupture ensue."[18]

The imminent danger of a united coalition of Indigenous nations and all-out war along the entire frontier shaped the moment that policymakers were crafting the two foundational documents to create an American republic and empire. The Constitution and the Northwest Ordinance would do little to shore up and perpetuate a union that could not pay its debt, control its territory or citizens, or even field an army. In the end, while there was extensive violence in 1787 and beyond, the "general war" Congress feared did not come to pass that summer or ever, although an Indigenous confederacy did succeed in thwarting the US invasion of the Ohio Valley through the mid-1790s. The important fact, however, was the intensity of the fear that summer that war was imminent. Even without full-scale warfare, however, as Secretary Knox reported, the United Indian Nations threatened the ability of the United

States "to establish the possession and facilitate the surveying and selling of those ... lands which have been so much relied on for the reduction of the debts of the United States." The Enlightenment ideals of republican governance and the delicate negotiations over representation, slavery, taxation, and federalism would be words on paper, interesting historical artifacts, if "general war" broke out along the entire western frontier or if the United Indian Nations were successful in protecting their homelands from invasion, seizure, and sale. How, delegates in Philadelphia and New York asked themselves, were they going to make any of this new framing stick? Congress urgently instructed the newly appointed governor of the Northwest Territory, Arthur St. Clair, that he was to make "every exertion ... to defeat all confederations and combinations among the tribes" using "every means in your power," including bribery. But a bribe here and there was entirely inadequate to the scale of the problem. With no funds, and barely any army, the United States needed a mechanism for conquest and colonization.[19]

That was where the Ohio Company entered the scene. The company's purchase from Congress of 1.5 million acres along the Ohio River was the fourth transformative event of the summer of 1787, an interlocking piece alongside the Constitution and Northwest Ordinance building a foundation for future national stability. Organized in March 1786, the Ohio Company of Associates was a joint-stock company composed largely of New Englanders who were former soldiers and officers in the Continental Army. Although a speculative land company, the Ohio Company assured Congress that it was not trying to make a quick buck but would foster orderly, compact settlement consistent with the ideals contained in the Northwest Ordinance. Persistent and canny lobbying by former officers and minister Manasseh Cutler had by the summer of 1787 gained substantial political allies. Cutler promised that the Ohio Company would pursue "regular" and "judicious" settlement, "a wise model for the future settlements of all the federal lands ... leaving no vacant lands exposed to be seized by such lawless banditti as usually infest the frontiers of countries distant from the seat of government."[20]

Still, as late as July 14, the day after the Northwest Ordinance had been passed, some congressmen continued to prefer to offer Ohio land directly to purchasers rather than bundle off so much territory to a speculative company. Then, on July 18, the speech from the United Indian Nations was read in Congress. The looming threat of all-out war encompassing the entire western frontier from north to south ended any more hesitation on the part of Congress. It decided it wanted to sell the land.[21]

But there was a new problem: it wanted to unload more land than the Ohio Company could afford with the capital it had thus far raised. One congressman, for example, dreamed of selling six million acres, entirely out of the capacity of the Ohio Company. The deal was saved by a fairly hushed partnership with land speculator William Duer. Serving as Congress's Board of Treasury secretary, Duer promised to help Cutler get the votes in Congress that he needed if Cutler attached an option for another 3.5 million acres. The shady cooperative to take on this land became known as the Scioto Company and included financier Duer and several members of Congress. The Scioto Company sold title to this land, primarily to purchasers in France, but without first having paid Congress, and acquired full title to the land: the company was thus selling land it did not yet own. In the long term, these tactics resulted in a logistical nightmare and the financial ruin of the Scioto Company. In the short term, however, the partnership with Duer facilitated the Ohio Company's purchase. "Ye Ohio Company could not have completed their payment," Cutler admitted. "We are beholden to ye Scioto company." The radical expansion of the amount of land purchased and the alliance with Duer, who made no pretensions to promoting orderly and community-based settlement but acted openly as a profit-maximizing (and ultimately unscrupulous) speculator, marked the urgency with which Congress now wished to cash in on quick land sales in the Ohio Valley.[22]

The sale to the Ohio Company accomplished many benefits in a single stroke. It raised funds for the US government and off-loaded land that would fall in value if there were a war with Indigenous nations (particularly if that war were lost, in which case the value of the land might plumet to zero). At the same time, it planted a settlement dominated by war veterans in a militarily sensitive region, increasing the chances the United States could hold the line and at the same time buffering White American settlements farther east and south. Finally, it opened the door as well to less conscientious operators: first William Duer and his Scioto Company, linked irrevocably with the Ohio Company, and later in the summer of 1787 John Cleves Symmes, a New Jersey judge who convinced Congress to sell him two million acres between the Great and Miami Rivers. The Ohio Company, with its high-minded minister-lobbyist and prominent army veterans, had offered Congress hope that the orderly,

"Compact and progressive Seating" George Washington had advocated all along might in fact be realized. But when that first sale had been made, solving at once the problem of how to populate and profit off the land, Congress wanted more. When the Constitutional Convention had opened in May, no western land claimed by the federal government had been sold. By the time the signatories to the US Constitution inscribed their names to that document in September, Congress had struck deals to sell seven million acres, most of it to the very speculators Washington had once warned against. They would just as decisively shape the future of Ohio as would the Ohio Company.[23]

* * *

In 1785 Ensign John Armstrong had seen firsthand the imminent collapse of United States empire beyond the Appalachian Mountains and had sounded the call "that if the honorable Congress do not fall on some speedy method" to impose order in the Ohio, it would soon be entirely out of federal control. Nationalists responded to the threat. The "method" policymakers cobbled together two years later was neither "speedy" nor easy. It emerged out of and responded to a host of constraints, problems, and political commitments.[24]

The Constitution, Northwest Ordinance, threat of war with a powerful Indigenous confederacy, and sale of lands to the Ohio Company and other speculative land companies were mutually constitutive events in the summer of 1787. Together they transformed the political possibilities for American empire. To read any of these events separately from the others is to miss important context about the constitutional origins of the United States. The Constitution established a stronger national government while at the same time elevating and empowering "the people," imagining such people (for the time being) to consist of White, male, property-owning heads of households. However, too often the document has been read in isolation from the other critical events taking place alongside and during the famous Philadelphia convention. Much of the analysis of the Constitution operates from the vantage point of the existing seaboard states that sent representatives and voted to ratify the document. Such a perspective is of course important, but it is not the entire story.

The Constitution left essential work undone. It left more than half the territory claimed by the United States without political organization and a clear path toward statehood or inclusion in the union. And while it created a more robust central government, it did nothing in itself to lift the nation out of debt or secure its most valuable imaginable asset: the trans-Appalachian homelands of Indigenous nations. The document was written, moreover, under what contemporaries thought were the gathering storms of a vast, pan-Indian war threatening the frontier from the Great Lakes to the Gulf of Mexico. The war did not break out at that time, or ever, at the feared scale, but the threat influenced the predictions and actions that summer of Congress, the Continental Congress, and speculative land companies alike.

It was the Northwest Ordinance that extended American republican government to new territories and offered them a progressive track to statehood. This mechanism, which applied to all the states carved out of the Northwest Territory—Ohio, Indiana, Illinois, Michigan, and Wisconsin—extended as well to all other territories organized after 1789, including the future states of Tennessee, Louisiana, Mississippi, Alabama, Arkansas, Iowa, and Minnesota. It created these entities not initially as sovereign units but as the creations and colonies of Congress, ruled undemocratically until certain benchmarks had been reached. Notwithstanding temporary colonial governance, the Northwest Ordinance extended the promise of full political equality to new states and proved sufficient incentive over time to entice White western settlers to remain loyal to the United States rather than break off into separatist states or ally with Spanish Louisiana or British Canada.

That first essential land sale to the Ohio Company of Associates, negotiated alongside and always mindful of the Northwest Ordinance, marked an important step toward flooding the Ohio Valley with permanent White settlers. If the Ohio Company marketed itself as fostering the orderly settlement Congress wished for, its competitors in what became southwest Ohio made fewer claims to answer the public rather than private good. Each, however, raised desperately needed capital for the national government and transferred responsibilities to others for surveying and selling the land, privatizing the market risk and transaction costs of western settlement for millions of acres. Moreover, speculators offered land to White settlers in smaller (more affordable) parcels than direct sales from the government. In both senses, the work these land companies did, then, aided the resource-strapped federal government to profit off and resettle the West.

The future of American empire or Ohio was by no means settled after that summer of 1787. Much work remained to be done, particularly in the violent task of dispossessing Indigenous people from their villages and fields. In this work, public and private resources aided one another, and John Armstrong was once again in the thick of it. He was part of General Harmar's 1790 and Governor St. Clair's 1791 expeditions against the Indigenous Confederacy, but retired from the army in 1793 before Anthony Wayne's more successful venture in 1794. He settled in Columbia, Ohio, near Cincinnati, and in 1796 became the treasurer of the Northwest Territory. In eleven short years he had moved from hustling settlers off Ohio Valley lands to becoming one of the most trusted and respected political leaders of their permanent settlement. By the time of his death in 1816, at Armstrong Station, a settlement he had founded himself on the Ohio River, the foundation laid in 1787 had proven durable indeed.[25]

Notes

1. Treaty of Fort McIntosh, January 21, 1785, Ohio History Central, accessed January 31, 2023, https://ohiohistorycentral.org/w/Treaty_of_Fort_McIntosh_(1785)_(Transcript).

2. John Armstrong to Josiah Harmar, 1785, and Josiah Harmar to Richard Henry Lee, May 1, 1785, in *The St. Clair Papers: The Life and Public Services of Arthur St. Clair,* ed. William Henry Smith (Cincinnati: Robert Clarke, 1882), 2:3–5, 4n; "John Armstrong," *Dictionary of American Biography* (New York: Charles Scribner's Sons, 1936). On Ross's return after being removed, see Andrew R. L. Cayton, *The Frontier Republic: Ideology and Politics in the Ohio Country, 1780–1825* (Kent, OH: Kent State University Press, 1986), 10. Josiah Harmar to John Dickinson, February 8, 1785, *Pennsylvania Archives,* Ser. 1, 10:406.

3. Josiah Harmar to Henry Knox, October 22, 1785, and "Advertisement," March 12, 1785, *The St. Clair Papers* 2:12, 5n, 5; and Cayton, *Frontier Republic,* 9. No record survives to testify to whether Emerson's convention ever met, but meetings that spring alarmed local officers and policymakers back east.

4. Council at Wakitumikee, May 18, 1785, Add MS 24322, ff. 112–13, British Library; Report of the Secretary at War to Congress, July 10, 1787, *The Territorial Papers of the United States,* comp. and ed. Clarence Edwin Carter (Washington DC: Government Printing Office, 1936), 2:31–35;

Sami Lakomäki, *Gathering Together: The Shawnee People through Diaspora and Nationhood, 1600–1870* (New Haven, CT: Yale University Press, 2014), 122; And see "Address of the Chiefs of the Six Nations and Western Confederacy to Gov. St. Clair," quoted in Lisa Brooks, *The Common Pot: The Recovery of Native Space in the Northeast* (Minneapolis: University of Minnesota Press, 2008), 134.

5.   "Report of the Secretary at War to Congress," July 10, 1787, in *Territorial Papers,* 2:31. Knox's use of the word "savage" here is a racial slur against Indigenous Americans and requires contextualization. With this word choice, he participated in a long project by European colonizers to frame Indigenous society and modes of occupying land as inferior to that of Europeans, who, by contrast, were posited to be uniquely civilized among peoples of the world. Today we do not accept this racist language or set of cultural assumptions.

6.   Max M. Edling, *A Revolution in Favor of Government: Origins of the U.S. Constitution and the Making of the American State* (Oxford: Oxford University Press, 2003), 149–53; and George William Van Cleve, *We Have Not a Government: The Articles of Confederation and the Road to the Constitution* (Chicago: University of Chicago Press, 2017), 52–57.

7.   Hugh Williamson to George Washington, February 19, 1785, *The Papers of George Washington,* Confederation Series, ed. W. W. Abbot (Charlottesville: University Press of Virginia, 1992), 2:371–73; and *Journals of the Continental Congress, 1774–1789,* ed. Worthington C. Ford et al. (Washington, DC, 1904–37), 32:239.

8.   George Washington to Hugh Williamson, March 15, 1785, *The Papers of George Washington,* Confederation Series, July 18, 1784–May 18, 1785, ed. W. W. Abbot (Charlottesville: University Press of Virginia, 1992), 2:439–40; Timothy Pickering to Elbridge Gerry, March 1, 1785, in Octavius Pickering, *The Life of Timothy Pickering* (Boston, 1867), 1:504; Peter Onuf, *Statehood and Union: A History of the Northwest Ordinance* (Bloomington: Indiana University Press, 1987), 1–43; and Michael A. Blaakman, "The Marketplace of American Federalism: Land Speculation across State Lines in the Early Republic," *Journal of American History* 107, no. 3 (2020): 583–608.

9.   Onuf, *Statehood and Union,* 1–43; Peter S. Onuf, "State-Making in Revolutionary America: Vermont as a Case Study," *Journal of American History* 67 (1981): 797–815; and Jessica Choppin Roney, "1776, Viewed from the West," *Journal of the Early Republic* 37, no. 4 (2017): 655–701.

10. John Armstrong to Josiah Harmar, 1785, *The St. Clair Papers,* 4n.

11. "By the Last Southern Mail [dated July 12, 1787]," *Independent Chronicle,* July 19, 1787.

12. Article IV, Sections 3 and 4, "The Constitution of the United States: A Transcription," US National Archives and Records Administration, https://www.archives.gov/founding-docs/constitution-transcript. In 1787,

North Carolina and Georgia continued to claim their land to the Mississippi River but had done little to organize them politically. Eventually, both states ceded their western claims to the national government. The present-day state of Kentucky was the only trans-Appalachian space with much US political organization, but its settlers wanted separation and independence from Virginia.

13. William Blount to Richard Caswell, July 10, 1787, Benjamin Hawkins to Richard Caswell, July 10, 1787, and Richard Henry Lee to Francis Lightfoot Lee, July 14, 1787, *Letters of Delegates to Congress, 1774–1789,* ed. Paul H. Smith et al. (Washington, DC: Library of Congress, 1976–2000), 24:350–52, 354–56.

14. Northwest Ordinance, July 13, 1787, The Avalon Project: Documents in Law, History, and Diplomacy, accessed October 28, 2014, http://avalon.law.yale.edu/18th_century/nworder.asp.

15. Cayton, *Frontier Republic,* 70; and Mark A. Peterson, *The City-State of Boston: The Rise and Fall of an Atlantic Power, 1630–1865* (Princeton, NJ: Princeton University Press, 2019), 425.

16. "An Act for the Government of the Territory of the United States, South of the River Ohio," May 26, 1790, *Statutes at Large,* 1st Cong., 2nd Sess., 1:123; "An Act for an Amicable Settlement of Limits with the State of Georgia, and Authorizing the Establishment of a Government in the Mississippi Territory" (1798), *Statutes at Large,* 5th Cong., 2nd Sess., 1:549–50; and "An Act to Divide the Territory of the United States Northwest of the Ohio, into Two Separate Governments" (1800), *Statutes at Large,* 6th Cong., 1st Sess., 2:58–59.

17. Lisa Brooks, *The Common Pot: The Recovery of Native Space in the Northeast* (Minneapolis: University of Minnesota Press, 2008), 106–62.

18. *Journals of the Continental Congress,* 31:891; Richard Caswell to Evan Shelby, May 21, 1787, in *Annals of Tennessee to the End of the Eighteenth Century,* ed. J. G. M. Ramsey (Charleston, SC, 1853), 366–67; Report of the Secretary at War to Congress, July 10, 1787, *The Territorial Papers of the United States,* 2:31–35; and "Speech of the United Indian Nations, at their confederat Council held near the Mouth of the Detroit River between the 28th Novr. and 18th. Dec.r 1786," Continental Congress Papers, Letters from Major General Henry Knox, vol. 1, April 1785–October 1787, 381–87. The speech of the United Indian Nations had occurred months before in December 1786 in Detroit, but the news only arrived in New York in mid-July 1787.

19. *Journals of the Continental Congress,* 31:89; and "Instructions to the Governor of the Territory of the United States Northwest of the River Ohio, Relative to an Indian Treaty in the Northern Department," October 26, 1787, *American State Papers: Indian Affairs,* Class II (Washington, DC, 1832), 1:29.

20. *Journals of the Continental Congress,* 32:368, 427–30; Manasseh Cutler, *An Explanation of the Map Which Delineates That Part of the Federal Lands* (Salem, MA, 1787), 14; Michael Blaakman, "The Heart of the Deal: Corruption and Conquest in David McCullough's *The Pioneers," Journal of the Early Republic* 41, no. 2 (Summer 2021): 185–96; Cayton, *Frontier Republic,* 16–17, 24; and R. Douglas Hurt, *The Ohio Frontier: Crucible of the Old Northwest, 1720–1830* (Bloomington: Indiana University Press, 1996), 156–59.

21. *Journals of the Continental Congress,* 32:427–30; and Blaakman, "The Heart of the Deal," 192–93.

22. Richard Henry Lee to George Washington, July 15, 1787, *Letters of Delegates to Congress,* 24:356–57; Cutler quoted in Cayton, *Frontier Republic,* 41; *Journals of the Continental Congress,* 33:427–30; Cayton, *Frontier Republic,* 41; Hurt, *Ohio Frontier,* 160, 190–93; and Blaakman, "The Heart of the Deal," 193–94.

23. Hurt, *Ohio Frontier,* 154–55, 168–69; Blaakman, "The Heart of the Deal," 192–93; and George Washington to Hugh Williamson, March 15, 1785, *Papers of George Washington,* Confederation Series, 2:439–40. Congress had attempted to survey and sell land on its own account in the "Seven Ranges," and these sales began in September 1787 directly to the public but were disappointing. Less than seventy-three thousand acres were ever paid for. In the end, objectionable as many found speculators, they did provide a valuable service. They sold the land for a higher price than the government, but in smaller, more affordable parcels (e.g., 50–75 acres) than the minimum requirement of 640 acres from the government.

24. John Armstrong to Josiah Harmar, 1785, *The St. Clair Papers,* 4n.

25. "John Armstrong," *Dictionary of American Biography.*

5

Selective Migration and the Production of Ohio's Regional Cultural Landscapes

A Genealogical Geography

TIMOTHY G. ANDERSON

The Treaty of Paris, signed in late 1783, not only ended the Revolutionary War and recognized the United States as a sovereign, independent state. It also codified the political boundaries of the new republic, formally transferring hundreds of millions of acres between the Appalachians and the Mississippi River from Great Britain to the United States. In a geopolitical sense, from the outset the new federal government faced a number of complex issues related to the control, administration, and disposition of such a vast space, compounded later by the addition of even more territory as a consequence of the Louisiana Purchase (1803) and the Mexican-American War (1846–48). First, although many Euro-Americans at the time considered these lands to be largely unoccupied, they in fact comprised the ethnic homelands of hundreds of Indigenous population groups who had occupied the continent for thousands of years. Indeed, as evidenced in other chapters, one of the federal government's most vexing and ineptly handled challenges was addressing the issue of territorial claims on the part of these groups. Second, because some of the earliest "sea-to-sea" colonial charters recognized the Pacific Ocean as their western boundary, Congress had to manage conflicting claims to territory west of the Appalachians by several eastern states. Third, because the commercialization of land formed the basis of European and American attitudes and laws regarding land tenure and subdivision, a central goal was to "alienate" these public lands (collectively referred to as the "public domain" or "Congress lands") into the hands of private individuals. The first two Congresses wrestled with the challenges of how to achieve this in an orderly and "practical" way.[1]

Regarding Indigenous territorial claims, the sad and violent history of the forced removal of Native Americans from their ancestral homelands is well documented. The American government essentially advocated a policy of "expulsion" of Indians from their territorial homelands through a combination of military ventures and quasi-legal treaties that ultimately resulted in the cession of virtually all ancestral territories.[2] The relatively recent concept of "settler colonialism" aims to reframe this history by casting Anglo-European and Anglo-American settlers as central actors in Indian dispossession. In his comprehensive summary of this new paradigm, Walter Hixson contextualizes settler colonialism as a set of processes through which settlers replaced Indigenous "ethnic and national communities" with their own, including the creation of structured legal and cultural frameworks for achieving the end goal of permanent occupation of Indian lands. At the same time, settler colonialism seeks to better articulate the actions of Indigenous peoples, as "Indians participated at every level of the colonial encounter and, contrary to settler fantasies, the indigenes did not 'vanish.'" In doing so, settler colonialism assigns agency to Indigenous peoples as central actors—rather than passive participants—involved in a triangular relationship between settlers, the state, and Indigenes.[3]

This dynamic dovetails with a second story concerning what would happen with the land claims in the interior of the continent by eastern states, especially those areas north and west of the Ohio River (collectively referred to as the "Northwest Territory"). In return for federal assumption of the states' Revolutionary War debts, Congress eventually won the concession of nearly all these claims after a complex (and often contentious) series of negotiations. These territories subsequently became known as the "public domain." In order to satisfy land warrants issued to militiamen and war veterans, however, two states negotiated the "reservation" of portions of their claimed territory in what is now Ohio. The Virginia Military District (1784) comprised around 4.2 million acres in southern Ohio between the Scioto and Little Miami Rivers, while the Connecticut Western Reserve (1786) encompassed some 3.5 million acres in northern and eastern Ohio. The federal government also reserved a "military district" (1796) of around 2.5 million acres in the central part of Ohio to satisfy land warrants that had been issued to Revolutionary War veterans.[4]

Finally, the challenge of negotiating an orderly transfer of public domain lands into the hands of private individuals required the federal government to ultimately adopt a systematic and standardized system of land survey and subdivision tied to the geographic grid of latitude and longitude. The value and utility of its public domain lands changed over time, but initially the federal government envisioned them as means of replenishing the treasury through sale to individuals and speculators. Authorized by the Land Ordinance of 1785, Congress initially opted to sell land directly to individuals at public auctions. This act also implemented the first federal land survey system, the Public Lands Survey System (PLSS), also known as the "township and range" system. The PLSS was first applied in the so-called Seven Ranges in eastern Ohio and subsequently implemented throughout the country in thirty-seven different surveys undertaken as new territories and states were added. A committee headed by Thomas Jefferson in 1784 had drafted a plan for the survey of public domain lands into one-hundred-square-mile tracts, further subdivided into one-square-mile lots that would be sold at public auction for one dollar per acre. Disagreement among members of Congress, especially over the ideal size of lots, resulted in a basic grid of thirty-six square miles instead, but the fundamental characteristics of Jefferson's system were retained, namely a rectilinear survey grid and square subdivision of land.[5] Sales of land on the Ohio frontier under the 1785 Ordinance were quite modest, most likely because it only allowed for the sale of whole one-square-mile sections (640 acres), and the auctions took place in far-off New York City. In response, the federal government turned to private ventures, selling off millions of acres in Ohio to private companies, including the Ohio Company of Associates, based in Massachusetts, and the Symmes Company, headed by John Cleves Symmes, a resident of New Jersey. Most of these private schemes, however, never sold enough land to repay the government for their deeds, and much of this land reverted back into the public domain as stipulated in the 1785 Ordinance.[6]

In response, the federal government again turned to direct sales, but under much different terms than originally proposed in 1785. Laws introduced in 1796 and 1800 refined the township-and-range system by instituting thirty-six-square-mile townships as the base survey unit, which could be further subdivided into one-square-mile "sections." These laws also established land offices in the Ohio territory and authorized land sales on credit, allowing buyers five years to complete their purchases. Furthermore, under the Indiana Act of 1804, settlers were allowed to purchase smaller fractions of land in rectangular parcels of 320-acre half sections or 160-acre "quarter" sections. These modifications to how land was sold to private individuals enacted between 1796 and 1804 made the public domain more accessible to migrating settlers and resulted in significant increases in land sales.[7]

As more US citizens pushed into Ohio, it became a proving ground of sorts for innovative strategies aimed at disposing of the public domain. At the same time, with the possible subsequent exception of Texas, the variety of different land survey systems that were employed in Ohio is unmatched anywhere else in the country. In the Connecticut Western Reserve and the US Military District, privately hired surveyors subdivided both tracts (largely prior to large-scale settlement) into twenty-five-square-mile townships, distinguishing both tracts from the federal system of thirty-six-square-mile townships. In the Virginia Military District, surveyors employed an irregular metes-and-bounds system that had been common in colonial Virginia to delimit and legally record property boundaries. The tangible effects of these different survey systems remain observable in Ohio's contemporary landscapes in the form of property boundaries and transportation patterns, as well as in administrative patterns such as county and township boundaries. As a result of this distinctive settlement history, Ohio (again, with the important exception of Texas) has the largest variety of land subdivision and survey systems of any state (fig. 5.1).[8]

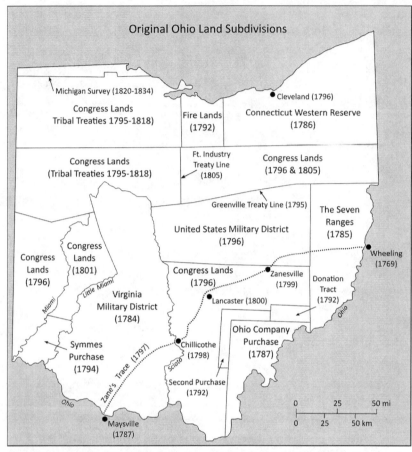

FIG. 5.1. Original eighteenth-century land subdivisions in Ohio. Cartography by author. Source: Sherman, *Original Ohio Land Subdivisions.*

Regional Origins of Ohio's Earliest Anglo Populations

It was into this new geopolitical setting that Euro-American and European immigrant settlers arrived in the Northwest Territory during the early Federal era. From where did these early Ohioans hail? To answer this, we can turn first to the United States census. In 1850, the federal government began recording the place of birth of each person enumerated in the decennial census. For the first time, a relatively accurate "official" record of the geographic origins of each state's population became available. A close examination of nativity as recorded in the 1850 census schedules reveals that Ohio's Euro-American population was, from the outset, highly diverse in terms of ethnicity and geographic origins. Perhaps the most striking detail is the fact that out of a total population of just under 2 million, fully 66 percent had been born in Ohio. Given that the Euro-American population of the state in 1790 was at most 10,000, this rapid and substantial population increase is most likely explained by high rates of in-migration and high birth rates. A close inspection of the birthplaces of the non-Ohio-born population reveals clear patterns with regard to state, regional, and international nativity. Of the 669,588 persons not born in Ohio, some 49 percent were born in the mid-Atlantic region, especially the states of Pennsylvania (190,396) and New York (75,442); 15 percent were born in the Upland South, especially Virginia (83,300) and Kentucky (11,549); and about 9 percent were born in New England, especially Connecticut (20,478) and Massachusetts (16,437). Just under 10,000 were born in states outside of these three regions. In addition, the 1850 census recorded 145,992 persons born outside of the United States, about 75 percent of whom hailed from German lands. The census also recorded 25,279 African Americans, but this figure is likely an undercount due to the use of varying categories by census takers to record members of this population group ("black" and "mulatto," e.g.).[9]

When the nativity of the non-Ohio-born population recorded in the 1850 census is mapped at the civil township level, it is evident that early Anglo settlers from distinctive regions in the East tended to put down roots in different areas of Ohio (fig. 5.2). Comparing figure 5.1 with figure 5.2, it appears that the unique subdivision of Ohio's early settlement landscape and early routes of ingress into Ohio, such as Zane's Trace, the National Road, the Ohio River, and Lake Erie, played critical roles in affecting the regional settlement patterns noticeable in figure 5.2. Transplanted New Englanders, for example, were the most numerically dominant population group in the Connecticut Western Reserve. Likewise, Upland Southerners from Virginia, and to a lesser extent Kentucky, congregated in and around the Virginia Military District in the south-central regions of the state. Settlers from the mid-Atlantic region, especially Pennsylvania, came to dominate the population in most other regions of early Ohio, but were especially overrepresented in central and east-central portions of the state.[10]

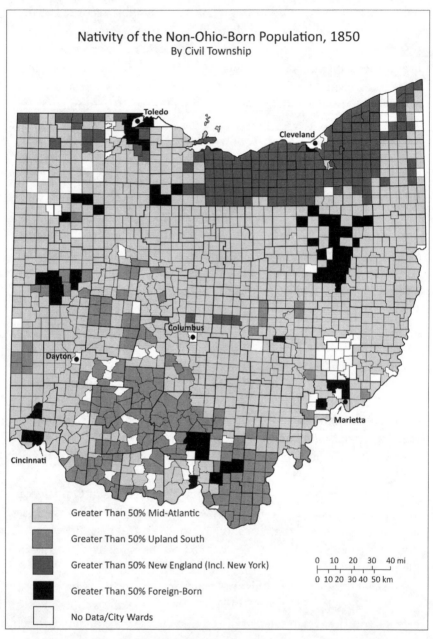

FIG. 5.2. Nativity of the non-Ohio-born population, 1850. Cartography by author. Source: 1850 Federal Population Census Schedules; Wilhelm, *The Origin and Distribution of Settlement Groups.*

The noted cultural geographer Wilbur Zelinsky asserted some decades ago that the first group to establish a "viable, self-perpetuating" society in a previously unsettled territory (or in an area from which Indigenous populations have been removed) will produce a significant and lasting influence on the nature of that territory's cultural landscapes, no matter how small such a group may be. Zelinsky labeled this notion the Doctrine of First Effective Settlement, arguing that, especially in the case of America's colonial landscapes, "in terms of lasting impact, the activities of a few hundred . . . initial colonizers can mean much more for the cultural geography of a place than the contributions of tens of thousands of new immigrants a few generations later."[11] This concept is not without its detractors. For example, it largely dismisses and fails to explain the contributions of Indigenous societies to the nation's cultural landscapes. Even more problematic is its underlying assumption that social change is largely "exogenous rather than endogenous." Furthermore, it relies on the now heavily critiqued position that human culture is essentially "superorganic" in nature in that it operates as an entity with causal powers whose totality is greater than the sum of its individual parts.[12] Even with such critiques in mind, the concept of first effective settlement nevertheless helps to explain the tangible, conspicuous variations observed in Ohio's regional cultural landscapes.

Principal Migration Streams and the Production of Ohio's Regional Cultural Landscapes in the Federal Era

American historical geographers have devoted considerable attention to the documentation of spatial patterns and processes associated with the settlement of North America by numerous population groups. Prior to roughly 1970, many of these studies focused on the documentation and assessment of changes in the cultural landscapes of specific regions resulting from successive episodes of settlement. Such research tended to be preoccupied with rural landscapes and emphasized the recording and mapping of material culture features such as folk houses in order to uncover processes at work in the formation of regional culture areas.[13] A subsequent generation of cultural and historical geographers shifted their attention to a more thorough and nuanced assessment of the spatial processes underlying the production of the national and regional patterns identified by an earlier generation of geographers. A persistent theme in the scholarship of this period was the documentation and evaluation of cultural transfer that took place during the European and African settlement of eastern North America and the analysis of cultural "divergence" in the interior of the continent during the Early National period. Often informed by detailed examination of archival documents and data, a central goal of such research was a more thorough understanding of how "American" cultural landscapes and settlement systems evolved from earlier Old World antecedents.[14]

One of the most prevalent themes in this line of research has been the identification and documentation of interregional migrations from East Coast colonial culture areas to interior locales to more fully understand how such migrations influenced the production of varying regional cultural landscapes in the trans-Appalachian West. A number of studies have employed places of birth recorded in the 1850 census to document and map the geographical origins of populations at the multicounty or state level.[15] But, as previously mentioned, the analysis of census data alone provides only a partial picture of the nativity and geographical origins of the population of a given place because this information was recorded at only the state (or national) scale. For this reason, researchers interested in a fuller understanding of the regional origins of frontier populations or looking to shed light on larger-scale social and historical processes at work in interregional migrations have turned to other data sources to fill the gaps in the census record. One such resource is the biographical sketches of residents found in county histories published in the late nineteenth century. These histories often included several hundred biographical sketches of the county's residents, including sometimes very specific information at the county or local level related to place of birth. Although these histories contain inherent biases—women and those of modest financial means are highly underrepresented—they are nevertheless rich sources for determining the place and date of birth of significant numbers of frontier settlers. In his study of nearly thirty-two thousand biographical sketches contained in 175 county histories from twelve midwestern states, John Hudson produced highly detailed birthplace maps for the two hundred earliest residents of each county that revealed distinctive migration fields. Employing both statistical and cartographic techniques, Hudson fashioned isolines connecting places of birth with places of death, demonstrating that migrations from East Coast colonial regions (New England, the mid-Atlantic, and Virginia) to midwestern locales were largely latitudinal (i.e., east–west) in nature.[16]

Most recently, advances in technology over the past three decades have facilitated the compilation of very large electronic databases of genealogical and genetic data that can be accessed and shared by both academics and the general public. Working within a new genre that has been coined "genealogical geography," geographers and demographers have been especially proficient in exploiting these databases containing hundreds of millions of names to revolutionize our understanding of the migration geographies of multiple generations of people linked by kinship and ancestry.[17] Some of the most detailed scholarship of this kind has been carried out by Samuel Otterstrom, a geographer at Brigham Young University. Working from the base premise that "individuals are tied together in time and space by their biological connections," Otterstrom and his coauthor Brian Bunker have developed a spatial-temporal model of intergenerational migration across North America utilizing detailed statistical algorithms and GIS mapping technologies that queries the New FamilySearch genealogical database of over eight hundred million names.[18] In a subsequent monograph-length study, Otterstrom employs this model to detail the geographical origins and migration pathways of thousands of mostly Mormon pioneers to Northern California during the gold rush era.[19]

Using these and similar tools allow us to identify five primary migration streams that resulted in the population patterns illustrated in figure 5.2. The result is a generalized genealogical geography of the earliest "pioneer" settlement groups in Ohio. To depict these geographies in space and time, the "lifepaths" of representative families from these migration streams are mapped across three to four generations from places of birth to places of death. Limitations on space preclude detailed discussions of each migration map here, but a more in-depth analysis of the first—the migration of upland southerners to south-central Ohio—is offered first below.

Virginia to Southern Ohio

The middle Scioto Valley of southern Ohio was one of six early "extensions" of the Upland South into the trans-Appalachian frontier during the last half of the eighteenth century. Settlers from Virginia and the Maryland Tidewater were chief among the first Anglo populations to settle in each of these extensions—the South Branch of the Potomac Valley, the upper Shenandoah River valley, the Watauga eastern Tennessee Valley region, the Nashville Basin, and the Bluegrass Basin. County histories and genealogical data, as well as earlier scholarly research, have established that Hardy County, Virginia (now West Virginia), was the most significant source region for the earliest settlers of Ross and Pickaway Counties in the middle Scioto Valley of Ohio. That was especially true when considering cultural landscape features, the establishment of a significant cattle industry, and their role in the politics of early Ohio.[20] Early knowledge about the Scioto Valley by Virginians most certainly stems from Christopher Gist's two exploratory expeditions into the Ohio Country in the early 1750s, commissioned by the Virginia Assembly on behalf of Governor Dinwiddie. Gist and his party traveled throughout much of what is now Ohio and Kentucky and submitted reports containing glowing descriptions of a wide, fertile valley in the vicinity of the Shawnee capital, Chillicothe.[21]

This valley was similar in many ways to another region settled by elite Virginia planters several decades earlier in far western Virginia, the South Branch of the Potomac Valley in what is now Hardy County, West Virginia. Here, as early as the 1730s, a number of wealthy families established one of the earliest extensions of the Virginia/Maryland Tidewater plantation elite system, itself an extension of the manorial estate system of southern England featuring a ruling gentry-elite landholding class and a quasi- or full-on coerced system of labor control characterized by sharecropping or, in the United States, slavery. While tobacco was the focus of production on estates in the Tidewater region of Virginia and Maryland, the planter elites of Hardy County focused their efforts on the production of cattle for growing urban markets such as Philadelphia, New York, and Boston. Extensive research by Paul Henlein, Terry Jordan, and John Hudson (cited above) has shown that an altogether new system of cattle production emerged here in the mid-eighteenth century. That system was then taken to the Scioto Valley in the 1790s and came to define the Corn Belt agricultural system in the lower and upper Midwest by the middle of the nineteenth century. Known today as stocker feeding, the system borrowed some aspects of ancient transhumance (the seasonal movement of herds between highland and lowland pastures) methods from western Scotland and Ulster, especially with regard to shorthorn breeds. It also involved significant innovation, as it came to be focused on driving fattened cattle to distant markets.

The stocker-feeder industry in Hardy County came to be dominated by a relatively small number of wealthy families from diverse ethnic lineages, whose large, Georgian mansions with classical features dominated the region's cultural landscape. Fort Pleasant, just north of Moorefield, for example, was the estate of Garret Van Meter, the largest cattle producer in the valley. Of Dutch descent, Garret's father, Isaac, was born in New Jersey but later moved to the lower Hudson Valley and then to Hardy County around 1730, where Garret was born. Willow Wall was the ancestral home of the McNeill family, another prominent family instrumental in establishing the Hardy County stocker-feeding system in the Scioto Valley. The McNeill's were of Scots-Irish heritage and were among the first families from Hardy County to move to Ohio (fig. 5.3).[22]

Beginning in the late 1790s, members of several of the leading South Branch planter families began to move to the middle Scioto Valley and expanded the South Branch stocker-feeding system in both scope and

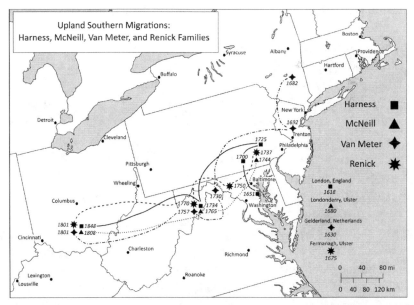

FIG. 5.3. Lifepaths of selected Upland Southern families to Ohio, 1651–1848. Cartography by author. Sources: Ancestry.com; Henlein, *Cattle Kingdom*; MacMaster, *The History of Hardy County*.

value. Three primary cattle-producing areas emerged in what was to become Ross and Pickaway Counties: the Darby Bottoms along the lower Darby Creek near its confluence with the Scioto, the Pickaway Plains between Circleville and Chillicothe, and the so-called High Bank south and east of Chillicothe. By 1815, some fifteen hundred cattle were being fattened in the Scioto Valley, expanding to five thousand just five years later. During the decade of the 1840s, anywhere between seven thousand and fifteen thousand cattle were driven across the Appalachians to eastern markets, such as Baltimore, Philadelphia, and New York. By the late 1840s there were thirty-five thousand beef cattle in these two counties alone. The industry began to wane by midcentury, however. Demand from distilleries in the 1850s led to an increase in the price for corn, and railroad transportation engendered competition from grazers in Indiana and Illinois who had adopted the stocker-feeder system. By the 1860s, only fourteen thousand cattle were fed annually in the Scioto Valley. Thereafter, the number of cattle continued to decline, generally replaced by hogs, which were transported via the Ohio River to processing plants in Cincinnati, at the time known as "Porkopolis."[23]

Two primary landscape elements comprise the Upland South cultural landscape in the middle Scioto Valley: distinctive folk architecture features and Upland South settlement patterns. With regard to architectural elements, the most distinctive features are transverse crib barns, Virginia I-houses, and a number of extant planter-elite mansions. Transverse crib barns are the most common barn type in the study region. They are usually rather small compared to other midwestern barn types and are typified by a gable entrance and three bays consisting of a central bay with two adjacent crib bays. The size and design of such barns reflect an agricultural system in which a barn is needed primarily for grain and hay storage rather than as shelter for livestock. A number of extant nineteenth-century I-houses, many with Federal ornamental features, comprise a second element of the region's distinctive cultural landscape. A fine example is the Isaac Van Meter house near Piketon, dating from 1821 (fig. 5.4). Finally, a number of nineteenth-century planter mansions remain a part of the Scioto Valley landscape. Paint Hill, the George Renick estate, is another good example of a classic Virginia I-house, as is Mount Oval, the estate of William and Jane Boggs Renick, with both neoclassical and Federal stylistic features. The Renick family figured prominently in the history of both

FIG 5.4. Isaac Van Meter house (1821), near Piketon, Pike County, Ohio. Photo by author.

the South Branch and Scioto Valleys. The family was of German and Irish heritage, and it was brothers George and Felix who drove the first herd of five hundred fattened cattle from the Scioto Valley to Boston in 1805, and who established a thriving cattle-breeding business, importing English shorthorn breeds to Ohio. A second highly distinctive element of the Upland South cultural landscape in southern Ohio was the use of an irregular metes-and-bounds survey system that stands in stark contrast to the rectilinear township/range system employed in most other regions of the state. The old Military District is the only region in the state in which the metes-and-bounds system continues to be used, and its effect on property boundaries is clearly evident from the air and in modern transportation arrangements as well.[24]

African American and Multiethnic Settlements in Rural Ohio

The significant contributions of African Americans to the frontier-era settlement of the trans-Appalachian West and to the production of the region's cultural landscapes has until recently been rather neglected.

Fortunately, renewed academic interest over the past two decades in documenting such contributions, especially with regard to African American farming communities in the Midwest, has begun to shed light on this long-overlooked history.[25] The 1850 federal census recorded 13,957 "black" and 11,039 "mulatto" persons living in Ohio. These two groups accounted for just over 1 percent of the entire population of the state, but it is likely that the total Black/mulatto population of 24,996 represents an undercount given that census takers applied a limited number of racial categories. What is striking is that almost 45 percent of the "black" population was identified as "mulatto," what today would be referred to as "multiethnic" or "multicultural." Indeed, genealogical information and oral histories for these early communities indicate that they were, from the beginning, multiethnic in nature (including significant Native American ancestry), or what an earlier generation of scholars referred to as "tri-racial isolate" or "Melungeon" populations.[26]

In southern Ohio, five primary multiethnic settlement regions emerged between 1819 and 1843 (fig. 5.5). In fact, this migrant population

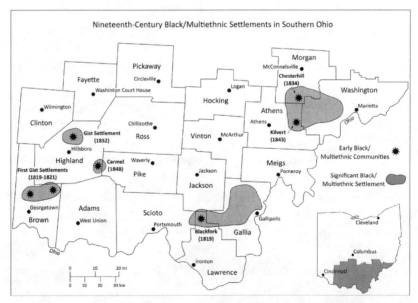

FIG. 5.5. Nineteenth-century Black/multiethnic settlements in Southern Ohio. Cartography by author. Sources: Vincent, *Southern Seed, Northern Soil;* Kessler and Ball, *North from the Mountains;* Wright, *Gist's Promised Land.*

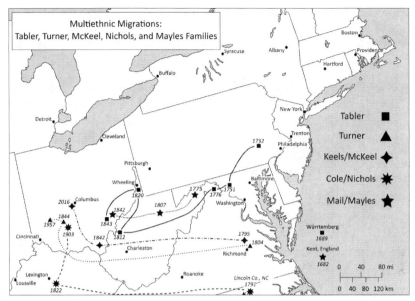

FIG. 5.6. Lifepaths of selected African American / multiethnic families to Ohio, 1732–2016. Cartography by author. Sources: Ancestry.com; Kessler and Ball, *North from the Mountains;* Trotti, "Freedmen and Enslaved Soil"; Adams, *Ancestors of the Tablers.*

can be considered part of the greater migration from the Upland South to southern Ohio. In 1850, of the 14,325 persons in this population group not born in Ohio, 7,727 (54 percent) were born in Virginia, 1,360 (9 percent) were born in North Carolina, and 1,008 (7 percent) were born in Kentucky. The lifepaths of members of five prominent families in each of these settlement regions, gleaned from genealogical sources, illustrates their origins in Virginia, North Carolina, and Kentucky (fig. 5.6). A common denominator among at least four of these settlement regions is that they were initially established by groups of former slaves who had been manumitted by plantation owners in Virginia and North Carolina, and who were willed land in Ohio upon the plantation owners' deaths.[27] Today, the cultural landscapes of these settlements are highlighted by rural churches of denominations historically affiliated with African American communities (African Methodist Episcopal, Church of God, Baptist), together with associated cemeteries, which often contain examples of distinctive folk art and motifs, and heritage and memorial landscapes, including Underground Railroad historical sites and historical markers.

New England to the Western Reserve

A third migration stream linking New England with the Western Reserve in northeast Ohio emerged in the first decade of the nineteenth
century. Reserved by Connecticut in part to satisfy land warrants issued
to Revolutionary War veterans and civilian victims of British atrocities
during the war, the Western Reserve began as a trans-Appalachian extension of New England "culture" and landscapes in the West. By 1850,
a clear majority of the civil townships in the Reserve were numerically
dominated by settlers either born in Connecticut or Massachusetts
or of New England ancestry (fig. 5.2). A close analysis of biographical
sketches in county histories and genealogical entries on Ancestry.com
from the area of Tallmadge and Stark County, one of the earliest-settled
regions of the Reserve, reveals a migration field in western Connecticut,
focused in and around the town of Litchfield (fig. 5.7).[28] As the western-
most portion of "New England extended," many aspects of the cultural
landscapes of this part of Ohio reflect the New England origins of most
of the region's first Anglo-American settlers. Examples include historic
Congregational (now United Church of Christ) churches dating from

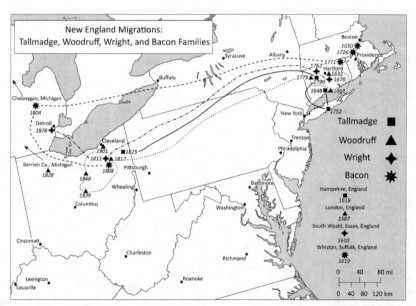

FIG. 5.7. Lifepaths of selected New England families to Ohio, 1632–1901.
Cartography by author. Sources: Ancestry.com; Carley, *Litchfield*.

FIG. 5.8. First Congregational Church (1825), Tallmadge, Summit County, Ohio. Photo by author.

the early nineteenth century (fig. 5.8), "saltbox" and Cape Cod folk houses in some small towns, New England place-names, and distinctive settlement patterns such as village "greens."

Pennsylvania-Germans to Central Ohio

The earliest significant Germanic population group in Ohio consisted of Pennsylvania-Germans from southeastern and southern Pennsylvania, who began migrating to the central and eastern portions of the state as early as 1797. While members of various Anabaptist sects tended to settle in the rural areas just south of the Western Reserve, Lutherans and members of German Reformed denominations clustered along Zane's Trace in the rich agricultural lands north and west of the glacial divide in portions of five counties, centered on Fairfield County and its county seat, Lancaster. By 1850, just under one-half of the population of those five counties not born in Ohio had been born in Pennsylvania. When the birthplaces of so-called prominent citizens of Fairfield County, whose biographical sketches are included in the 1877 county history, are

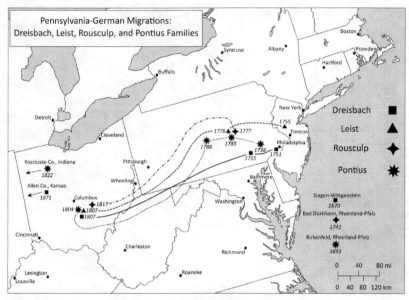

FIG. 5.9. Lifepaths of selected Pennsylvania-German families to Ohio, 1738–1817. Cartography by author. Sources: Ancestry.com; Anderson, "Creation of an Ethnic Culture Complex Region."

compared with genealogical information gleaned from Ancestry.com and mapped, a migration field focused on southern and southeastern Pennsylvania emerges (fig. 5.9).

The distinctive Pennsylvania-German cultural landscape that emerged here came to be dominated by three sets of features: Pennsylvania bank barns, Federal-style brick I-houses, and rural churches and cemeteries. The most iconic of these is the Pennsylvania bank barn, a form introduced from the Upper Rhine Valley by immigrants during the colonial era. There are at least eighty-five extant examples in this five-county region of Ohio, composing the densest concentration of this type of barn outside of southeast Pennsylvania. The agricultural system brought by Pennsylvania-German migrants was extensive, commercially oriented, and focused on the production of both crops and livestock. This barn form served the needs of both, with an upper section containing grain cribs, hay mows, and a threshing floor, and a lower section containing livestock stanchions. The Rousculp barn near Somerset in Perry County, likely constructed in the early 1820s, is an excellent example of a log bank barn (fig. 5.10). A second common feature of the rural Pennsylvania-German

FIG. 5.10. The Rousculp barn (ca. 1822), near Somerset, Perry County, Ohio. Photo by author.

cultural landscape in Ohio is the presence of numerous examples of brick I-houses with Federal styling and ornamentation. This Georgian form was the most common form of folk housing in the colonial era and made its way west with streams of migrants during the Early National era, where popular Federal ornamentation features began to appear. There are also a few examples of the so-called Pennsylvania four-over-four house throughout the region. Finally, a third common feature of the Pennsylvania-German rural cultural landscape in Ohio is the presence of numerous rural churches and accompanying cemeteries. Lutheran and Reformed churches are the most common, but other denominations associated with Pennsylvania-Germans, such as the Church of the Brethren and the Evangelical United Brethren, are present as well. The cemeteries associated with these churches often contain gravestones that not only reflect national styles popular at the time, but are also fascinating examples of Pennsylvania-German folk art and motifs.[29]

German Immigrants to Western Ohio

Of the nearly 146,000 foreign immigrants recorded in the 1850 federal census, just under one-half—representing about 3.5 percent of the state's total population—were born in the German lands. Some of these immigrants were living in the state's emerging urban centers, especially Cleveland and Cincinnati, but most settled in several townships comprising small, close-knit rural communities. One of the most significant of these was a four-county region of western Ohio centered in Auglaize and Mercer counties. Here, German immigrants, primarily from the Oldenburger Münsterland, settled the fertile farmlands in the vicinity of the Ohio-Erie Canal beginning in 1832. The initial settlement of this area in the early 1830s resulted in the establishment of three towns in the three southernmost townships of Auglaize County: Stallowtown (later Minster), Bremen (later New Bremen), and New Knoxville. By 1850, just under twenty-five hundred of those enumerated in Auglaize County were German-born, including 85 percent of all heads of household in southern Auglaize County.

Detailed archival and genealogical research of this group has revealed that a large majority of the immigrant settlers hailed from villages within a forty-mile radius of the city of Osnabrück in northwestern Germany. This included the counties of Tecklenburg and Warendorf in the Prussian province of Westphalia; the District of Osnabrück in the western part of the Kingdom of Hannover; and the Oldenburger Münsterland, the southernmost parts of the Duchy of Oldenburg. The lifepaths of four prominent families from the area, mapped employing genealogical information, family histories, and German emigration records, confirms these origins and the fact that most of these immigrants traveled directly to western Ohio shortly after entry into the United States at Baltimore or New York (fig. 5.11).

One of the most fascinating aspects of this immigrant settlement cluster is how confessional differences in the relatively small sending region in Germany came to be remanifested in western Ohio and reinforced by subsequent migration chains. Minster was established in 1832 by a Catholic settlement society in Cincinnati and was made up almost wholly of immigrants from southern Oldenburg and several Catholic parishes in the neighboring District of Osnabrück. New Bremen was also founded in 1832, but by a Lutheran settlement society in Cincinnati, and was composed almost exclusively of immigrants from Protestant communities in the Duchy of Osnabrück and the nearby County of Diepholz, both part of the Kingdom of Hannover. New Knoxville, dominated by German Reformed Protestants, was established in 1838 and

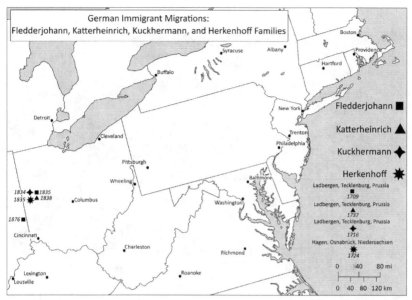

FIG. 5.11. Lifepaths of selected German immigrant families to Ohio, 1834–1876. Cartography by author. Sources: Ancestry.com; Höndgen, "Community Versus Separation"; Hoge, *From Ladbergen to America*.

was perhaps the most striking example of direct transplantation from Germany. Twenty-eight of forty German families and individuals were born in the small village of Ladbergen in northern Westphalia. Germanic cultural landscape elements in the Auglaize-Mercer County region are dominated by religious features such as churches and cemeteries and, to a lesser extent, Germanic place-names. The landscapes of eastern Mercer County, especially, feature a number of large Catholic churches and other Roman Catholic landscape features such as monasteries and convents (fig. 5.12).[30]

This overview of migration patterns to Ohio during the early, formative years of the young republic reminds us that there were *several* "pioneer" settlement groups in the Old Northwest, and that each group made significant contributions to the production of the region's diverse cultural landscapes. As the 1850 census returns illustrate, Ohio's population was from the outset rather diverse in terms of ancestry, ethnicity, and national origin. This is true for the numerically dominant Anglo-American population as well, as it itself comprised representatives from each of the three main East Coast colonial settlement regions—New England,

FIG. 5.12. St. Augustine Catholic Church (1849), Minster, Auglaize County, Ohio. Photo by author.

the mid-Atlantic, and the Upland South. So, too, family histories and genealogical information reveal that many of Ohio's African American pioneers were members of a diverse population with a fascinating mix of African, Indigenous, and Anglo-European ancestry. A close inspection of individual family histories and genealogies reveals that bonds of kinship tied people together across time and space, linking sending and receiving regions sometimes thousands of miles apart. Such ties are illustrated in this chapter by the lifepaths of representative families from five of Ohio's most significant pioneer population groups. Each of these groups left indelible traces—footprints, if you will—in the regions of the state in which they settled, especially when (and where) they were the "first effective settlers." Sometimes these traces in the cultural landscape are overt, conspicuous to even the most casual observer—a New England–style congregational church, an iconic Pennsylvania-German bank barn, a Virginia-style planter's mansion. Sometimes, however, they are less overt, relics that require a keen eye to spot—township boundaries that reflect a metes-and-bounds survey system, place-names that indicate the regional origins of those who named towns and physical features, a historical marker celebrating a rural area's Black pioneer settlers. Whether overt or hidden, such landscape features are physical manifestations of the diverse populations that shaped Ohio's history and geography.

Notes

1. Timothy G. Anderson, "Dividing the Land," in *North American Odyssey: Historical Geographies for the Twenty-First Century,* ed. Craig E. Colten and Geoffrey L. Buckley (Lanham, MD: Rowman & Littlefield, 2014), 221–23.
2. Donald W. Meinig, *Atlantic America, 1492–1800,* vol. 1, *The Shaping of America: A Geographical Perspective on 500 Years of History* (New Haven, CT: Yale University Press, 1986), 70–72.
3. Walter L. Hixson, *American Settler Colonialism: A History* (New York: Palgrave Macmillan, 2013), 4–5, 197. For an overview of settler colonialism and its theoretical foundations, see Lorenzo Veracini, "Settler Colonialism: Career of a Concept," *Journal of Imperial and Commonwealth History* 41, no. 2 (2013): 313–33.
4. Although now dated, the most comprehensive history of these early Ohio land subdivisions remains C. E. Sherman, *Original Ohio Land*

Subdivisions (Columbus: Ohio Department of Natural Resources, Division of Geological Survey, 1925).

5. For detailed studies of the history of the PLSS and its impact on the country's cultural landscapes, see William Pattison, *Beginnings of the American Rectangular Survey System, 1784–1800* (Chicago: University of Chicago, Department of Geography, Research Paper 50, 1957); Hildegard Binder Johnson, *Order upon the Land: The U.S. Rectangular Land Survey and the Upper Mississippi Country* (New York: Oxford University Press, 1976); Albert C. White, *A History of the Rectangular Survey System* (Washington, DC: Bureau of Land Management, 1983); Edward T. Price, *Dividing the Land: Early American Beginnings of Our Private Property Mosaic* (Chicago: University of Chicago Press, 1995); Nicholas Blomley, "Law, Property, and the Geography of Violence: The Frontier, the Survey, and the Grid," *Annals of the American Association of Geographers* 93, no. 1 (2003): 121–41; and Bill Hubbard Jr., *American Boundaries: The Nation, the States, and the Rectangular Survey* (Chicago: University of Chicago Press, 2009).

6. Ethan Bottone and Timothy G. Anderson, "National Discourses Materialized: Early Settlement and Land Tenure in Perry County, Ohio, 1801–1842," *Historical Geography* 45 (2017): 152–171.

7. Bottone and Anderson, "National Discourses Materialized," 156. For detailed discussions of frontier land sales, see Malcolm J. Rohrbaugh, *The Land Office Business* (London: Oxford University Press, 1968); and David T. Stephens and Alexander T. Bobersky, "Analysis of Land Sales, Steubenville Land Office, 1800–1820," *Pioneer America Society Transactions* 13 (1990): 1–9.

8. Anderson, "Dividing the Land," 223.

9. For an analysis of nativity in the 1850 Ohio census, detailed at the civil township level, see Hubert G. H. Wilhelm, *The Origin and Distribution of Settlement Groups: Ohio, 1850* (Athens, OH: Cutler Printing, 1982).

10. Timothy G. Anderson, "The Creation of an Ethnic Culture Complex Region: Pennsylvania-Germans in Central Ohio, 1790–1850," *Historical Geography* 29 (2001): 133–57.

11. Wilbur Zelinsky, *The Cultural Geography of the United States* (Englewood Cliffs, NJ: Prentice Hall, 1973), 13–14.

12. William B. Meyer, "First Effective Settlement: Histories of an Idea," *Journal of Historical Geography* 65 (2019): 1–8. For an overview of the humanistic critique, see James S. Duncan, "The Superorganic in American Cultural Geography," *Annals of the American Association of Geographers* 70, no. 2 (1980): 181–98; and Don Mitchell, "There's No Such Thing as Culture: Towards a Reconceptualization of the Idea of Culture in Geography," *Transactions of the Institute of British Geographers* 20, no. 1 (1995): 102–16.

13. Some classic treatises of this genre include Carl O. Sauer, "The Morphology of Landscape," *University of California Publications in Geography* 2,

no. 2 (1925): 19–54; Andrew H. Clark, *Three Centuries and the Island: A Historical Geography of Settlement and Agriculture in Prince Edward Island, Canada* (Toronto: University of Toronto Press, 1959); Fred Kniffen, "Folk Housing: Key to Diffusion," *Annals of the American Association of Geographers* 55, no. 4 (1965): 549–77; and Henry Glassie, *Pattern in the Material Folk Culture of the Eastern United States* (Philadelphia: University of Pennsylvania Press, 1968).

14. Examples include James T. Lemon, *The Best Poor Man's Country: Early Southeastern Pennsylvania* (Baltimore: Johns Hopkins University Press, 1972); R. Cole Harris, "The Simplification of Europe Overseas," *Annals of the American Association of Geographers* 67, no. 4 (1977): 469–83; Robert D. Mitchell, "The Formation of Early American Culture Regions: An Interpretation," in *European Settlement and Development in North America*, ed. James R. Gibson (Toronto: University of Toronto Press, 1978); Terry G. Jordan and Matti Kaups, *The American Backwoods Frontier: An Ethnic and Ecological Interpretation* (Baltimore: Johns Hopkins University Press, 1989); and Robert D. Mitchell and Warren Hofstra, "How Do Settlement Systems Evolve? The Virginia Backcountry during the Eighteenth Century," *Journal of Historical Geography* 21, no. 2 (1995): 123–47.

15. Examples include Terry G. Jordan, "Population Origins in Texas in 1850," *Geographical Review* 59 (1969): 89–103; William A. Bowen, *The Willamette Valley: Migration and Settlement on the Oregon Frontier* (Seattle: University of Washington Press, 1978); Wilhelm, "The Origin and Distribution of Settlement Groups"; Gregory S. Rose, "Major Sources of Indiana's Settlers in 1850," *Pioneer America Society Transactions* 6 (1983): 67–76; Gregory S. Rose, "Information Sources for Nineteenth-Century Midwestern Migration," *Professional Geographer* 37 (1985): 66–72; Russel L. Gerlach, *Settlement Patterns in Missouri: A Study of Population Origins with a Wall Map* (Columbia: University of Missouri Press, 1986); Gregory S. Rose, "Upland Southerners: The County Origins of Southern Migrants to Indiana by 1850," *Indiana Magazine of History* 82 (1986): 242–63; Douglas K. Meyer, *Making the Heartland Quilt: A Geographical History of Settlement and Migration in Early-Nineteenth-Century Illinois* (Carbondale: Southern Illinois University Press, 2000); and Anderson, "The Creation of an Ethnic Culture Complex Region."

16. John C. Hudson, "North American Origins of Middlewestern Frontier Populations," *Annals of the American Association of Geographers* 78, no. 3 (1988): 395–413.

17. For a rich collection of essays on this topic, see Dallen J. Timothy and Jeanne Kay Guelke, eds., *Geography and Genealogy: Locating Personal Pasts* (Aldershot, UK: Ashgate, 2008). Other standout examples include Zhongwei Zhao, "Chinese Genealogies as a Source for Demographic Research: A Further Assessment of Their Reliability," *Population Studies*

55 (2001): 181–93; Catherine Nash, "Geographies of Relatedness," *Transactions of the Institute of British Geographers* 30, no. 4 (2005): 449–62; Paul A. Longley, Richard Webber, and Daryl Lloyd, "The Quantitative Analysis of Family Names: Historic Migration and the Present Day Neighborhood Structure of Middlesbrough, United Kingdom," *Annals of the American Association of Geographers* 97, no. 1 (2007): 31–48; and Paul A. Longley, James A. Chesire, and Pablo Mateos, "Creating a Regional Geography of Britain through the Spatial Analysis of Surnames," *Geoforum* 42, no. 4 (2011): 506–16.

18. Samuel M. Otterstrom and Brian E. Bunker, "Genealogy, Migration, and the Intertwined Geographies of Personal Pasts," *Annals of the American Association of Geographers* 103, no. 3 (2013): 544–69. The New FamilySearch database is maintained by the Church of Jesus Christ of Latter-day Saints.

19. Samuel M. Otterstrom, *From California's Gold Fields to the Mendocino Coast: A Settlement History across Time and Place* (Reno: University of Nevada Press, 2017).

20. Paul C. Henlein, *Cattle Kingdom in the Ohio Valley, 1783–1860* (Lexington: University of Kentucky Press, 1959); Robert Leslie Jones, *History of Agriculture in Ohio to 1880* (Kent, OH: Kent State University Press, 1983), 88–89; Terry G. Jordan, *North American Cattle-Ranching Frontiers: Origins, Diffusion, and Differentiation* (Albuquerque: University of New Mexico Press, 1993), 200–201; John C. Hudson, *Making the Corn Belt: A Geographical History of Middle-Western Agriculture* (Bloomington: University of Indiana Press, 1994), 66–73; and David Hackett Fischer and James C. Kelly, *Bound Away: Virginia and the Westward Movement* (Charlottesville: University of Virginia Press, 2000), 168–72.

21. Kenneth P. Bailey, *Christopher Gist: Colonial Frontiersman, Explorer and Indian Agent* (Hamden, CT: Archon Books, 1976), 32–41; and Hudson, *Making the Corn Belt,* 32–39.

22. Alvin Edward Moore, "History of Hardy County of the Borderland," *Moorefield Examiner and Hardy County News* (Moorefield, WV), 1963; and Richard K. MacMaster, *The History of Hardy County, 1786–1986* (Salem, WV: Walsworth Press, 1986).

23. Henlein, *Cattle Kingdom,* 49–60; and Hudson, *Making the Corn Belt,* 66–70.

24. For a highly detailed study of the tangible effects of the metes-and-bounds survey system on the cultural landscape of this part of Ohio, see Norman J. W. Thrower, *Original Survey and Subdivision: A Comparative Study of the Form and Effect of Contrasting Cadastral Surveys* (Chicago: Rand McNally, 1966).

25. Excellent examples include Stephan A. Vincent, *Southern Seed, Northern Soil: African-American Farm Communities in the Midwest, 1765–1900* (Bloomington: Indiana University Press, 1999); Cheryl Jennifer LaRoche,

Free Black Communities and the Underground Railroad: The Geography of Resistance (Champaign: University of Illinois Press, 2014); and Anna-Lisa Cox, *The Bone and Sinew of the Land: America's Forgotten Black Pioneers and the Struggle for Equality* (New York: Hachette, 2018).

26. For examples of such scholarship, see Edward T. Price, "The Mixed-Blood Racial Strain of Carmel, Ohio, and Magoffin County, Kentucky," *Ohio Journal of Science* 50, no. 6 (1950): 281–90; Edward T. Price, "A Geographical Analysis of White-Negro-Indian Racial Mixtures in Eastern United States," *Annals of the American Association of Geographers* 43, no. 2 (1953): 138–55; and Edgar T. Thompson, "The Little Races," *American Anthropologist* 74, no. 5 (1972): 1295–306; For more recent studies, see David Henige, "Origin Traditions of American Racial Isolates," *Appalachian Journal* 11, no. 3 (1984): 201–13; John S. Kessler and Donald B. Ball, *North from the Mountains: A Folk History of the Carmel Melungeon Settlement, Highland County, Ohio* (Macon, GA: Mercer University Press, 2001); and Melissa Schrift, *Becoming Melungeon: Making an Identity in the Appalachian South* (Lincoln: University of Nebraska Press, 2013).

27. For details on these histories, see Price, "The Mixed-Blood Racial Strain"; Alvin C. Adams, *Ancestors of the Tablers of Kilvert* [MS copy], 1993, Ohioana Special Collections, Ohio University Library; Michael Trotti, "Freedmen and Enslaved Soil: A Case Study of Manumission, Migration, and Land," *Virginia Magazine of History and Biography* 104, no. 4 (1996): 455–80; Kessler and Ball, *North From the Mountains;* Howard Bodenhorn, "Manumission in Nineteenth-Century Virginia," *Cliometrica* 5 (2011): 145–64; Paula Kitty Wright, *Gist's Promised Land: The Little-Known Story of the Largest Relocation of Freed Slaves in U.S. History* (Seaman, OH: Sugar Tree, 2013); Barb Drummond, *The Midas of Manumission: The Orphan Samuel Gist and His Virginian Slaves* (self-pub., 2018); and David Meyers and Elise Meyers Walker, *Historic Black Settlements of Ohio* (Charleston, SC: History Press, 2020).

28. For an excellent overview of the history and cultural landscapes of Litchfield, see Rachel Carley, *Litchfield: The Making of a New England Town* (Litchfield, CT: Litchfield Historical Society, 2011).

29. Anderson, "Creation of an Ethnic Culture Complex Region."

30. Much of the information in this section is derived from Anne Aengenvoort Höndgen, "Community versus Separation: A Northwest German Emigrant Settlement in Nineteenth-Century Ohio," in *German-American Immigration and Ethnicity in Comparative Perspective,* ed. Wolfgang Helbich and Walter D. Kamphoefner (Madison, WI: Max Kade Institute for German-American Studies, 2004), 18–43; and Dean Hoge, *From Ladbergen to America: The Heritage and the Migration* (Minster, OH: Globus, 2007).

6

(Re)tracing Zane

Zane's Trace and Production of
Space in the Ohio Country

WILLIAM M. HUNTER

A noted geographer once said that the holistic study of the cultural land-scape encourages us to draw from a variety of sources to uncover the totality of human-environment interrelations.[1] The notion was decep-tively simple: nature was the medium, culture the agent, and the cultural landscape was the result, and therefore, all landscapes held clues to the cultural ideals and traditions of the people who created them.[2] So, as a student, I selected what I thought was a relatively easy thesis subject in an old road called Zane's Trace. But the Zane's Trace that I encountered during seventeen days of fieldwork through ten Ohio counties raised more questions than it answered. It was the beginning of a career-long journey to better understand the fundamental geographic notions of landscape, place, and scale.

Zane's Trace was the first formally sanctioned nonmilitary road in the Northwest Territory. Settler-developers blazed the route from 1796 to 1797 from what is now Wheeling, West Virginia, to Maysville, Kentucky, through the interior of the Ohio Country. Roughly paralleling the ancient glacial moraine formed at the end of the last glacial period, the Trace followed the edge of the Ohio hill country, crossing the Muskingum, Hocking, and Scioto Rivers in a broad arc through a variety of landscapes. The routes of Zane's Trace played a role in the pattern of settlement and the development of circulation patterns. It was also an instrument of territoriality as it shaped settlement and directed trade. And Zane's Trace continues to constitute place along its route. This essay explores the evolution of the cultural landscape along its route, finding unity amid a diversity of culture areas, property systems, and natural landscapes to provide one avenue of insight into the processes of exploration, delineation, and subdivision—the essential elements of the settler project. It explores how this route was implicated in dispossession as it shaped settlement until it was made remote by the shifting scales of transportation, political machinations, and westward settlement. Yet, the current fragmentary landscape not only demonstrates the persistence of Zane's Trace through time, but also points to powerful historical processes that influenced its development, disillusion, commemoration, and now designation as a historic resource.

Ebenezer Zane was a significant historical figure in his own right, a veteran of the Revolutionary War, founder of Wheeling, Virginia, and developer with a clear view of the Ohio Country and a desire to see Wheeling reign as the gateway.[3] Ebenezer Zane's petition to Congress to locate an overland route to and from the Ohio River opposite Kentucky, and the conditional acceptance of his petition, provides insight into the nature of the initial idea. Zane was apparently satisfied with the commercial opportunities presented by the traffic on the route. He petitioned Congress for no other compensation for his trouble, nor any reimbursement of his expenses, than the right to locate his military bounty holdings at the crossings of the Muskingum, Hocking, and Scioto Rivers.[4] Notably, Zane supported his petition by citing a savings in time and money in the travel of emigrants and mail from Philadelphia to Fort Washington (Cincinnati) and Frankfort, Kentucky. This approach appears to have satisfied the political and military interests of Congress, as on May 17, 1796, a bill authorizing the blazing of the Trace was approved. As we will see, this fixation on saving time and money—the need to "annihilate space by time"—had grave implications for the people and places along its route. Zane, his family, Native guides, and, in all likelihood, enslaved people brought to what was then a remote corner of

Virginia, blazed the trail along the most suitable route between Wheeling and Maysville. The exact route was at Zane's discretion, restricted only by prior land claims, salt springs, and the interests of transportation.[5] The Trace was impressed directly onto the landscape—never surveyed, mapped, or formally recorded for Congress—as an articulation of the initial idea of Zane's Trace on the land. Thus, Zane's Tracts—surveyed by none other than the Ohio Company's Rufus Putnam and located on the site of present-day Zanesville, Lancaster, and Chillicothe—were the last of the pre–Congressional Survey land grants. Each evolved into important territorial administrative centers that guided the expression of state power in the unorganized interior.[6]

Zane's Trace was articulated in an already rich cultural environment. Long before the first contact, the landscape of the Ohio Country was transformed from the natural to the cultural. The mounds, extensive geometric forms, and burial works are testaments to the long precontact occupation and reveal enduring long-distance relationships: a dense network of meaningful places across the landscape. Humans have occupied the Ohio Country for at least fifteen thousand years. Archaeological evidence suggests that Ohio's prehistoric inhabitants engaged in extensive long-distance travel and trade, necessitating a network of long-distance footpaths and traces.

By the mid-seventeenth century, disease, famine, and warfare—the disruption of livelihood systems by imperial and colonial vectors—had ended that long occupation, as it opened space for an array of Native refugees to the "middle ground" of the Ohio Country.[7] New Native spaces and geographic knowledge evolved relative to an ever-present world economy. Indeed, the Trace evolved through this vast network of ancient places, trails of traders, and the war roads established from the imperial expansion through the tumult of the 1780s and 1790s, absorbing the Ohio Country into a capitalist world-system, all the while transmitting imperfect geographic knowledge of the country back to the metropole.[8] The location of roads and routes evolved into a spine of speculation, an essential band of an "interlocking web of exchange flows that absorbed most Appalachians within the pervasive reach of global commodity chains."[9]

The Trace loosely follows the terminal moraine of the glaciers, so the initial idea was expressed through a variety of landforms within three distinct physiographic sections: the Lexington Plain near the southern reaches, the Glaciated Appalachian Plateau in the central portion, and the Unglaciated Appalachian Plateau in the eastern and south-central portions. Each physiographic region presented different possibilities for cultural expression and the location of the initial and eventual routes of the thoroughfare. The road pattern is not as affected by the topography in the Lexington Plain as it is elsewhere in the unglaciated plateau, and settlement nucleation generally occurs on the cleared interfluves. The Glaciated Appalachian Plateau presents an entirely different physical possibility for cultural expression. Glacial deposition and erosion have broadened and flattened the valleys and rounded the hills and ridges. Located between the rugged hill country to the west and the gentle Till Plains to the east, the region is physically and culturally "in-between" the Appalachian East and agricultural Midwest.[10]

The highly dissected, rugged topography of the Unglaciated Appalachian Plateau limits the possibilities for route location and determines the location of settlement nucleation. The generation of dry, level, and direct overland routes has been suggested as originating with the migratory movement of animals and the extensive trade and long-distance travel routes of Native Americans, overwritten by the evolving transportation network of an expanding world-system. These routes generally followed ridges and were analogous to a braided stream, constantly shifting to avoid impassable ground.[11] The ridges offered the driest and least eroded courses, were windswept of snow and some debris, and provided a prospect from which to view the surrounding landscape.[12]

The conditions of 1796 allowed Zane to locate his route free (for the most part) from the encumbrances of private property, although property interests—his among them—undoubtedly shaped its location. Zane's Trace is expressed within four different cultural overlays in the form of land survey districts: the Virginia Military District, the Congressional Lands, the United States Military District, and the Seven Ranges. The survey systems determined not only the subdivision of land but also the location, period, and method of land sale and distribution.[13] The relationship between the land survey system and the settlement patterns of eastern migrants has long been recognized, the general route of the Trace having been demonstrated as directing the settlement of Ohio by early Anglo-Americans.[14]

Both the type of land survey and the timing of Anglo-American settlement influenced the form of the actual routes of the Trace and shaped the initial cultural character along its route. In some places like the Seven Ranges, the Trace was established after formal survey; in other places, such as the United States Military District, it accompanied formal survey; and in the Congress lands, it preceded survey. These contrasting land systems had an enormous effect on the cultural landscape that followed in its wake.

The irregular metes-and-bounds system of the Virginia Military District suggested an organic method of land alienation; in contrast, the regularity of the township-and-range surveys expressed a rational method of land alienation. The relation with natural features typical of the Virginia Military District survey greatly reduced public expenditure on infrastructure improvement and maintenance, at the cost of extensive litigation wrought by conflicting land claims.[15] This system of land alienation ensured that absentee owners restricted settlement in a large portion of the Virginia Military District.[16] To the traveler, the impression of the Virginia Military District is dramatically different from that of the regularly (i.e., rectilinearly) surveyed Congress lands. The largest proportional concentration of southern, mostly Virginian, migrants were expected to be found in the townships of the Virginia Military District. Indeed, census data from 1850 indicate a slight plurality of southern migrants in the Virginia Military District, with an important exception: high concentrations of Pennsylvania settlers near its southern terminus in Adams County, illustrating the effects of both the Trace and the Ohio River in channeling settlement both down- and upstream. By midcentury, the African American presence along the Trace was concentrated in the vicinity of the larger cities of Chillicothe (11.6 percent of the total population); Lancaster (4 percent); and a portion of Zanesville (Springfield Township, 4 percent of the total population, 2.9 percent in Zanesville).

The settlement convergence of culturally diverse migrant groups produced acculturation, but certainly not total assimilation, and the route of the Trace produced distant regional flavors. Virginia land barons, Pennsylvania settlers, scattered Yankees, and large African American communities clustered in river cities and in some farming settlements all reflected the relationship between the Trace, land survey systems, and the pattern of settlement. Zane's Trace served as a great interior artery from the northern heartland to the southern interior, a conduit of migration and an agent of landscape change until the expansion of the National Road when the axis of trade and traffic shifted west. As curves were straightened and grades flattened, the initial expression of Zane's Trace began to fade from the landscape.

So, how to engage—much less understand—the swirl and complexity of such a cultural landscape? To get past the myths, the misunderstandings, the erasures? To see through to the real? In the spirit of geographic exploration, I decided to approach people and the land along Zane's Trace directly and on their terms: to experience space in real time through direct and sustained interaction over seventeen days, retracing Zane by following its landscape signatures—traces, homes, taverns, stars, and signs—by hiking its 230-mile route. Fortunately, the people and the land along Zane's Trace could be approached directly, and on their terms. The feature of the Trace, which was initially expressed and functioned as a footpath, invites low locomotion that keeps intercourse down to a human scale, allowing time to "recognize forms that express function and process, to see problems implicit in location and areal extension, to think about joint or disjunct occurrence" through "being afoot, sleeping out . . . seeing the land."[17] A feature such as the Trace allowed me to experience space in real time while being keenly aware of my particular situatedness and the liberties for travel that it allowed. Movement across space, even in the Old Northwest, was conditioned and regulated relative to categories of race and class well into the modern era, and the present day.

Perhaps the most compelling of the landscape signatures is the actual remnant of the Trace, the relic features of the long-forgotten road (fig. 6.1). Found along the length of the route in many forms, these elements express the processes of landscape change directly associated with the changing relationship of society to technology, and therefore, society to space and time. As curves were straightened and grades flattened, the initial expression of Zane's Trace began to change in function and form, and it began to fade from the landscape. Yet, across the edge of Appalachian Ohio, township and property boundaries, farm lanes and wood lots, clearly express the initial idea of Zane's Trace. The most vivid relic features of the initial idea were cast by the thousands of anonymous travelers—human and nonhuman alike—simply by the act of movement across space, as migrants, settlers, and drovers and their herds join commercial traffic and mail, representing vernacular control of siting and road maintenance.[18] Yet these travelers were following a general course determined by the processes of the global economy and the actors who held a stake in the creation of landscapes. But so much is absent in the

FIG. 6.1. Relic braid of Zane's Trace, Liberty Township, Adams County, Ohio. Photo by author.

visible landscape—hundreds of features, sites, homes, and places—true traces that are long missing from the scene: spectral elements, neither material objects nor stern absences, that are challenging to recognize, let alone interpret and address.[19] For example, Eagle Creek, the site of the momentous revivals of the Second Great Awakening, or the African American hamlet of Cherry Fork, wiped off the map, go unseen but still reside in place.[20]

Next to the traces, the most abundant clues to culture are homes: folk, vernacular, popular, and high-style buildings reflecting and re-creating the historical processes channeled through the Trace over time. Folk types of domestic architecture are reinvented across time and space, while popular and high-style forms of architecture are more suggestive of a place in time. Early forms of architecture are often of and by the land, constructed of local materials arranged according to a traditional plan and local situation reflecting the traditions of East Anglia and Saxony via Pennsylvania and Virginia. As the powers of the market encroach across space, materials appear from distant places, shaped by elite fashions hundreds or thousands of miles away. The Kirker Farmstead in Adams County near the southern terminus illustrates several critical themes associated with the landscape of Zane's Trace. A native of Ireland raised in the heart of the Pennsylvania Culture Area who moved to Kentucky at the cusp of the revolutionary transition of the Ohio Country, Thomas Kirker was placed at the confluence of many critical social, political, and religious narratives. The southern folk I-house, the Irish stone cottage, and the Pennsylvania barn exemplify the fusion of cultures.

Likewise, the remaining taverns are perhaps the most useful landscape signatures for locating and understanding the early route of the Trace and for situating ourselves in relation to time and space relationships. They were the seminal outposts of market capitalism, geographically expressing the arrival of the capitalist world-system to the Ohio Country.[21] The travelers' inns were generally situated at logical points based on distance relationships, first on foot and bridle travel, and later on stagecoach travel. The very location of such relic features is a testament to forgotten notions of space and time (fig. 6.2). The Treber Inn is the archetype of the frontier tavern. Marylander John Treber built his iconic tavern on Brush Creek in 1797 in what would become Adams County. Well built in log and supplemented by a limestone wing, the building was designed as a commercial space oriented to a much larger economic network. The first structure on the site was constructed as a residence, but the volume of pedestrian traffic soon brought a change in function, and thus a subsequent change in the interior design of the structure.[22]

FIG. 6.2. The Eager Inn Tavern, Morgantown, Benton Township, Pike County, Ohio. Photo by author.

The subdivision of the interior, particularly the use of multiple hearths built into a triangular chimney and the unusual room arrangement on the second floor, reflects the function of the tavern. The commodious one-and-a-half-story rear addition is constructed of locally quarried rough-cut limestone, and like the cottage component of the Kirker Place, a fusion of folk and popular architectural forms.

Fortunately, along the routes of the Trace there is an abundance of signs—actual signs—demarcating the route, representing the course for commercial and civic purposes, and reshaping the local understanding of place. The signs range from the official representation of a state historical marker, the local representation of historical societies, the commercial representation of the business entities (there were two Zane Trace Bed and Breakfasts, for example), and the informal representations by interested individuals. Physical markers—cairns, slabs of rock, entrance gates, directional arrows—are generally less obtrusive than written signs. Cairns and gates simply make us aware of historical features, whereas words on signposts function both as physical objects and as linguistic symbols requiring appraisal and an assessment of their veracity. Even the least conspicuous marker on the most dramatic site drastically alters the context and the flavor of the historical experience.[23] Signs were also considered to include the assemblages of personal memorials found marking individual or community grave sites, which also marked the route of the Trace.[24] The collection of graves did not order the land, but they ordered people's perception of the land and of their communities, serving to perpetuate the cumulative idea of Zane's Trace.[25] An example of a grave that clearly marks the route is the well-kept military headstone of Zechariah M. Crane, a private soldier in the Thirteenth Regiment, Kentucky Mounted Militia, who died and was buried on the route home from the War of 1812; it marks the Trace in place and time, even as the thousands of unmarked graves along its route go unseen.[26]

Finally, good luck would allow me to meet those rare souls who are the preservers of local wisdom—the "stars," in folklorist Henry Glassie's opinion. As the Trace is part of the local mythology of the towns and countryside along the way, the features constitute an integral component of the local understanding of place. In each town or village, there are those who possess an extraordinary understanding and perpetuate the cumulative idea through writing, stories, and chat. For example, the late Gleena Blackburn, a retired teacher and storyteller, offered an immense

amount of information through the compressed narrative of the mag-
nificently told story. Sitting along the roadside, we spoke for well over
an hour as she shared a collage of geography, memory, and sentiment
welded together and burnished by art and imagination.[27] She was amazed
that I found her, a guide, in such a remote place, and mapped out the
route of the Trace through her personal geography.

And that brings us to the ultimate lessons of Zane's Trace. Careful
study of the Trace reveals a confused jumble of scales and spatial relations
assembled, amended, shattered, and reformed in order to annihilate
space by time—to speed the mail.[28] Therefore, a revolution in temporal
and spatial relations often entails not only the destruction of ways of life
and social practices built around preceding time-space systems but the
"creative destruction" of a wide range of physical assets embedded in
the landscape.[29] The sudden shifting of scale is a form of violence that
entails the destruction not only of ways of life and social practices built
around preceding time-space systems but of real material landscapes as
well.[30] Until the expansion of the National Road into the Ohio Country,
Zane's Trace served as a great interior artery from the northern heartland
to the southern interior, a critical adjunct to the Ohio and Mississippi
river systems, for a time. The funding of the Maysville Road, an extension of the Trace to Lexington, and the plans for the establishment of a
National Road from Zanesville to Florence, Alabama, and New Orleans
was an issue of national debate and local consequence. When the national
Republican dream of a federal transportation system died with Andrew
Jackson's 1830 veto of the Maysville Road bill, the peripheral nature of
the southern route of Zane's Trace was assured.[31]

A sequence of maps of any section of the Trace speaks to the manifes-
tation of changing distance relationships that characterized the transition
of part of the Ohio Country from periphery to core, to semiperiphery
of a dynamic world economy. Each succeeding map conveys important
clues to the place of Zane's Trace in time, expressing the rise and fall of
its significance as the interior of Ohio developed, as well as the methods
of transportation that reordered distance relationships. Cartographic
sources, however, exclude the meaning of the distance relationships
that maps symbolize. For example, the once-prosperous village of Jacksonville, built on Zane's Trace at a key river crossing, was established
and grew relative to a frame of geographic scale related to animate
long-distance travel and trade. By 1900, the once-prosperous village of

folk architecture, local lumber, and local materials "was declining in population and commercial importance from its proximity to the new town of Peebles."[32] Peebles represents the movement of a place into the core; the streetscape of Jacksonville represents the atrophied landscape of the periphery. Large portions of the Virginia Military District, removed from access to rail transportation, represent this condition. Platted at the intersection of the Maysville Turnpike and the Norfolk and Western Railroad line, the Main Street of the railroad town of Peebles represents a landscape of national architecture, milled lumber, and mass production in stark contrast to the tavern towns such as Jacksonville.

With the shifts in scale and ongoing improvements, the original Zane's Trace had quickly lost its initial identity. Yet the Trace was constantly re-created and re-presented over time. "It was known by the name of Zane's road, the Limestone road, and the Limestone and Chillicothe Road . . . afterward the 'New State Road,'" as it was called, laid out over the same general line, but so changed and altered in many parts as to form a new road.[33] With slippery scales and constant technological innovation, the function of Zane's Trace was transformed: portions were reconstructed in the medium of the era and hardened just as other portions faded away, proving the maxim that there is no such thing as a stationary highway. Indeed, the Trace was the precursor to the western-oriented landscapes of the National Road, within which it was quickly subsumed between Wheeling and Zanesville. For example, near an iconic S-bridge on the National Road alignment west of New Concord, one can see the remnants of the Trace and National Road, the B&O railroad, and US 40 and Interstate 70, all within a quarter of a mile of one another, reflecting five distinct scaler relationships that were determined by economic and technological factors far beyond any local control.

Indeed, due to rapidly changing economic and technological innovation, the function of Zane's Trace was transformed: portions of the route were reconstructed in the medium of the era—the National Road, US 40, Interstate 70—just as other portions were made remote. It is a story of how the changing nature of transportation systems greatly affected the cultural environment, increasing the prominence of some places and relegating others to obscurity or destruction—a testament to the ephemeral character of even the most important aspects of our collective history. Each successive landscape developed during subsequent technical regimes relative to this broad initial imprint, which persisted in a highly selective and uneven manner, depending on the processes of accumulation and the struggle over property and power that played out in that place.[34] If power entails the creation and manipulation of social signification, the making of meaning, then history and landscape are avenues of power. By re-creating landscapes, filling them with signs, preserving some artifacts and destroying others, historians, activists, and preservationists produce meaning on the landscape, thereby affecting the everyday behavior of the people who call these subtly manufactured places their homes.[35] The question of why some historical events resonate and others fade is answered in both the inherent duplicity of landscape and by the way in which conflicts are constructed into historical events or consigned only to the memories of participants.

The Trace was found to be more than a sum of artifacts, not a single route or a place but rather a cumulative idea that is constantly re-presented in a postindustrial era that simply cannot grasp the distance relationships that were expressed in the initial articulation. Perhaps the lesson is that we should confront such fragmentary landscapes by engaging with their history, nature, myth, and transitoriness, not as some anomaly but as illuminating a fundamental aspect of our culture and our economy.[36] Above all, Zane's Trace calls us to engage the complexity of the Ohio County in its totality, to subvert the tyranny of scale, and make time to see through that "shallow screen that intervenes between our present lives and our history" to reveal a more democratic, honest, and inclusive history of dispossession, settlement, and the production of space in the Ohio Country.[37]

Notes

1. Hubert G. H. Wilhelm, *Landscape and Culture Course Book* (Athens: Ohio University Department of Geography, 1996); and William M. Hunter, "Landscape, the Cumulative Idea and the Cultural Geography of Zane's Trace" (master's thesis, Ohio University, 1998).
2. Carl O. Sauer, "The Morphology of Landscape," in *Land and Life: The Writings of Carl Ortwin Sauer,* ed. John Leighly (Berkeley: University of California Press, 1965).
3. Clement L. Martzoloff, "Zane's Trace," *Ohio Archaeological and Historical Publications,* vol. 13 (Columbus, OH: Fred T. Herr, 1904).
4. Martzoloff.

5. Martzoloff, 313; and John B. Ray, "Zane's Trace, 1796–1812: A Study in Historical Geography" (PhD diss., Indiana University of Pennsylvania, 1968), 40.
6. Christopher E. Sherman, *Original Ohio Land Subdivisions: Being Volume III—Final Report* (Columbus: Press of the Ohio State Reformatory, 1925), 116.
7. Richard White, *The Middle Ground: Indians, Empires and Republics in the Great Lakes Region, 1650–1815* (Cambridge: Cambridge University Press, 1991).
8. Wilma A. Dunaway, *The First American Frontier: Transition to Capitalism in Southern Appalachia, 1700–1860* (Chapel Hill: University of North Carolina Press, 1996).
9. Dunaway, 246.
10. Nancy R. Bain, "Change on the Edge of Ohio," in *A Geography of Ohio,* ed. Leonard Peaceful (Kent, OH: Kent State University Press, 1996).
11. Ray, "Zane's Trace."
12. Archer B. Hulbert, "The Indian Thoroughfares of Ohio," *Ohio State Archaeological and Historical Quarterly* 8 (1900): 262–66; and Jay Appleton, *The Experience of Landscape.* (London: John Wiley, 1975).
13. Norman J. W. Thrower, *Original Survey and Land Subdivision: A Comparative Study of the Form and Effect of Contrasting Cadastral Surveys* (Chicago: Rand McNally, 1957).
14. Hubert G. H. Wilhelm, "The Pennsylvania-Dutch Barn in Southeastern Ohio," in *Man and Cultural Heritage, Geoscience and Man,* vol. 5, ed. H. J. Walker and W. G. Haag (Baton Rouge: Louisiana State University, 1974); and Hubert G. H. Wilhelm and Allen G. Noble, "Ohio's Settlement Landscape," in *A Geography of Ohio,* ed. Leonard Peaceful (Kent, OH: Kent State University Press, 1996).
15. Thrower, *Original Survey and Land Subdivision;* and John F. Hart, *The Look of the Land* (Englewood Cliffs, NJ: Prentice-Hall, 1975).
16. Andrew R. L. Cayton, *The Frontier Republic: Ideology and Politics in the Ohio Country, 1780–1825* (Kent, OH: Kent State University Press, 1989).
17. Carl O. Sauer, "The Education of a Geographer," in *Annals of the American Association of Geographers* 46, no. 3 (1956): 287–99.
18. John R. Stilgoe, *Common Landscapes of America, 1580 to 1845* (New Haven, CT: Yale University Press, 1982).
19. Deryck Holdsworth, "The Archives and the Landscape: Texts for the Analysis of the Built Environment," in *Vision, Culture, and Landscape,* ed. Paul Growth (Berkeley: Department of Landscape Architecture, University of California, 1997); and Anne Mosher, "Low Bridge, No Bridge: Public Memory and Creative Destruction along the Erie Canal" (paper presented at the annual meeting of the Association of American Geographers, Chicago, March 7–11, 2006).

20. Nelson W. Evans and Emmons B. Stivers, *A History of Adams County, Ohio* (West Union, OH: E. B. Stivers, 1900); and Richard H. Schein, "The Normative Dimension of Landscape," in *Everyday America: Cultural Landscape Studies after J. B. Jackson,* ed. Chris Wilson and Paul Groth (Berkeley: University of California Press, 2003).

21. Dunaway, *The First American Frontier.*

22. Evans and Stivers, *A History of Adams County, Ohio.*

23. David Lowenthal, "Age and Artifact," in *The Interpretation of Ordinary Landscapes,* ed. D. W. Meinig (Oxford: Oxford University Press, 1979), 110.

24. Lowenthal, 123.

25. Stilgoe, *Common Landscapes of America.*

26. Lowenthal, "Age and Artifact."

27. Yi-Fu Tuan, *Space and Place: The Perspective of Experience* (Minneapolis: University of Minnesota Press, 1977), 729.

28. N. Brenner, "The Limits to Scale? Methodological Reflections on Scalar Structuration," *Progress in Human Geography* 25 (2001): 591–614.

29. David Harvey, *The Condition of Postmodernity* (Cambridge: Blackwell, 1989), 453.

30. David Harvey, *The Limits to Capital* (Chicago: University of Chicago Press, 1982).

31. Charles Sellers, *The Market Revolution: Jacksonian America, 1815–1846* (New York: Oxford University Press, 1991), 316.

32. Evans and Stivers, *A History of Adams County, Ohio,* 445.

33. Ray, "Zanes's Trace," 57.

34. D. Hayden, *The Power of Place: Urban Landscapes as Public History* (Cambridge, MA: MIT Press, 1995).

35. Richard Peet, "A Sign Taken for History: Daniel Shay's Memorial in Petersham, Massachusetts," *Annals of the Association of American Geographers* 86 (1996): 21–43.

36. R. A. Salerno, *Landscapes of Abandonment: Capitalism, Modernity and Estrangement* (Albany: State University of New York Press, 2003).

37. Robert Hewison quoted in Harvey, *The Condition of Postmodernity,* 87.

7

Ice Water Baths and Rising Waters

*Dudley Woodbridge Jr.'s Commercial
Connections along the Ohio and Its
Tributaries in the Early Republic*

KIM M. GRUENWALD

The title of David McCullough's final book, *The Pioneers: The Heroic Story of the Settlers Who Brought the American Ideal West,* leaves readers in no doubt about his thesis as he chronicles the early history of Marietta, established by the Ohio Company in 1789. On a snowy evening in January of 1790, a group of settlers held a meeting to debate those very ideals. Four possible topics were put up to a vote. One involved the security of property: "Is the Police of the City of Marietta equal to the good Gov of the same." Another involved a moral question: "Whether Capital punishment ought ever to be instituted." The third focused on the very organization of society itself: "Is the popular opinion true that the Interests of the farmer, the mechanic & the merchants are one & the same inseparably connected." But the men chose instead the first one listed: "Whether the Am States have contravariant to the regulations of the Span Govt a right founded in the Customs & Laws of Nations to navigate the Mississippi from its source to its mouth." That, in a nutshell, was what it was all about. Would they be able to get their crops to market down the Ohio and Mississippi Rivers through New Orleans, then controlled by a foreign power?[1]

The Ohio River begins where the Allegheny and Monongahela merge at Pittsburgh in western Pennsylvania. Marietta sits at the mouth of the Muskingum River, about 170 miles southwest of the Ohio's source, and 130 miles further on lies the Big Sandy River at the boundary of present-day West Virginia and Kentucky. Another sixty miles brings travelers to Cincinnati, but thereafter things get complicated. There is a break in navigation where the Ohio flows over a series of rapids, dropping twenty feet in elevation over three miles. That might not sound like much, but the so-called Falls of the Ohio wreaked havoc with shipping schedules for decades, and Louisville businessmen stood ready to facilitate the flow of goods from Pittsburgh six hundred miles upriver to New Orleans on the Gulf of Mexico, with warehouses that stored goods waiting for the river to rise. All told, eighteen major tributaries and many more minor ones drain over two hundred thousand square miles in the Ohio Valley before arriving at Cairo, Illinois, to make the Mississippi mighty nearly one thousand miles from its source.[2]

The settling of early Ohio is all about the rivers—what Americans called the western waters. The era of Marietta's founding has a unique place in the story of the expansion of the United States. When historians study colonial America, they look at the Atlantic World of oceangoing ships and the settling of the coast to the fall line of rivers, the furthest point of navigation upstream from the coast. Backcountry settlers on the frontier sold crops and bought goods at towns along the fall line. Much of the story of the settling of the plains beyond the Mississippi River during the nineteenth century is about overland journeys, culminating in the building of railroads. But it is no wonder that the Lewis and Clark Expedition set out to explore the new Louisiana Purchase along the Missouri River, for Americans had been relying on rivers to stake their claim to North America from the 1750s through the first decades of the founding of a new nation. Marietta's history is part of that story of life on the western waters.

McCullough's cast of characters includes Ohio Company founders, Revolutionary War veterans, and professional men. What is missing, though, or at any rate assigned to the periphery, are the settlement's men of business. Although Connecticut merchant and judge Dudley

Woodbridge established one of the first stores in Marietta, it would be his son who established the family's far-reaching commercial connections from Philadelphia to Pittsburgh to the Ohio River and beyond in the years that followed. Those were the kinds of connections that bound West and East together and helped a new nation begin the task of establishing a continental empire. In January of 1797, Dudley Woodbridge sent his son to Philadelphia to purchase some goods for their store. The eighteen-year-old had safely crossed the Ohio but ran into trouble on one of the river's tributaries south of Wheeling. "I attempted to ford Grave Creek, rode in, the current very swift my horse swam and could not get up the opposite bank, wheeled about, I jumped off and the current carried me about 7 rods before I could make the shore, my boots being full of water and my clothes heavy, I got hold of a twig which gave way and I went in head and ears but finally got out, rode 12 miles to Wheeling Creek and dryed myself." Thus did Dudley Woodbridge Jr. survive his baptism in western waters and his initiation into the hazardous life of making one's living on the Ohio River.[3]

Dudley Woodbridge arranged for his son to serve as a merchant's apprentice in Philadelphia at the age of sixteen, then brought him west to run his store a year later. The path to success did not always run smoothly as Dudley Woodbridge Jr. dealt with a critical father, partnered for a time with Harman Blennerhassett (which led to testifying in Aaron's Burr trial), and grieved for his first wife, who died shortly after the birth of their daughter. A letter from his sister-in-law to her son who served as a clerk for a short time gives us a second-hand view of how Dudley Woodbridge Jr. believed a merchant should conduct business. Forging connections meant developing skills in handling people. A merchant could not be quiet, bashful, or reserved, and should always be polite and obliging when dealing with customers. Running a business in the West required a talent for speculation and a willingness to take risks, as well as attention to detail and knowledge of markets. His nephew apparently turned his back on the work as "drudgery," but Woodbridge thrived on it.[4]

Dudley Woodbridge Jr. used the rivers to establish Marietta as a sub-regional hub for the region in the opening decades of the nineteenth century. Goods came from Philadelphia to Marietta, and then on to other places along the Ohio and its tributaries, both north and south of the river. Marietta merchants then shipped flour, whiskey, and other goods south to New Orleans and on to the Atlantic World. There were three orders of towns in the early West. First were the largest—the ports of entry for the region like Pittsburgh, Cincinnati, and Lexington. Lower in the hierarchy were medium-sized towns like Marietta, where merchants gathered produce from their own hinterlands and provided eastern goods in exchange. The small, local communities in Marietta's hinterland made up the last order, and might house only a mill and a local store where people from the area could meet and exchange news.[5] Commercial connections between these three orders of towns on both sides of the Ohio; connections between Ohio, the East Coast, and the Gulf of Mexico; and connections between people north and south of the river's course laid the foundation for a new continental empire.

The first connections needed to build a subregional hub were local. Dudley Woodbridge Jr. employed a few young men as clerks to run the store and take messages to other stores up the Muskingum and elsewhere when he was absent. Woodbridge also sent them on the occasional run to Pittsburgh for supplies. On one such trip, Woodbridge instructed Henry Mills to take charge of goods that had been sent from Philadelphia and make sure that all the packages had arrived and were undamaged. The Pittsburgh merchant who had stored the goods had already paid the wagon drivers who had delivered them, so Mills had only to bring the bill back home. The clerk needed to procure a boat, load the goods, buy nails, and head downriver. On the way, Woodbridge wanted the clerk to stop in Steubenville for flour and in Wheeling for a trunk of books that had gone missing a while back.[6]

Woodbridge began in 1799 by simply supplying local traders with goods such as whiskey, powder, and lead in exchange for furs, skins, cash, and salt. In July and August, he told Silas Bingham and James White that they were to return anything they did not sell in the fall and he would give them 20 percent of the sales they did make. But within a few years, he supplied shopkeepers in smaller towns with hardware, textiles, tools, and anything else they wanted from the East. A contract from 1804 with Increase Matthews states:

> Our terms follow: provided you send a memorandum of the principal articles wanted before the goods are purchased and the money is paid in Philadelphia, at the time of purchase we should charge 10% of the cost and carriage or we will furnish you with groceries at 60 days credit for 15 percent

advance on cost and carriage, and dry goods on 6 months
credit for 20% advance . . . should the money be remitted
to Philadelphia before due, interest will be allowed at 1%
advance for paying the money in Philadelphia.

Most agreements were more general and involved a broad selection of
goods. Woodbridge supplied shopkeepers in towns along the Muskingum
and Little Muskingum Rivers, Duck Creek, Wolf Creek, and the Little
Hocking River in Ohio, as well as the Little Kanawha River and other
creeks south of the Ohio in western Virginia.[7]

Country stores in smaller towns were not always large or well stocked.
In the early years, a trader with a couple of chests of goods might call
his place a store. One traveler wrote about three "warehouses" at the
confluence of the Ohio and Little Miami Rivers, at least one of which
was simply a single room full of European goods. Bostonian John May
rented half of a building in Wheeling in 1789, and another trader ran his
own business at the opposite end. May opened for business in the middle
of August and recorded that the first week or so, he had folks from the
area coming in to look but not buy. Near the end of his second week, a
group of women came in and bought goods with cash, and that Satur-
day, he was very busy exchanging goods for furs and deerskins, which
he had plenty of time to prepare and pack the following week because
business was slow. Over the next few months, he pickled peaches from
his landlord to sell in Marietta, bartered local butter, and traded goods
for deerskins and ginseng. May also outfitted boats for people heading
downriver, including "a Mrs [Dudley] Woodbridge and young family
from Norwich." By early November he had sold almost all his goods, so
he headed home with his pelts and medicinal plants for sale back east.
May's experiences show that some weeks were tediously slow, only to
be followed by a flurry of activity at the end. There was some cash to be
had, but most of the trade was for things he intended to sell elsewhere.[8]

The next ring of local connections involved branch stores in the
third order of western towns. Dudley Woodbridge Jr. set up stores in
partnerships with his most trusted associates in towns located at the
head of navigation along Ohio tributaries like the Hocking River. James
Converse and Woodbridge established a store in Lancaster, one of the
sites originally granted to Ebenezer Zane. When Zane blazed a trace from
Wheeling in western Virginia to Limestone (Maysville) in Kentucky in

1796 and 1797, he asked for a section where the route crossed the rivers that ran north at the farthest point a keelboat could go on the largest tributaries. By 1811 the population of Lancaster was only perhaps 350, but farmers in the area could barter for goods in the Woodbridge store, and then Converse sent their crops seventy miles south to the Ohio and on to New Orleans.[9]

One other local connection involving waterways deserves to be noted—the partnership between merchants and farmers. In February of 1806, the citizens of Marietta organized a lottery to raise funds for a bridge over the Little Muskingum River to make it easier to get to town from the countryside. Most of those who subscribed pledged corn, whisky, and labor at under five dollars apiece. Merchants and professionals pledged cash, with most of it coming from the Woodbridge family. Merchants and farmers both wanted to facilitate trade.[10]

In 1807 Woodbridge's brother William wrote to their uncle back east that "our little place continues to increase in wealth & population Thanks be to the unremitting activity of our commercial people." When Dudley Woodbridge Jr. first took over his father's business, the firm's ledgers recorded many customers by location only—Catts Creek, Duck Creek, Wolf Creek, and Bull Creek, among others. But by 1811, the vast majority of customers were listed by town and township. Marietta's population had grown to nearly six thousand, who tended more than four times that number of livestock and who had improved seventeen thousand acres of fields and orchards. Washington County towns supported tanneries, distilleries, gristmills, and sawmills, and Marietta itself boasted the county's only carding machine and ropewalk, as well as concerns that manufactured nails, hats, and tin plating. Most of this manufacturing was probably for local consumption, but clearly the county had a well-established commercial community within twenty years or so of its founding.[11]

Merchants needed to make national connections to bring goods to Ohio from Philadelphia. The first step for that is clear from an ad placed in a Chillicothe newspaper from one H. Fullerton in March of 1807: "I wish to start to Philadelphia the first of April for a supply of goods, and from experience find it necessary to have money when I start; therefore I request all those indebted to me to be punctual in discharging their accounts before that time as no further indulgence will be given." Once they reached Philadelphia, Woodbridge, his brother John, or one of his agents would spend a week comparing prices, looking for deals, and purchasing goods. Woodbridge warned Thomas Pierce that "a great deal of time and running about will be necessary to obtain goods on tolerable terms." Asa Runyon, another western merchant, wrote that prices differed from shop to shop and might rise 10–15 percent over a day or two. Joseph Hough of Hamilton, Ohio, wrote that it took three months to ride a horse to Philadelphia, purchase goods, then return with wagons to Pittsburgh, keelboats to Cincinnati, and with wagons north to Hamilton. Faced with poor roads and inclement weather, Hough wrote, "Those three months were months of toil and privation and of exposure of every kind."[12]

Dudley Woodbridge Jr. typically arranged two buying trips per year. Here is what one such trip from 1804 looked like: Woodbridge spent approximately $6,000—$1,800 in cash, $4,200 on credit. The grocer accounted for about 40 percent of the final tally (tea, sugar, coffee, snuff, tobacco, pepper, wine, soap, chocolate). The hardware dealer accounted for about 15 percent of the total (buttons, gimlets, brass cocks, whips, saddles, bridles, and bits). Much smaller amounts went to a crockery merchant and a merchant who sold stationary. At the store of one dry goods merchant, Woodbridge spent almost 10 percent of his funds (for some basics for making coats). Thus, nearly 70 percent of the business, mostly on credit, went to five trusted suppliers. The other $1,800, mostly cash, went for all sorts of fabrics from a variety of merchants around the city in amounts ranging from $25 to $400. For all trips during the opening decade of the nineteenth century, dry goods, mostly textiles, would comprise 40–60 percent of the bills, with one large order bought on credit and the rest spread around in smaller lots paid with cash. Woodbridge had all the suppliers send the purchased goods to the grocer, who then packed them for shipment to Pittsburgh by wagon where it was stored in warehouses until the river rose high enough to make the journey down the Ohio.[13]

Dudley's brother Jack made the trip in the fall of 1805; a blotter lays out the details of the trip. Jack purchased $2,819.70 worth of goods on credit and spent $1,103.23 in cash. He reported $109.37 in personal expenses. Shipping the goods cost $6.66 in coppering and portage, $447.29 in wagon bills, $30.00 in freight charges to shift the cargo from Wheeling to Marietta, and $2.50 to shift the goods from shore to store. Thus, freight and expenses accounted for $595.82 out of a grand total of

$4,518.55, or a little less than 15 percent. It looks like a high mark up of prices would indeed lead to a good profit—at least if the customers could pay in a reasonable amount of time, but that did not always happen.[14]

What did all this look like from the Philadelphia point of view? For that we can turn to the ledger of a merchant named Samuel Meeker covering the years 1807 to 1810. It contains 550 accounts, seventy-seven of them in the West—so about 15 percent. He sent supplies to seven firms in Pittsburgh, thirteen in Ohio, and one in Indiana. Fifty-seven of the firms (nearly 75 percent) did business south of the Ohio, including thirty-one in Kentucky and seventeen in Tennessee. Just over half of the customers were in the largest towns—Pittsburgh, Lexington, Cincinnati, Natchez, and New Orleans—with just under half in the second order of towns, the subregional hubs like Marietta. Clearly, westerners south of the river had ties just as strong as those to the north, and the entry ports to the region wielded considerable influence. Anyone from the West seeking credit would need a letter of introduction from someone the Philadelphian knew and trusted. In the early 1800s, eastern merchants sent agents west once or twice a year to collect debts. Between 1807 and 1810, Meeker sold goods on credit to western merchants sixty-nine times. Just over half of the transactions were under $500, just over 20 percent involved sums between $500 and $1,000, and nearly 25 percent were for orders of over $1,000. Meeker's ledger does not indicate the kinds of goods he specialized in, but Dudley Woodbridge Jr.'s totals would have put him in the upper half of such sales.[15]

In addition to risking an ice water bath crossing the Ohio's tributaries, what were some of the other hazards and obstacles merchants faced? First, they could only ship goods for a short time twice a year. During the summer, the river might run so low that nothing but the smallest boats could pass, and in the winter, the river could be choked with ice. The only reliable time to ship goods came with the fall rains and with the rising waters from melting snow in the spring. Here is an account of one of Woodbridge's clerks in March of 1818: "Before you receive this, you will probably hear of the river having been high, it continued rising til it overflowed the town, and several feet higher than the last fresh, measuring two feet on the store floor. The goods I secured by hoisting part aloft and part on the counter, the water got off the floor this morning so I have been able to clean out and get the principal part of the goods to their places today." But it was so dry during the fall of

1816 that Joseph Hough and his men had to unload the boat, scrape out the Ohio's channel, float the boat forward, and reload before continuing on several times.[16]

A second problem was related to the first—shipments of produce went down river at roughly the same time, meaning gluts on the market and falling prices in New Orleans. If the river ran low, delaying shipment, flour and pork spoiled, although the whiskey kept fine—one reason for shipping corn in that form. Even if shipments made it to New Orleans, they might spoil if they sat in warehouses waiting for higher prices. Prices for flour fluctuated wildly between a high of twelve dollars and a low of three dollars per barrel. One historian concluded that most profits came from marking up the goods that came from the East rather than selling their own shipments to good effect. Looking back later at his career, Woodbridge opined that retailing had kept him afloat when speculations in the fur trade and other ventures failed.[17]

Almost all goods were shipped east through New Orleans, but some goods justified the high transportation costs of going back east in wagons over the mountains instead: furs and skins, as expected, but also ginseng, highly sought in China at the time. The China trade began to open in Philadelphia in the 1780s, and by the early 1800s many an Ohio Valley farmer supplemented their income picking it in the wild both north and south of the river. In addition, a medicinal plant called snakeroot was in demand in France. The dried plants brought in much higher prices in relation to their weight than traditional agricultural goods. John May's venture chronicled above is one such example—he brought goods by wagon through the mountains from the East and headed back home the same way with wagons loaded with pelts and dried plants about three months later.[18]

Marietta's first local and national ties had been fairly linear and direct. But as the West's population grew, regional connections became more complex. An illuminating Ohio River travel account comes from a man named Fortescue Cuming in 1807. On a fine afternoon in July, he wrote:

> We proceeded from Marietta, accompanied by a Mr. Fry, a genteel and well informed lawyer, from the vicinity of Boston in search of an establishment in some part of this new country. We had also as a passenger, a countryman, by trade a house carpenter, who resided in Virginia, about 50 miles

lower down the river, and was returning home after a trip up and down the Muskingum as one of the crew of a keel boat. We landed on the right bank at Browning's Tavern, a good house and pleasant situation, almost opposite the Little Kanawha. Several travelers sat down with us to an excellent supper amongst them a merchant from Lexington, a traveling speculator and well digger from French Grant, and a Mr. Smith from Cincinnati who was deputized by the marshal of Virginia to collect evidence for the trial of Colonel Burr and his associates at Richmond.

In less than a day of traveling on the Ohio, then, Cuming encountered a lawyer, a land speculator, a carpenter, and a federal law enforcement officer, among others, and the men hailed from states north and south of the river, as well as from the East.[19] As the artery of trade and communication in the West, the Ohio River brought people together. During the first two decades of the nineteenth century, residents north and south of the river established a thriving commercial community centered on the Ohio and its tributaries, and so they called home "the Western Country."

Up until Jefferson's Embargo Act in 1807, most of Dudley Woodbridge Jr.'s letters had gone to merchants in Philadelphia and Pittsburgh, local traders and shopkeepers, and lawyers who collected debts in Cincinnati, Chillicothe, and Louisville. That changed over the next decade. A whole new wave of settlers came west in the 1810s, and the population rose fast as people bought federal land. The populations of Pittsburgh, Cincinnati, Louisville, and New Orleans surged as well. During the War of 1812, with European trade cut off, internal trade within the Ohio Valley itself expanded to include tools from Pittsburgh and glass from Zanesville, as well as cotton, tobacco, and salt from south of the Ohio. The largest western cities were now both markets for farmers and suppliers of manufactured goods.

Woodbridge's relationship with Pittsburgh reveals how western cities grew. After the disastrous end to his partnership with Blennerhassett and the death of his wife, he left his new baby in the care of his parents and sister and relocated to the Ohio's headwaters for a short time in 1809 and 1810. He kept buying groceries and dry goods from the same suppliers in Philadelphia, but also wrote to Lancaster merchants offering plows, axes, and sickles from Pittsburgh craftsmen and brought hemp, yarn, and tobacco east from Lexington. Yet he wrote home that he missed "the endearing chitchat of my little girl" and that he found the city to be a "bleak" place. He enjoyed the "bustle" of his current home but wanted "to get into a kind of business that would please [him]." The retail business needed to be connected with "some other branch" to be profitable. He had been hearing good things about Ohio, and in the end, he returned to Marietta to operate as a wholesaler.[20]

Back home, Dudley Woodbridge Jr. began by ordering leather from tanners to supply Marietta shoemakers. Soon he was buying nails and wrapping paper in Pittsburgh rather than Philadelphia, as well. Hats and buttons began to appear in his correspondence, and he ordered iron from George Anschutz to sell to manufacturers in Zanesville, north of Marietta. By 1815, iron products made up a quarter of Pittsburgh's manufacturing output, and the city boasted nail factories, a rolling mill, and an air foundry. As its labor force grew, Pittsburgh residents began buying Ohio cheese, Kentucky pork, and salt from western Virginia.[21]

The expansion of Woodbridge's business can best be seen in his ties to Zanesville. Like the town of Lancaster on the Hocking, where Woodbridge had a branch store a decade earlier, Zanesville lay at the point of furthest boat navigation from the Ohio on the Muskingum River. Ebenezer Zane had established a ferry there for people following his trace to Kentucky. The town served as Ohio's state capital for a brief couple of years before the War of 1812, and the population doubled. It grew even faster after the war as land sales boomed north of town with the Muskingum providing access to the Ohio River. In addition to a branch store, Woodbridge supplied a handful of other storekeepers as well. He also provided the raw materials needed for the manufacture of glass, paper, cloth, and other goods. His wholesale business grew and thrived in southern Ohio and western Virginia.[22]

In supplying raw materials to Zanesville manufacturers, Dudley Woodbridge Jr.'s commercial connections also demonstrate connections between North and South in the Ohio Valley, although those connections had been there from the beginning. Ohio Company founder Manasseh Cutler had hoped to fill the new settlement with those from the North, but when he visited Marietta early on, he found worship services that catered to settlers on both sides of the Ohio on Sundays, and settlers trading with others on the opposite banks for meat and corn when supplies ran low. In addition, one of the most trusted local healers was a woman named Rebecca Williams, who lived across the river in what was then western Virginia.[23]

Merchants had wider-ranging connections. When a New Yorker came west in 1813, he carried letters of introduction from fellow merchants in New York, Baltimore, and Philadelphia to their counterparts in Russellville and Lexington, Kentucky, as well as Marietta. Three men established firms called Duncan, Dobbin and Company (Louisville), Forsyth, Dobbin, and Company (Wheeling), and Duncan, Forsyth and Company (Pittsburgh). Other examples abound, and one can trace the organization and dissolution of such businesses in local newspapers when partners advertised to collect debts whenever a firm called it quits. Other connections included helping each other when needed. In June of 1812, Dudley Woodbridge Jr. rode out to see about a boat that hit a snag and sank about ten miles below Marietta. He made sure that the packages were recovered and had been set out to dry, and then wrote to merchants in Limestone (Maysville) and Cincinnati about where they could recover their goods. In addition to tracking down wayward packages, merchants exchanged currency, forwarded letters to clerks, and agreed to come together to hear disputes between their fellow businessmen.[24]

Just as his ties to Pittsburgh manufacturing expanded, Dudley Woodbridge Jr. did more and more business with both manufacturers and producers of raw materials south of the Ohio. Before the War of 1812, he bought salt from an Ohio supplier, but switched to suppliers in western Virginia, and indeed with time Kanawha salt became a staple throughout the Ohio Valley. Woodbridge bought gunpowder and hemp from Lexington manufacturers and shipped it to Zanesville and Pittsburgh. He sold salt to a firm in Nashville in exchange for cotton. Woodbridge provided glass and pottery manufacturers in Zanesville with white and red lead from Ste. Genevieve in Missouri.[25]

In 1813, Dudley Woodbridge wrote twice looking for sugar and cotton to a firm called Baum and Perry in Cincinnati, which was one of the first companies to operate commercial barges on the Ohio and Mississippi Rivers. The barges could be up to one-hundred-feet long and carry one hundred tons of freight. Baum and Perry loaded them with whiskey, flour, and pork to send downstream and returned from New Orleans with sugar, dry goods, and coffee. Although the goods had to be hauled north against the current, the prices compared favorably to hauling such goods across the mountains from Philadelphia. There were only about two dozen barges operating five years later, but they proved to be the precursor to steamboats.[26]

On occasion, the western ties in the Ohio Valley did threaten the national ones that had been firmly established by Marietta's first merchants. When Robert Fulton sought exclusive rights to navigate the Ohio and Mississippi Rivers with the earliest steamboats in 1815, westerners erupted in protest. An editorial in a Cincinnati newspaper declared that rivers were "the *common highway* of the West," and any attempt at monopoly would limit freedom. In addition, there was never enough specie west of the Appalachians to satisfy needs, and the balance of trade had always favored the East. Bankers from Ohio, western Pennsylvania, western Virginia, Kentucky, and Indiana met in Steubenville and Cincinnati, Ohio, in 1816 and 1817 to discuss strategies for confronting eastern bankers over their policies, and East and West blamed each other for the Panic of 1819. In July, Daniel Southard of Louisville reported that merchants from Kentucky and Tennessee had been jailed for not paying debts, and some Philadelphia merchants called for the prosecution of "everyone from the west."[27]

The united front over steamboats and banks would be the high point of unity in the West, however. The economy of the canal era did not diminish trade down the Ohio, but the Erie Canal brought in a wave of new residents who settled in the north and middle parts of the state and sent their crops east by way of Lake Erie. When abolition sentiment spread, many Ohioans who had never depended on the ties along the Ohio River heeded its call. The Ohio River became one route among many, and there was a new West to plan for across the Great Plains and on to California and Oregon—places northerners wanted to control free from slavery. The most iconic image of the Ohio River in American culture is the slave Eliza with a babe in her arms fleeing from dogs across the icy river to freedom. But the novel *Uncle Tom's Cabin,* published in 1852, says more about the polarization of the region from the 1830s onward than it does about the closing decades of the eighteenth century and opening decades of the nineteenth. The artery of trade became a true border between North and South long after the passage of the Northwest Ordinance.[28]

From the 1790s through the 1820s, the Ohio River kept the burgeoning West connected to the East through the commercial connections forged by merchants, and connections between North and South along the river were just as strong. The founders of the Ohio Company planted a portal between East and West, situating their town at a strategic place along a river system that would give them access to the interior of the continent. Dudley Woodbridge Jr.'s commercial activities made Marietta a subregional hub for southeastern Ohio and western Virginia. He imported goods from Philadelphia, supplied shopkeepers, and ran branch stores. When the valley's population surged in the 1810s, Woodbridge expanded his activities to include growing industries and markets in Pittsburgh, Cincinnati, Lexington, and Louisville. In later decades, the credit reporting agency of R. G. Dun and Company listed Dudley Woodbridge Jr. as "the oldest trader of the place" and "the best off in the co[unty]." He never made the transition to manufacturing as others in Marietta did, and although he began to suffer from migraine headaches later in life, he wrote his brother in 1841 that he could "still supervise my store." He died a dozen years later at the age of seventy-three.[29] Dudley Woodbridge Jr. and other residents of the region, north and south of the river's course, called the Western Country home. The history of the region starts with the Ohio River, and I urge everyone to come on in; the water's fine!

Notes

1. David McCullough, *The Pioneers: The Heroic Story of the Settlers Who Brought the American Ideal West* (New York: Simon and Schuster, 2019); and journal entry, January 27, 1790, Thomas Wallcut Papers, 1671–1866, Massachusetts Historical Society, Boston.

2. R. E. Banta, *The Ohio* (New York: Rinehart, 1949), 7–17; Chief of Engineers, United States Army, comp., *The Ohio River,* 5th ed. (Washington, DC: Government Printing Office, 1934), 1–2; and Robert L. Reid, introduction, and Scott Russell Sanders, "The Force of Moving Water," in *Always a River: The Ohio River and the American Experience,* ed. Robert Reid (Bloomington: Indiana University Press, 1991), esp. xii, 14–15.

3. Dudley Woodbridge Jr. to Dudley Woodbridge, February 2, 1797, box 1, folder 3, Backus-Woodbridge Collection, Ohio Historical Society, Columbus (hereafter BWC).

4. Sarah Backus to William Backus, August 24, 1819, box 2, folder 3, BWC; see also Dudley Woodbridge Jr. to William Woodbridge, July 5, 1841, and William Petit to William Woodbridge, December 3, 1816, William Woodbridge Papers, Burton Collection, Detroit Public Library, Michigan.

5. Edward K. Muller, "Selective Urban Growth in the Middle Ohio Valley, 1800–1860," *Geographical Review* 66 (1976): 178–99.

6. See letters from Dudley Woodbridge Jr. to Mr. Dyer, Royal Converse, Henry Mills, and Asa Davis in letterbooks, 1799–1801, box 24, folder 2, and 1804, box 36, folder 1, BWC. The letter to Mills detailed above is dated May 14, 1804.

7. See letters from Dudley Woodbridge Jr. to John Harris, Mr. Stone, Silas Bingham, Thomas Hart, and Increase Matthews in letterbooks, 1799–1801, box 24, folder 2, and 1804, box 36, folder 1, BWC; blotter, Woodbridge Mercantile Company Records, Regional History Collection, vol. 19, West Virginia University, Morgantown (hereafter WMCR).

8. Dwight L. Smith, ed., *The Western Journals of John May: Ohio Company Agent and Business Adventurer* (Cincinnati: Historical and Philosophical Society of Ohio, 1961), 155; and Francis Baily, *Journal of a Tour in Unsettled Parts of North America in 1796 and 1797*, ed. Jack D. L. Holmes (Carbondale: Southern Illinois University Press, 1969), 92–93.

9. John Bernard Ray, "Zane's Trace, 1796–1812: A Study in Historical Geography" (PhD diss., Indiana University, 1968), 32–55, 158–64; letterbook, Dudley Woodbridge Jr. to James Converse, February 3, March 22, April 2, and December 7, 1804, box 36, folder 1, BWC; John Melish, *Travels through the United States of America, in the Years 1806 and 1807, and 1809, 1810, and 1811* (New York: Johnson Reprint, 1970), 428–29.

10. "Muskingum Bridge," Western Reserve Historical Society, Cleveland, Ohio.

11. William Woodbridge to James Backus, June 21, 1807, box 2, folder 1, BWC; ledger, box 27, folder 1, and 2 ledgers, box 45, folder 1, BWC; Claire Prechtel-Kluskens, comp., *Third Census of the United States, 1810* (microform), US National Archive, Washington, DC; Muller, "Selective Urban Growth," 182–85.

12. "Notice," advertisement, *Fredonian* (Chillicothe, OH), March 14, 1807; Fred Mitchell Jones, "Middlemen in the Domestic Trade of the United States, 1800–1860," *Illinois Studies in Social Sciences* 21, no. 3 (1937): 1–14; Dudley Woodbridge Jr. to Thomas L. Pierce, November 16, 1811, letterbook, vol. 2, WMCR; Asa R. Runyon to Asa Runyon and Co., June 4, 1815, Runyon Family Papers, Filson Historical Society, Louisville, Kentucky; R. Pierce Beaver, "Joseph Hough, an Early Miami Merchant," *Ohio Archeological and Historical Quarterly* 45 (1936): 41–42.

13. Invoice book, box 35, folder 2, BWC; invoice book, vols. 23 and 100, WMCR. See letterbooks for the following letters from Dudley Woodbridge Jr. to Joseph Clark, June 5, 1800, box 24, folder 2, BWC; to Harvey and Worth, December 1, 1801, and Joseph Clark, December 1, 1801, vol. 1, WMCR; to Joseph Clark, May 8, 1804, and Mrs. Jourdan, July 9, 1804, box 36, folder 1, BWC; and to Richard Ashurst, August 18, 1818, and William Wilson, August 18, 1818, vol. 4, WMCR.

14. Jack also purchased nails worth $980, probably in Pittsburgh; vol. 23, WMCR.

15. Samuel Meeker Ledger, 1807–10, Historical Society of Pennsylvania, Philadelphia; Jones, "Middlemen in the Domestic Trade," 18.

16. Louis C. Hunter, "Studies in the Economic History of the Ohio Valley: Seasonal Aspects of Industry and Commerce before the Age of Big Business and the Beginnings of Industrial Combination," *Smith College Studies in History* 19 (October 1933–January 1934): 9; Waterman Palmer to John Mills, March 6, 1818, Cutler Collection, Dawes Memorial Library, Marietta College, Marietta, Ohio; R. Pierce Beaver, "Joseph Hough," 41–42.

17. Thomas Senior Berry, *Western Prices before 1861: A Study of the Cincinnati Market* (Cambridge, MA: Harvard University Press, 1943), 74, 367; R. Carlyle Buley, *The Old Northwest: Pioneer Period, 1815–1840* (Bloomington: Indiana University Press, 1950), 1:335–56; Daniel Preston, "Market and Mill Town: Hamilton, Ohio, 1795–1860" (PhD diss., University of Maryland, 1987), 69–74; see letters from Dudley Woodbridge Jr. to Joseph S. Lewis, Harman Blennerhassett, James Converse, Joseph Clark, and John Damon, 1799–1801, in letterbook, box 24, folder 2, BWC; and letters from Dudley Woodbridge Jr. to Benjamin Ives Gilman, William Robinson Jr., James C. McFarland, Gilman and Ammidon, and Mr. Hoskins, 1816, in letterbook, vol. 3, WMCR.

18. Jonathan Goldstein, *Philadelphia and the China Trade, 1682–1846: Commercial, Cultural, and Attitudinal Effects* (University Park: Pennsylvania State University Press, 1978), 2–3, 21, 30; Robert D. Mitchell, ed., *Appalachian Frontiers: Settlement, Society, and Development in the Preindustrial Era* (Lexington: University Press of Kentucky, 1991), 159, 222, 264; see letters from Dudley Woodbridge Jr. to Benjamin Ives Gilman, William Robinson Jr., James C. McFarland, Gilman and Ammidon, and Mr. Hoskins, 1816, in letterbook, vol. 3, WMCR; and Dudley Woodbridge Jr. to Jack, September 7, 1820, vol. 4, WMCR.

19. Fortescue Cuming, "Sketches of a Tour of the Western Country," in *Early Western Travels, 1748–1846,* ed. Reuben Gold Thwaites (Cleveland: A. H. Clark, 1904–7), 4:126–27.

20. Dudley Woodbridge Jr. to Benjamin B. Howell, Charles Copeland, and others, January–August 1810, in letterbook, box 43, folder 1, BWC; Dudley Woodbridge Jr. to William Woodbridge, December 12, 1809, William Woodbridge Papers; Dudley Woodbridge Jr. to John Woodbridge, April 20 and September 11, 1810, and to Tilford, April 23, 1810, in letterbook, box 43, folder 1, BWC; William Woodbridge to Dudley Woodbridge Jr., box 2, folder 1, BWC.

21. Dudley Woodbridge Jr. to Andrew Miller, Thomas and Jonathan Cromwell, William Hays, G. and S. Anschutz, and James and Thomas Sinclair, 1811–13, letterbook, vol. 2, WMCR; ledger, box 45, folder 2, BWC;

Richard C. Wade, *The Urban Frontier: Pioneer Life in Early Pittsburgh, Cincinnati, Lexington, Louisville, and St. Louis* (Chicago: University of Chicago Press, 1964), 43–48; Catherine Elizabeth Reiser, *Pittsburgh's Commercial Development, 1800–1850* (Harrisburg: Pennsylvania Historical and Museum Commission, 1951), 4–15.

22. Ray, "Zane's Trace," 51–54, 76–77, 108, 165–73; William T. Utter, *The Frontier State, 1803–1825* (Columbus: Ohio State Archeological and Historical Society, 1942), 127; receipt books, box 47, folder 2, and box 49, folder 3, BWC; warehouse books, vols. 123 and 124, WMCR, and box 51, folder 1, and box 55, folder 3, BWC; and letters to Zanesville merchants in letterbook, vol. 2, WMCR.

23. Manasseh Cutler to Winthrop Sargent, April 20, 1786, Manasseh Cutler to Nathan Dare, March 16, 1787, and Cutler journal, August 1788, in *Life, Journals, and Correspondence of Rev. Manasseh Cutler, LL.D.,* ed. William Parker Cutler and Julia Perkins Cutler (Cincinnati: R. Clarke, 1888), 1:189, 194, 412–13, 419; Andrew R. L. Cayton, "Marietta and the Ohio Company," in Mitchell, *Appalachian Frontiers,* 187–200; S. P. Hildreth, *Pioneer History* (Cincinnati: H. W. Derby, 1848), 352–59.

24. L. Loomis to R. J. Meigs, March 31, 1813, J. L. Robinson to Joseph Ficklin, March 31, 1813, Kearney Wharton to Samuel Roberts, April 2, 1813, Benjamin B. Howell to John W. Hunt, April 9, 1813, and Benjamin B. Howell to Abraham S. Barton, April 9, 1913, in the Isaac H. Jackson Papers, Cincinnati Historical Society, Cincinnati, Ohio. Leonard Dobbin to Holderman Pearson and Co., February 6, 1821, in the John W. Hunt Papers / Holderman Pearson and Co., Filson Historical Society, Louisville, Kentucky; Daniel Preston, "Thomas Kelsey, Hardluck Entrepreneur," *Ohio History* 104 (1995): 130–41; and Lewis A. Atherton, *The Frontier Merchant in Mid-America* (Columbia: University of Missouri Press, 1971), 115–23; Dudley Woodbridge Jr. to Thomas Boal and Co., Samuel January, Scudder and A. Hart, and Ebenezer Buckingham, 1812, in letterbook, vol. 2, WMCR; Dudley Woodbridge Jr. to Daniel Conner, 1802 and 1803, in letterbook, vol. 1, WMCR; and Dudley Woodbridge Jr. to Daniel Conner and Joseph Pierce, 1804, in letterbook, box 36, folder 1, BWC.

25. Dudley Woodbridge Jr. to Mr. Stone, July 15, 1799, letterbook, box 24, folder 2, BWC; Woodbridge to Nathan Kinne, December 12, 1803, letterbook, vol. 1, WMCR; Woodbridge to William Steele, Donnally Steele and Company, and Richard Beale, 1813–20, letterbook, vol. 4, WMCR; Dudley Woodbridge Jr. to Trotter, Scott and Company, George Trotter, and J. and D. Maceoun, 1812–13, letterbook, vol. 2, WMCR; Dudley Woodbridge Jr. to S. Cantrell and Cantrell and Read, 1811–12, letterbook, vol. 2, WMCR; Marietta Jennings, *A Pioneer Merchant of St. Louis, 1810–1820: The Business Career of Christian Wilt* (New York: Columbia University Press, 1939), 84, 89–90; Utter, *Frontier State,* 183–87, 260.

26. Dudley Woodbridge Jr. to Baum and Perry, May and December 1813, vol. 2, WMCR; Utter, *Frontier State,* 183–87.

27. Louis C. Hunter, *Steamboats on the Western Rivers: An Economic and Technological History* (Cambridge, MA: Harvard University Press, 1949), 3–14, quotation on 11; Utter, *Frontier State, 1803–1825,* 281–85; Buley, *Old Northwest,* 1:132, 577–85; Harry N. Scheiber, "Preface: On the Concepts of 'Regionalism' and 'Frontier,'" in *The Old Northwest: Studies in Regional History, 1787–1910,* ed. Harry N. Scheiber (Lincoln: University of Nebraska Press), xii; Daniel R. Southard to David Starr, July 1, 1819, David R. Southard Papers, Filson Historical Society, Louisville, Kentucky.

28. Harry N. Scheiber, *Ohio Canal Era: A Case Study of Government and Economy, 1820–1861* (Athens: Ohio University Press, 1987); Erik F. Haites, James Mak, and Gary M. Walton, *Western River Transportation: The Era of Early Internal Development, 1810–1860* (Baltimore: John Hopkins University Press, 1975). The best current work about the ambiguous relationship between the Northwest Ordinance and the Ohio River as a boundary between slavery and freedom is Matthew Salafia's *Slavery's Borderland: Freedom and Bondage along the Ohio River* (Philadelphia: University of Pennsylvania Press, 2013).

29. Credit report of Dudley Woodbridge, Ohio, vol. 193, p. 122, R. G. Dun and Company Collection, Baker Library, Harvard Business School, Boston; Dudley Woodbridge Jr. to William Woodbridge, July 5, 1841, William Woodbridge Papers.

8

Johnny Appleseed and Apple Cultures in Early Ohio

WILLIAM KERRIGAN

Johnny Appleseed is part of the American origin story. Every school child in the Midwest, and in most of the nation, learns the story of the wandering apple tree planter in elementary school. The versions of the legend vary in their retellings, but the key elements of the story are consistent. Johnny Appleseed was a pious man, committed to a life of benevolence and frugality. He brought the gift of the apple to the American wilderness, helping Euro-American frontier families transform a "savage" wilderness into a productive and domesticated landscape. Across Ohio and the Midwest, many communities claim the first apple trees planted in their locality were planted by the legendary apple seed planter. Some versions of the legend have him bringing apples much farther west, to Missouri and even the Pacific Northwest. In legend, at least, Johnny Appleseed was a hybrid of St. Francis and St. Nicholas—a person of extraordinary gentleness and generosity, but also of extraordinary reach.[1]

The myth of Johnny Appleseed is based upon the life of a real historical person, one whose activities were unusual enough to draw the attention of many people who encountered him. John "Appleseed" Chapman was born in Leominster, Massachusetts, in 1774 and as a young man migrated to northwestern Pennsylvania in the late 1790s. There he began establishing apple nurseries from seeds he had gathered from the discarded pomace behind cider mills farther east. In the first years of the nineteenth century, Chapman shifted his area of operation to Ohio and made establishing seedling nurseries the focus of his energy. In the first four decades of the nineteenth century, Chapman established seedling apple nurseries across Ohio, with his primary focus on the areas of the upper Muskingum watershed. In his final years he shifted the locus of his activities to the region known as the Great Black Swamp in northwestern Ohio and northeastern Indiana. He died in Fort Wayne, Indiana, in 1845. John Chapman was not the first to bring apple trees to Ohio, and he was just one of many human agents in the spread of the apple tree. To understand the meaning and significance of John "Appleseed" Chapman's horticultural activities in Ohio, we need to shatter myths that give him both primacy and universality in the story of Ohio apple growing.

This requires us to widen our view and look at Ohio's *other* horticulturalists. But we also need to pause to explain a bit of the history and science of apple propagation. The apple's origins are in the mountains of Kazakhstan, near Almaty, whose name is derived from a word meaning "apple mountain" or "full of apples." The apple tree has proven to be a remarkably hardy and adaptable plant, and humans soon carried the apple tree far from its original site, east to China, and west across Southwest Asia, Turkey, North Africa, and Europe. But the seed of an apple carries all the genetic diversity of the first central Asian trees, and the fruit borne on seed-grown apple trees is unlikely to resemble in shape, color, or taste that of its parent apple. Most seed-grown apple trees will produce crabbed and bitter fruit, but occasionally one will emerge with fruit of exceptional quality. Until recently, the primary method of reproducing apples with the same qualities of the parent tree was to take cuttings from the tree and graft them onto new apple rootstock. Over time and across the landscape, apple-growing cultures propagated and spread desirable apple cultivars through the practice of grafting.[2]

When European powers began establishing colonies in the Americas, they brought apple trees with them. Native Americans, like so many peoples before them, came to love this hardy, sweet fruit and became important agents of the apple's migration into the North American interior. Fruit was a part of the diet of the Native peoples who occupied

Ohio before the arrival of Europeans, much of it gathered from the surrounding landscape. Native Americans of the Great Lakes region enjoyed a variety of wild fruit in season, including native crab apples, several species of plums, may-apples, pawpaw, wild grapes, and a wide variety of berries. Plucked from the forest or growing in informal orchards that sprung up where Indians discarded fruit stones and seeds, this fruit could be consumed fresh, dried and baked into breads, or, in the case of tart crab apples, roasted in the fire or marinated in maple syrup. Long before the arrival of Europeans, Native peoples exchanged fruit stones with other tribes, spreading regional varieties of plums, for instance, well beyond their natural range and thereby enhancing the variety of wild fruit available to them. But they did not appear to practice grafting, nor were formal orchards in well-defined places part of their subsistence strategy before the arrival of the Europeans.[3]

Intensive cultivation of tree fruit was a Eurasian innovation, but some tribes, notably the Seneca, embraced orchard agriculture early. Orchard agriculture and labor-intensive methods of production through grafting and pruning was one element of Old World mixed husbandry agriculture, the third leg of a stool that included keeping livestock and raising annual crops such as grains. Cultivated orchards mirrored some of the fundamental elements of the European economy and society. They reflected ideas about property rights, as a well-ordered orchard was a visible cue of landownership. They also mirrored the dominant European subsistence strategy of fixity, as opposed to mobility, on the land. An orchard represented a long-term investment in a well-defined place. The initial labor invested in planting and pruning it would not pay off for several years but then might yield sustenance and wealth for decades. Cultivated orchards were also compatible with the emerging European market economies. The ability to reproduce fruit of consistent qualities of color, size, shape, sweetness, and firmness through grafting made it possible for the market to assign apple varieties a monetary value. Consumers of grafted apple varieties, whether purchasing them by the bushel or the peck, would have a reasonable understanding of the eating and keeping qualities of the fruit they purchased. Nevertheless, some Euro-American migrants, most notably the poorer ones, eschewed the practice of grafting and often planted seed-grown "wild" apple trees as part of their subsistence strategy. Their reasons for doing so will be explored later.[4]

Human societies have always adopted new commodities, subsistence strategies, and foodways from others when they found them useful. As the apple made its epic journey from its central Asian home across the globe, peoples who encountered it for the first time often adopted not just the fruit but also the practices for propagating the varieties they prized. North America's Indigenous people did so too. The first apples to reach the Ohio Country were almost certainly carried by Native Americans. Most likely, the Wendat, who acquired them from the French in Canada, deserve the credit, but they were not the only Native peoples to bring apples into Ohio. The Lenape, who acquired them from the early Delaware Valley colony of New Sweden, brought apples with them as they were pushed west by aggressive Anglo-American migrants. The Shawnee, who returned to Ohio in the early eighteenth century, may have also carried apples and peaches with them, and the mid-eighteenth-century migrant Senecas, often referred to as the Mingo, almost certainly did, as the Seneca had established large orchards in upstate New York by that time. John "Appleseed" Chapman, who first set foot in the Ohio Country in the last years of the eighteenth century, was a relative latecomer to apple propagation in Ohio.[5]

The Anglo-American migrants who began to establish settlements in Ohio in the years after the American Revolution brought with them a way of getting a living from the land that they had employed for generations. A mixed husbandry system that included annual and perennial agriculture and the raising of domesticated livestock rooted them to fixed pieces of property. Perennial fruit orchards were a part of this system, and these required staying in place. Peaches and apples were not the only fruit they cultivated, but they were the most common and most important ones. Yet within the broad Anglo-American migrant class, the strategies they employed in starting orchards, and their reasons for establishing them, were not uniform. In various locations in early Ohio, these newcomers understood orchards as a method of establishing their high social standing, as potential sources of a profitable and marketable commodity or, for the most resource-starved migrants, as simply a strategy of eking out a living. To understand the significance and meaning of John "Appleseed" Chapman's apple-planting activities, it is necessary to look at how the apple emerged in other new communities in the state.

Horticulture had emerged as a popular hobby among the eastern elite before the American Revolution. "Cultivating gentlemen" and prosperous men in post-Revolutionary American society formed horticultural societies, carried out experiments on their own lands, traded plants, and shared what they learned with others through their social networks and publications dedicated to agricultural subjects. While the term "horticulture" encompasses a broad swath of agricultural activity—from cultivation and improvement of edible fruits, nuts, seeds, and vegetables to ornamental plants, flowers, and even turf grasses—fruit cultivation received particularly strong interest in the first decades after the Revolution. Horticultural societies emerged in northern states early, with members dedicated to sharing knowledge to improve cultivation of a number of crops, including apples.[6] For Virginia's slave-owning gentry, who commanded abundant pools of labor, gardens and orchards provided an opportunity to demonstrate their education and their gentility, and to show off their wealth. To be able to offer guests the finest freshly picked dessert fruits at the end of an opulent dinner, and to show off the extensive collection of rare plants in their gardens and orchards, was of great importance to men like Thomas Jefferson and George Washington.[7]

The wealthy Virginians who began occupying the Scioto Valley at the end of the nineteenth century, including Thomas Worthington and Edward Tiffin (both early governors of the state), and Nathaniel Massie, had ambitions to become the Jeffersons and Washingtons of their new home. They quickly established large estates by exploiting their access to large numbers of laborers they brought to Ohio with them. Most of these laborers had been their slave "property" in Virginia, but as the Northwest Ordinance had banned the importation of slaves into the region, they were now deemed servants under the law. Some may have been bound to long-term indentures. These men and women cleared the land, plowed the fields, built their fine estates, and set out large orchards of fine, grafted fruit trees, which these gentlemen had carried with them from Virginia.[8] Worthington, Tiffin, and Massie modeled themselves on the Virginia gentry they so admired. Emulating Jefferson, Worthington even imported German redemptioners who were experienced horticulturalists to care for his fine orchards. Once mature, these orchards provided him an abundance of dessert fruits he could serve to guests at the home he called Adena, his own Monticello built upon a Scioto Valley hilltop. When Virginian William Henry Harrison was appointed territorial governor of Indiana, he emulated Worthington and other wealthy Virginia transplants by surrounding the Vergennes estate he called Grouseland with fine orchards. For these men, large orchards of fine fruit helped established them as gentleman of high standing.[9]

East of the Scioto Valley, the well-connected New Englanders who established the first official settlement at Marietta also made fruit cultivation a part of their plan. The descriptor "Founders" is often applied to both the Virginia gentry who established a presence in the Scioto Valley and to the New Englanders who established the town of Marietta. The latter were the focus of a book by popular historian David McCullough, *The Pioneers: The Heroic Story of the Settlers Who Brought the American Ideal West*. McCullough's narrative does not depart from earlier generations of Ohio historians in celebrating and centering the state's origins in this small settlement.[10]

The heroes of McCullough's book include two prominent founders of the Marietta colony, Rufus Putnam, a New Englander of modest beginnings who rose to prominence as a result of military achievements during the Revolutionary War, and Yale-educated Reverend Manasseh Cutler, a scholar of some renown who had, in McCullough's words, "succeeded in becoming three doctors in one, having qualified for both a doctor of law and doctor of medicine, in addition to doctor of divinity."[11] Between them, Cutler and Putnam possessed substantial social capital. Through military service, Putnam had established personal relationships with George Washington and many of the nation's first leaders. When Cutler traveled to Philadelphia to lobby Congress for a sizable grant of land for their planned colony north of the Ohio River, "he carried with him letters of introduction from the governor of Massachusetts, the president of Harvard College, and some forty others."[12] He was very well connected indeed. The assemblage of men Cutler and Putnam gathered to fill out the New England Associates brought additional political, social, and financial capital to the enterprise. All had served as officers in the Revolutionary army.

The colony they established at the confluence of the Muskingum and Ohio Rivers had the backing of the national government, and was carefully planned and well-resourced. The New England Associates brought with them the men and supplies they would need to quickly establish an orderly town. They built a fort, Campus Martius, and carefully laid out the streets of the new town. In describing Rufus Putnam, Marietta's first apple tree champion, McCullough notes that on his second journey to the town, Rufus Putnam returned to the new colony with "wagons . . . loaded with as many as fifty varieties of apple seeds."[13] But here McCullough is in error. It certainly would not have required even a solitary wagon to carry tens of thousands of apple seeds, which would take up minimal space on a westward journey, and as explained above, apple seeds do not come in "varieties." In truth Putnam employed his substantial resources to carry young, grafted trees, and freshly cut grafts with their cut ends dipped in beeswax to keep them moist and living. Keeping the fragile trees and grafts viable on this long journey would have required substantial effort. Poorer migrants could not have spared the wagon space necessary to carry out this task.

Rufus Putnam no doubt carefully chose the varieties he brought to Ohio. The trees, of course, had to produce apples large and sweet enough to be attractive to anticipated customers, but also, because of Marietta's isolation, they must have good keeping qualities. Among the varieties he returned with was the Roxbury Russet—rebranded the Putnam Russet in Ohio, an apple renowned for its ability to remain crisp and desirable even after very long journeys packed in barrels. Many of early Ohio's first apple exports had to travel by flatboat all the way down to New Orleans and remain in sellable condition. Rufus Putnam's nurseries of known commercial grafted trees would serve as an important source of grafted apple trees in the state in its first decades, and no doubt brought commercial returns.

John Chapman's family migrated to the Marietta region in the winter of 1804–5, but the legendary apple seed planter received only a brief mention in McCullough's story. McCullough noted that John Chapman, "like Rufus Putnam . . . had a great, lifelong love of apple trees."[14] The two had little else in common, and families like the Chapmans are largely absent from McCullough's version of Ohio's origins. This was a distortion, because for every pioneer like Rufus Putnam and Ephraim Cutler, there were dozens of families more like the Chapmans—down on their luck, arriving with meager supplies and threadbare resources, and scratching out a living often on land they did not own, on the settlement's margins.

The Chapmans arrived in Ohio in the middle of winter and settled on lands along Duck Creek just north of Marietta. John's father, Nathaniel Chapman Sr., was in poor health when he arrived, and he never acquired title to any land in the region. It is probable that the family squatted on one of the many unclaimed parcels in the lower Duck Creek Valley, a land of steep slopes and narrow, flood-prone bottom lands, making it some of the least desirable land open for settlement. The Chapmans may have selected this land precisely because they had no money and they expected to be left alone there.[15] Another possibility is that the Chapmans settled on a tract owned by some more successful cousins who had migrated to Ohio much earlier.[16] Whether the Chapmans were squatters or charity tenants on a cousin's tract in these early years, it appears that the family was barely getting by, making a living on some of the most isolated and unpromising lands in the region. The property was seven miles from the nearest neighbor, according to one early account. Just two years after they arrived, John Chapman's father passed away, and the family was so poor that they could not afford a proper burial for him. Two of the older sons walked seven miles to the nearest sawmill, acquired a few cut boards, and borrowed the tools needed to make a rude coffin, which they carried back to the homestead. They buried their father in an unidentified grave somewhere on the property.[17]

Surviving evidence of John Chapman's apple-planting activities suggests that despite family connections in the Marietta region, he did not spend much time planting seedling apple trees in the area, and this is not surprising. Marietta's location on the Ohio River and its early establishment of grafted orchards meant that there was little need for John Chapman's seedling apple trees. He would find more customers for his wild seed-grown trees in more isolated communities.

John Chapman had developed a far different strategy from Rufus Putnam for getting apple trees to the places where his poorer customers needed them. Having gathered apple seeds from the discarded pomace behind eastern cider mills, Chapman then carried them by packhorse or canoe or on his back into areas he anticipated would in just a few years be filling up with new White migrants. Planting these seeds in makeshift nurseries on land he did not own, he could offer newly arrived newcomers two-to-three-year-old seedlings—a head start on a productive orchard—for just a few cents per tree. In the central Ohio region where he spent much of his life, he appears to have established dozens, perhaps hundreds, of small nurseries along creeks, spaced roughly ten miles apart, making them a reasonable walk to any newcomer who agreed to purchase them.

The seedling trees John Chapman peddled formed the basis of an apple culture that was distinct from those established by the likes of the Worthingtons and the Putnams, one that might be called "cider culture."

Cider culture was characterized by small, resource-poor farms, often remote from markets, where both labor and cash were scarce commodities. Seedling apple orchards were just one element of a diversified production strategy, their primary advantages being that they could be established relatively easily and demanded little of the family's scarce labor to be useful. The bulk of the fruit from these scraggly orchards was used to fatten hogs or pressed into cider. Most cider in the Early Republic was consumed in its fermented state; the term "new cider" was sometimes used to refer to fresh cider not yet fermented, and the famous circuit-riding Methodist preacher Peter Cartwright recalled a stop at a frontier tavern where he and his companion had a dinner of hot bread and new cider, only discovering that the cider was not so new when they left the tavern and attempted to remount their horses.[18] The practice of distinguishing fermented cider as "hard cider" did not take off until the phrase was made famous by Harrison's "Log Cabin and Hard Cider" campaign of 1840, discussed later in this chapter.

Naturally fermented cider might contain only about 5 or 6 percent alcohol and was therefore subject to spoiling. To extend its life, some families fortified the cider by adding corn whiskey, or they left barrels of fermented cider out in the cold in the winter, removing the ice that formed on top. As alcohol had a lower freezing point than water, what remained in the barrel—sometimes called "applejack"—would have higher alcohol content, and thus could keep longer. Families with more resources might opt to distill large quantities of cider into concentrated apple brandy, which they could keep indefinitely, and could be sold in distant markets. Contemporaries often commented on the low quality of America's home-produced cider, claiming that Americans tossed even rotten and worm-eaten apples into the cider press.[19]

Decades later, when cider culture was in decline, and the aging Johnny Appleseed had become, to a more comfortable generation of Ohioans, a curiosity, some would write off seedling apple culture as a practice of the improvident, the unambitious, the superstitious, or the lazy. One story that circulated about Johnny Appleseed in his later years was that he believed the act of taking cuttings from one tree and grafting them to another was wicked and in defiance of God's will.[20] In a post–cider culture world, where grafted trees were cheap and abundant, people quickly forgot the benefits of the seedling apple tree. Planting and propagating apple trees from seeds was a smart strategy for Ohio's resource-poor and isolated migrants. First, by planting from seed, a kind of natural selection occurred within these primitive nurseries, as those seedling trees that thrived proved to have the qualities necessary to do well in the soils and microclimate from which they sprung. Many young, grafted trees carried from the East Coast at great expense might still wither and fail in their new environment, a risk Ohio's poorest migrants could not afford to take. John Chapman's hardy seedlings, to be sure, produced mostly crabbed and bitter fruit. But an orchard of one hundred seedlings was likely to produce at least a few trees with sweet fruit. A single mature apple tree with good, fresh eating apples could provide more sweet fruit annually than a family could consume. And the rest of the trees in this seedling orchard still had great utility for a poor family living on the margins, most commonly for producing a crude cider or for fattening hogs. Paying a few cents for John Chapman's two- or three-year-old seedlings and then transplanting them in an orchard on one's own farm meant shortening the time to having a productive orchard. Furthermore, it would not be too many years before traveling apple grafters might arrive in the community, offering to graft reliable commercial varieties to these wild trees, which might then in just a year or two begin producing fruit of known qualities that they could sell in emerging local markets. Planters of seedling apple orchards were not forever destined to a strategy of just getting by. Nevertheless, migrants whose farms had seedling orchards were marked in the same way those who could not afford to cover their crude log cabins with clapboards. They were the poor.

To really understand Chapman's customers and the value of his trees, it is worth taking a closer look at the experience of just one of these families. John Williams was only eleven when he migrated to eastern Ohio with his mother and two siblings in 1800. Turning forest into farm was no easy task, as Williams recalled: "Emigrants poured in from different posts, cabins were put up in every direction, and women, children, and goods tumbled into them. The tide of emigration flowed like water through the breach in a milldam. Everything was bustle and confusion, and all at work that could work."[21] The first task was building a primitive shelter. Then they girdled the mature beech trees on their property to keep them from leafing out, cleared away the small brush, and scratched up soil still permeated with tree roots before planting corn among the dying giants. "We were weak-handed and weak-pocketed—in fact, laborers were not to be had," Williams noted, and the hands of every member of the family were needed just to get by. In August, the Williams family finally found time to plant turnips. In the fall, they spent time in the woods gathering walnuts and hickory nuts. "These, with the turnips, which we scraped, supplied the place of fruit," he remembered.[22] The family planted some peach stones as well, as peach trees grew fast and bore fruit in just a few years. But in those first years, sweetness could only be found in a turnip or a walnut, or by gathering the delicate indigenous pawpaw that filled the woods. But change happened fast in emerging Ohio communities. Williams noted that in just a few years, stone-grown peaches were so abundant that "millions of peaches rotted on the ground." Eventually, the Williams family found the time to plant apple trees, but in the meantime, the tart-sweet tang of an apple occasionally could be had, for a boy willing to work for it. "We sometimes went to Martin's Ferry, on the Ohio, to pick peaches for the owner, who had them distilled. We got a bushel of apples for each day's work in picking peaches. These were kept for particular eating," John Williams recalled, "as if they had contained seeds of gold."[23]

Poor, "weak-handed" families like the Williamses were John "Appleseed" Chapman's typical customers. The seedling apple trees he sold cheaply could be quickly planted and then ignored while attention was turned to the many other labor-intensive tasks that converting forest to farm required. As commercial grafted orchards like the one at Martin's Ferry grew and matured, grafts from these could be more easily acquired, and it is possible that the Williams family eventually did this. But home cider production and consumption remained high in the early decades of the state, and seedling apples were perfectly fine for producing this beverage. For that reason, many families opted to retain their seedling orchards in their wild state for decades. Cider production in early Ohio was highly decentralized, with each family pressing their own, or paying a neighbor for the use of their cider press. While newspapers frequently listed the going prices of grafted apples, prices for cider were less frequently published, suggesting that most of Ohio's cider was consumed on the farm or in the neighborhood in which it was produced. Quality control appeared to be a problem, as many contemporaries commented on the awful state of American cider.[24]

Yet many families like the Williamses were not content to be just getting by on a self-provisioning farm. They hoped their hard labor would produce real value that they stood some chance of redeeming if necessary. Lands families like those the Williams family settled upon were typically sold by the government for $2.00 an acre on payments, or $1.64 for cash up front, and land prices rose quickly as more migrants arrived in an area.[25] Even squatter families who could not scratch up the cash to purchase the land they settled were sometimes able to sell their improvements to others before vacating. One early Ohio visitor noted that by 1810 "a log house, a peach, and perhaps an apple orchard, together with from ten to thirty or forty acres of land, enclosed, and partially cleared" could be sold to another newcomer for $50 to $100, independent of the value of the land.[26] The cider culture families, with their scraggly wild orchards, far outnumbered apple growers like Rufus Putnam and Thomas Worthington, and arguably had a greater impact in shaping Ohio's landscapes, economy, and culture than their more famous counterparts.

But cider culture did not last forever. When, precisely, to date the end of the cider culture era is complicated. One historian of apples identifies a decline in cider culture beginning in New England in the 1820s.[27] Cider culture no doubt persisted in the western interior, and among the poorest classes, for a longer time. The transition from cider culture to market-oriented orchards was aided by improvements in transportation, most notably better roads, improved river navigation, and the development of canals. Expensive grafted orchards would not be profitable if it were difficult to get much of the perishable crop to potential buyers. When Adlard Welby traveled through John Williams's neighborhood in the late summer of 1819, roughly two decades after the Williams family had arrived, he and his party found an abundance of good-quality fresh apples and peaches selling very cheaply. "We bought here, out of a waggon load, half a peck of peaches for six cents . . . the peach and apple orchards are literally breaking down with fruit; every morning we stop at the first orchard to take in as many apples as we want for the day."[28] The abundance of fruit and cheap prices suggests that the region's transportation infrastructure was still a hindrance for farmers seeking to maximize their incomes.

In his later years, John Chapman slowed his westward movement, and the world around him was changing. By the 1830s, the counties in the upper Muskingum River valley watershed where he had resided for decades were experiencing massive population growth. Roads were improving, and a navigable canal now stretched across eastern Ohio from

Cleveland down to Marietta. It was much easier for the region's farm families to access grafted apple trees and to get their goods, including grafted apples, to markets. Chapman's continued practice of peddling seedling apple trees appeared increasingly quaint and outdated, and he became the subject of stories and tall tales. It should be no surprise, then, that in the 1830s Chapman began to shift his base of operations to the Great Black Swamp, which stretched between Toledo and Fort Wayne, a region that remained isolated and relatively poor until it was drained in the second half of the nineteenth century. Ohio's cider culture was retreating into the swamps.

The emergence of hard cider as a theme in the 1840 presidential election was a sign that for most Americans, cider had become a nostalgic symbol of an old way of life. The election pitted incumbent Democrat Martin Van Buren against elderly war hero and Ohio resident William Henry Harrison. A Democratic newspaper suggested Harrison was too old for the job, sneering "give him a barrel of hard cider, and settle a pension of two thousand a year on him, and my word for it, he will sit the remainder of his days in his log cabin by the side of his 'sea coal' fire, and study moral philosophy."[29] Savvy Whigs turned the insult to their advantage, embracing the new populist politics of the era, dubbing Harrison "the Log Cabin and Hard Cider candidate," and suggesting the man who was born into immense privilege on the Berkeley plantation in Virginia was of humble origins. The ambitious young Virginian who had gone to great expense to establish orchards of fine grafted fruit trees at Grouseland in an effort to bolster his social standing was now reinvented as a simple backwoods farmer who lived in a log cabin and drank homemade hard cider. That cider by 1840 had become a symbol of nostalgia was evident in one of the campaign songs sung at Harrison rallies, which included these lines:

Should Good Old Cider Be Despised and ne'er regarded more?
Should plain log cabins be despised, our fathers built of yore?
For the true old style my boys, for the true old style
Let's take a mug of cider now, for the true old style.
We've tried experiments enough, of fashions new and vain.
And now we long to settle down to good old times again.
For the good old ways, my boys, for the good old ways!
Let's take a mug of cider now, for the good old ways![30]

The campaign worked, and Harrison was victorious, perhaps because an ongoing economic depression made voters responsive to the message of celebrating simpler times. But while Ohio voters might have sung about "the good old ways," they were not really going back to them. Ohioans were embracing new technologies and new methods to improve the productivity of their farms, including their orchards, and every year they became more deeply enmeshed in a market economy. The increasing importance of an apple orchard as a cash crop on a family farm became more evident by the 1830s, when newspapers began to regularly record the prices fresh and dried apples were fetching in cities like Cincinnati. The emergence of county agricultural societies across Ohio in the 1830s and 1840s, dedicated to improvement of commercial crops, including fruit, was another sign that the farm orchard had moved beyond its self-provisioning functions.

A few events in 1845 make it a fitting endpoint for Ohio's cider culture. In January of that year, the *Ohio Cultivator,* a new periodical dedicated to advising farmers on how to improve their yields and profits, was launched. One of the first issues the *Ohio Cultivator* took up was the campaign to criminalize the common practice of travelers plucking apples from roadside orchards. The movement to criminalize apple plucking was a powerful sign that the age of commercial apple production had arrived in Ohio. For decades, Ohio had been producing more apples than its transportation infrastructure could get to markets, and everyone assumed that a large portion of an annual apple crop was destined for the cider mill or hog pen. As a result, many people did not consider the act of stopping by roadside orchards and gathering a shirtful of ripe apples as inflicting harm on the orchard owner. By the 1840s, the common practice had become a major irritant to those orchardists who had the wherewithal to get all their fruit to market. More Ohio farmers had invested in commercially popular grafted varieties of fruit, especially late-keeping "winter apples," which would command a higher price at market after the season was over. These farmers began to see the practice of apple plucking as theft, and they lobbied their state legislature to define it as such. In April of 1845, John Chapman passed away in Fort Wayne, not far from his Great Black Swamp seedling nurseries. Just one week after his death, the Ohio state legislature criminalized apple theft, essentially declaring the end of Ohio's cider culture. At first the law applied only to orchards in the region around Cleveland, but within a year it was extended across the state.[31]

Stories and tall tales of the peculiar man known as Johnny Appleseed began circulating in the Ohio communities where Chapman planted his seedling trees during his lifetime, but he only became an American icon decades after his death. His place in the American—and Ohio—origin story seems quite secure. The Native American apple tree planters who preceded him have been largely erased from the story, and so have the progenitors of the distinct "cider culture" Chapman represented. Popular histories continue to focus on "great men" like Rufus Putnam and Thomas Worthington as "founders" of Ohio, granting them credit for creating the state's culture and institutions, and pushing the stories of other Ohioans to the margins. As commercial orchards of grafted fruit expanded across the Ohio landscape in the middle decades of the nineteenth century, the old cider culture may not have completely disappeared from Ohio memory, but the logic of that culture certainly had.

Notes

1. Some of the information and ideas presented in this essay I first explored in William Kerrigan, *Johnny Appleseed and the American Orchard: A Cultural History* (Baltimore: Johns Hopkins University Press, 2012); and William Kerrigan, "Apples on the Border: Orchards and the Contest for the Great Lakes," *Michigan Historical Review* 34, no. 1 (2008): 25–41.
2. Joan Morgan and Alison Richards, *The New Book of Apples* (London: Ebury Press, 1993), 9–11; Frank Browning, *Apples: The Story of the Fruit of Temptation* (New York: North Point Press, 1998), 36–38.
3. Kerrigan, "Apples on the Border," 25–41; William N. Fenton, ed., *Parker on the Iroquois: Iroquois Uses of Maize and Other Food Plants* (Syracuse, NY: Syracuse University Press, 1968), 94–95; John Heckewelder, *History, Manners and Customs of the Indian Nations Who Once Inhabited Pennsylvania and Neighboring States* (Philadelphia: Historical Society of Pennsylvania, 1876), 194; Donald Culross Peattie, *A Natural History of Trees of Eastern and Central North America* (Boston: Houghton Mifflin, 1991), 377–79.
4. For an extended examination of Indian and European subsistence strategies in colonial New England, and the implications of mobility and fixity, see William Cronon, *Changes in the Land: Indians, Colonists, and the Ecology of New England* (New York: Hill and Wang, 1983).
5. For more about the Native American carriers of the apple to the interior, see Kerrigan, "Apples on the Border," 25–41.

6. Important works on the cultural history of horticultural in the early American Republic include Tamara Plakins Thornton, *Cultivating Gentlemen: The Meaning of Country Life among the Boston Elite, 1785–1860* (New Haven, CT: Yale University Press, 1989); Philip Pauly, *Fruits and Plains: The Horticultural Transformation of America* (Cambridge, MA: Harvard University Press, 2008); Ericka Hannickel, *Empire of Vines: Wine Culture in America* (Philadelphia: University of Pennsylvania Press, 2013); and Cheryl Lyon-Jenness, *For Shade and Comfort: Democratizing Horticulture in the Nineteenth Century Midwest* (West Lafayette, IN: Purdue University Press, 2004).

7. On Jefferson, Washington, and other founders' obsessions with fine gardens and orchards, see Andrea Wulf, *Founding Gardeners: The Revolutionary Generation, Nature, and the Shaping of the American Nation* (New York: Alfred A. Knopf, 2011); and Peter J. Hatch, *The Fruits and Fruit Trees of Monticello: Thomas Jefferson and the Origins of American Horticulture* (Charlottesville: University Press of Virginia, 1998).

8. Thomas Worthington has often been portrayed as having strong anti-slavery views, and it is implied that the formerly enslaved workers he brought to Ohio came voluntarily and that they were fully free in Ohio. This is probably an oversimplification, as they could not stay in Virginia once emancipated, and they may have continued to be bound to Worthington by long-term indenture contracts. See Matthew Salafia, *Slavery's Borderland: Freedom and Bondage along the Ohio River* (Philadelphia: University of Pennsylvania Press, 2013), 67–68; Andrew R. L. Cayton, *Ohio: The History of a People* (Columbus: Ohio State University Press, 2002), 4.

9. Alfred Byron Sears, *Thomas Worthington: Father of Ohio Statehood* (Columbus: Ohio State University Press, 1998), 19–28, 33; David Mead Massie, *Nathaniel Massie: A Pioneer of Ohio* (Cincinnati, 1896), 62; Ben F. Sager, *The Harrison Mansion* (Vincennes, IN: Francis Vigo Chapter, D.A.R., 1928), 12–13.

10. The story presented in David McCullough, *The Pioneers: The Heroic Story of Settlers Who Brought the American Ideal West* (New York: Simon and Schuster, 2019), is not new. Most textbooks on the state of Ohio tell a similar story, centering Marietta as part of the state's origin story. An Ohio history school text from the 1930s declared that "perhaps no colony in America was ever planted under more favorable auspices, for these Marietta pioneers were the flower of New England's sturdy stock. 'I know many of the settlers personally,' wrote Washington, 'and never were men better calculated to promote the welfare of a community.'" William M. Gregory and William B. Guitteau, *History and Geography of Ohio* (Columbus, OH: Ginn and Company, 1935), 20. George W. Knepper, *Ohio and Its People* (Kent, OH: Kent State University Press, 2003), calls those who arrived in Ohio before the Marietta settlement

"illegal settlers, or squatters," and comments that they "were a constant problem on the American frontier" (p. 55). After noting that these people were widely viewed in a negative light by the elite, Knepper writes that "for every drifter or loser among them there were many of strong character who were simply too poor to purchase land legally" (p. 55). When turning to Marietta's founders, Knepper describes them as "aggressive and resourceful New England war veterans" (p. 60) and Manasseh Cutler as "one of those multitalented individuals so often brought forth by the Revolutionary generation" (pp. 60–61), and notes that the Ohio Company of Associates "proceeded to take up their lands in an orderly fashion" (p. 61). The most recent college textbook on Ohio history, Kevin F. Kern and Gregory S. Wilson, *Ohio: A History of the Buckeye State* (Malden, MA: John Wiley, 2014), corrects many of the biases found in earlier accounts, noting that "by 1785, more than 2,200 families were illegally living north of the Ohio River" and taking the time to tell the story of Joseph Ross and his family, who persistently resisted removal by the US Army (p. 113). For lack of a better alternative, the authors default to the descriptor "illegal settlers" to describe such people, and both terms in the phrase are probably deserving a rethink. In introducing the topic of Marietta's founding, Kern and Wilson make those invisible in McCullough's account visible, noting that "despite the presence of thousands of Native Americans and thousands more white squatters at the time of its founding, Marietta has traditionally held the distinction of being the first official American settlement in Ohio" (p. 114).

11. McCullough, *The Pioneers*, 5.
12. McCullough, 3.
13. McCullough, 82.
14. McCullough, 150.
15. W. E. Peters, *Ohio Lands and the History*, 3rd ed. (Athens, OH: W. E. Peters, 1930), 183–84.
16. The US Federal Census, 1810, Fearing Township, Washington County, Ohio, lists John Chapman's stepmother Lucy Chapman living with two children, alongside Parley, living with his wife and one child. Oral tradition places the family further north near Dexter City in present-day Noble County, and Parley Chapman is buried there. Fearing Township is about fifteen miles south of the grave of Parley Chapman.
17. W. M. Glines, *Johnny Appleseed by One Who Knew Him* (Columbus, OH: F. J. Beer, 1922), 8.
18. Peter Cartwright, *Autobiography of Peter Cartwright* (New York: Abingdon Press, 1956), 141.
19. Hatch, *Fruits and Fruit Trees*, 64–66; Ben Watson, *Cider, Hard and Sweet: History, Traditions, and Making Your Own* (Woodstock, VT: Countryman Press, 1999), 169–73.
20. Kerrigan, *Johnny Appleseed*, 142.

21. John A. Williams, "Our Cabin; or, Life in the Woods," *American Pioneer: A Monthly Periodical* 2, no. 10 (October 1, 1843): 442–43, American Periodical Series Online (APS).
22. Williams, 445, 451–55.
23. Williams, 454–55.
24. Hatch, *Fruits and Fruit Trees,* 66; Kerrigan, *Johnny Appleseed,* 148.
25. George Knepper, *The Official Ohio Lands Book* (Columbus, OH: Auditor of State, 2002), 37; Transcript of the Harrison Land Act of 1800, Ohio History Central, https://ohiohistorycentral.org/w/Harrison_Land_Act_of_1800_(Transcript).
26. John Bradbury, "Travels in the Interior of America in the Years 1809, 1810, and 1811," in *Early Western Travels,* ed. Ruben Gold Thwaites (Cleveland: Arthur H. Clark, 1904), 5:281–2.
27. John Henris, "Apples Abound: Farmers, Orchards, and the Cultural Landscapes of Agrarian Reform, 1820–1860" (PhD diss., University of Akron, 2009). Henris's dissertation, which focuses on apple growing in New England in this era and in the Yankee diaspora in the Ohio Valley, is a fine example of the direction the study of America's horticultural history needs to go, bridging the gap between the writings of horticultural reformers and the practices of local farmers. I am very much indebted to Dr. Henris's work, which has shaped my thinking about horticultural transformation in the Ohio Valley.
28. Adlard Welby, "A Visit to North American and the English Settlements," in Thwaites, *Early Western Travels,* 2:205.
29. Quoted in Daniel Walker Howe, *What God Hath Wrought: The Transformation of America, 1815–1848* (New York: Oxford University Press, 2007), 90.
30. Irwin Silber, ed., *Songs America Voted By* (Harrisburg, PA: Stackpole Books, 1971), 40.
31. See Kerrigan, *Johnny Appleseed,* 148–50, 167.

9

What If Manasseh Cutler Were Black?

The History of the Diverse Pioneers Who Created Ohio

ANNA-LISA COX

In his 2019 book, *The Pioneers,* David McCullough noted that an African American man by the name of Christopher Malbone voted in 1802 in territorial Ohio. Malbone voted for the man he wanted to see represent him as a delegate to the Constitutional Convention. What McCullough does not mention is that Malbone had the right to vote under the 1787 Territorial Ordinance, which never mentioned the color of a man's skin when proscribing voting rights in the region. What McCullough does note, however, was that "it was considered to have been the *first* vote cast by a black African in the Northwest Territory."[1]

After *The Pioneers* was released, I discussed it with Ms. Fay Williams. Ms. Williams was in her eighties, and an influential African American lawyer and community leader in Indianapolis. I shared my frustration with her about the various ways in which successful and entrepreneurial African Americans are described by historians. She leaned forward and said with great conviction, "I am so tired of the *F* and the *O!*" I was a bit taken aback and asked her what the *F* and the *O* meant. She responded, "The *first* and the *only*," adding that historians often use this designation when talking about anyone who has accomplished something of note, who also happens to not be a Protestant White man.

When historians argue that someone who is not a White Protestant man is the first or the only, it blinkers the reader and other historians, for it is a subtle yet powerful message that we should not look further back in time, we should not look for more, and we should certainly not look for many. To be sure, some historians—especially African American historians—use these terms as a way of bringing attention to truly heroic individuals in the past who have long been overlooked. However, these African American historians, especially local historians and preservationists working to preserve sites that bear witness to the success of African Americans in early Ohio, are working under the weight of these prejudiced tropes and myths, which also claim that the relics and evidence revealing the history of African Americans in early Ohio are rare and hard to find. There is an assumption of poverty, of lack, in records pertaining to the history of midwestern antebellum African Americans. Ironically, when David McCullough used this argument to defend his lack of narratives about women and Native Americans in *The Pioneers,* the interviewer never asked him about the lack of narratives in the book concerning African Americans, possibly because the interviewer assumed there were no African Americans for McCullough to trace in the region and the period he was covering.[2]

However, the evidence of African American settlement and success is hiding in plain sight. Indeed, the biggest challenge when writing *The Bone and Sinew of the Land,* a book on the Black pioneers in the Northwest Territory, was not the dearth of evidence, but the preponderance of it. By my conservative estimation, the number of African American rural communities in Ohio that were home to propertied farmers of African descent before the Civil War is well over ninety. Indeed, the table in the appendix, listing hundreds of African American propertied farmers living in antebellum Ohio, barely scratches the surface. There were many more propertied and successful African American entrepreneurs in Ohio who were foundational settlers, including blacksmiths, sailors, barbers, masons, general store owners, preachers, and others who came early and worked hard to make Ohio the state it is today. Many of them were literate, and there is a wealth of documentation surrounding their lives in Ohio, even in its earliest territorial days.[3]

William Kenny was among these early settlers to territorial Ohio. Kenny had been living in bondage in British-held Fort Detroit in the 1790s. Kenny was literate and may well have heard of the 1772 Somerset Case back in England, which had all but abolished slavery on English soil. Yet here he was being held against his will because Detroit was a colony and thus exempt from any laws abolishing slavery on British soil. Kenny freed himself, fleeing south to the Ohio territories. Literate, world-traveled, bright, and determined, Kenny was quickly hired to work for a territorial Judge in Ohio. Once he was settled, William Kenny wrote a letter to his former enslaver, Alexander McKee, firmly informing him that he would never be returning to bondage. Kenny was obviously well accustomed to the formalities of letter writing, whereby writers sign off as "Your obedient servant." But instead of this formality, Kenny ended his letter to his former enslaver in Detroit with some irony, writing, "No More at Present But still remains Your Ob't Servant."[4]

It is important to note that the region that would become Ohio, as well as the state itself, is known for Underground Railroad activities. This did not mean, however, that it was free from racism or slavery. In its early days, this region was a frontier where much happened, both good and bad. The historical tropes concerning this region continue to be strongly influenced by what occurred decades into the future, including the Civil War. In its early colonizing days, however, there was no North or South, and there was slavery everywhere. The Quakers, now known as leaders in the Underground Railroad in Ohio, held thousands of people enslaved across the colonies in the 1700s.

True, the 1787 Northwest Territorial Ordinance was written, and it made clear that slavery was not allowed in the region. However, enslavers from the eastern states, including the Northeast, found many ways to get around that document out on the Ohio frontier. Indeed, the abolitionist John Brown, who would become famous for his leadership of the Harpers Ferry uprising, experienced his transformative moment with slavery in Ohio. During the War of 1812, John Brown, who was about twelve years old, and his father stayed with a respected White landowner who would later become a United States marshal. The man held a boy illegally enslaved, who was very close in age to the young Brown. The future abolitionist would later describe the enslaved child as "very active, intelligent, & good feeling." While John was treated kindly by the White landlord, the enslaved child was brutally abused by his enslaver. The boy was "badly clothed, poorly fed; & and *lodged in cold weather* [emphasis added by John Brown]: and beaten before his eyes with Iron Shovels or any other thing that came first to hand." John Brown would later recount that he was horrified by this case and "the wretched, hopeless condition, of Fatherless & Motherless slave children: for such children have neither Fathers nor Mothers to protect & provide for them."[5] Brown's story is also a reminder that, despite what some historians have argued, slavery in the Midwest was not less harmful or abusive just because there were fewer large plantations or fewer large groups of people held enslaved in the Old Northwest than in the South.[6]

While this chapter is most concerned with those who were propertied farmers in Ohio, there is not one narrative that can (or should) encompass the experience of people of African descent in the antebellum era. While there were some who were freedom seekers on the Underground Railroad, many came long free, some literate and others as veterans of the Revolutionary War or children of presidents. There were hundreds of freedom entrepreneurs—men and women who worked while enslaved to raise the money to purchase their own freedom and the freedom of their family members; they came from all over and were just as likely to come from the Northeast as the South.

Deborah Harris was one of the many who came into Ohio as a settler from the Northeast. Deborah married her husband, Enoch Harris, in her home state of Pennsylvania, around 1812. They then returned to Knox County, Ohio, where her husband had been investing in land and making good money in the Mount Vernon area as a frontier entrepreneur (fig. 9.1). Once they returned to Ohio, they were determined to settle a new portion of land, and Enoch convinced two White brothers, Peter and Nicholas Kile, to come out to see a likely portion of land he had discovered in Bloomfield Township. Once the three men arrived, the White men deferred to "the older Enoch" and mutually agreed "that they should choose in the order of their ages, beginning with the oldest." Enoch Harris picked the best piece of land with a sure source of good water, and the story ends with the words "each as satisfied with his selection, and all three went back to Mount Vernon to complete the purchase of their new homes."[7] What this later story does not note is that Deborah was helping with the homesteading, and would soon give birth to their son, Irad, in the new cabin they built in Bloomfield Township.[8]

FIG. 9.1. Case daguerreotype of Enoch and Deborah Harris, ca. 1850.
Source: Courtesy of Kalamazoo Valley Museum.

Of course, Ohio already had residents, people for whom this had been
home for millennia. The story of African-descended settlers in early
Ohio is a complicated one. Some of them had Indigenous roots as well
as African. Some of these African-descended settlers were involved in
violent conflicts with the First Nations of Ohio, although, as Tiya Miles
points out, people of African descent coming to this frontier were very
different from White pioneers. Many were refugees from racism and
enslavement, and not all were in conflict with local Native Americans.
Recently, the work of Roy Finkenbine and Diane Miller has uncovered

the rich history of Indigenous abolitionists in Ohio, and the ways in which they not only assisted freedom seekers but welcomed them as neighbors and kin in ways that few White abolitionists in Ohio did.[9]

Regardless of their relationship with the first peoples of Ohio, the Harrises, William Kenny, Christopher Malbone, and other early African-descended settlers certainly did not deserve to be repeatedly betrayed and attacked by many early White settlers and leaders of Ohio, and this is an important part of Ohio's history as well. Although propertied African-descended early settlers were voting for their representatives in the first state constitution of 1803, the majority of those White representatives decided to reverse the 1787 ordinance and insert the word "white" into the state's first constitution, thus stealing the right to vote from the Black Buckeyes who were helping to settle the state. They also added Black Codes laws, which became increasingly prejudiced over time. These legislations and state constitutions were driven by the genocidal and violently racist language and beliefs of White politicians. Indeed, Silvana Siddali found that the racist language advocating violence and even genocide against free people of African descent in the Old Northwest was much more common in state conventions than language aimed at Indigenous people. And this language came with very real consequences.[10]

One that deserves more research recognition is that when Ohio's much-lauded public school legislations were passed, African American property owners in Ohio were taxed for schools their children were banned from attending. When Ohio's African American families resisted this move by pooling their resources to start private schools for their children, the teachers' lives were often threatened and the schools burned.[11] These laws and legislations were passed despite the fact that without patriots of African descent, Ohio and the United States may not have won the War of 1812. African American sailors were an important part of the US Navy when the pivotal battle of Lake Erie was fought, with some historians estimating that as many as 20 percent of the crew members who risked and lost their lives on board those vessels were Black.[12]

While African Americans were officially banned from militias and army service during the War of 1812, a number of African Americans in the Midwest fought for their country, including an entire Black regiment who fought under William Henry Harrison in the Indiana Territories. In Ohio, Enoch Harris left Deborah and his young family to fight under Colonel Alexander Enos in the First Regiment of the Ohio Militia.[13]

Their stories are scarcely known, but without them we cannot fully understand Ohio's early history, or why Ohio looks the way it does today—from its cities to its farming communities. Some historians have argued that the number of these early settlers was statistically so small, they could not have had much impact on the attitudes or behaviors of the White settlers who moved in around them. This ignores, however, that these African-descended early settlers were a highly visible minority. True, William Kenny may have been just one African-descended man clerking for an Ohio territorial judge in the 1790s. Imagine, however, a White settler bringing a grievance to that judge and arriving to find a well-dressed Black clerk, speaking with a British accent, expertly writing the judge's decision in a flowing script, before handing it to the White settler. The impact of William Kenny was much larger than a statistical percentage of the population, as were the societal impacts of other African-descended early settlers and leaders. Yes, the Black population of early Ohio was small, but this was a highly mobile group of people of color who made themselves known through their many achievements during this period—achievements and accomplishments that were known of during their lifetimes, even if they still are largely unresearched. Yet there is no scarcity of evidence of African American settlement and accomplishment in antebellum Ohio. Instead, there is a scarcity of interest, there is a scarcity of funding, and there is a scarcity of attention being paid. This scarcity goes well beyond verbiage to the actual destruction of the monuments that bear witness to this buried past, a topic I will return to below.

First to language, and the semiotics that strengthen this erasure. There are many misuses of language that force these histories of African-descended people into external and peripheral positions. Olivette Otele points out in her book, *African Europeans,* that the concept of "exceptionalism" as applied to people of African descent in Europe fits within the context of a broader pattern of prejudice. Otele refers to Dienke Hondius's categorizations, which include "infantalization, exoticism, bestialization, distancing and exclusion," and ends most recently with exceptionalism. As Otele points out, however, sometimes that exceptionalism has little to do with the African Europeans' accomplishments but rather that "they have defied obscurity to be included in European accounts."[14]

Otele's point is an important one when thinking about the history of the settlement of early Ohio. For African Americans struggling to draw attention to their histories in the Midwest, the use of exceptionalism can become a tool to bring attention, visitors, and funding to sites that have been ignored and to histories that have been denied. The concept of exceptionalism and scarcity is thus utilized by these local African American preservationists to get around the many barriers that silence and erase African Americans' histories. The erasure of this history in Ohio, and the Old Northwest, is not just about how this history is written—it is also about how it is preserved. As Tsione Wolde-Michael, the curator of the 2021 exhibit on the Emmett Till sign at the Smithsonian's National Museum of American History wrote, "History is an active battleground. What we choose to remember, memorialize, and preserve as a society determines how we understand our present and imagine our future."[15]

While Wolde-Michael is writing about a sign that bears witness to violence and murder in the South, the racist violence in Ohio's past is linked to the more recent destruction of African American heritage sites. In Ohio's case, however, the places of interest that are being destroyed and allowed to decay memorialize African American success, not their murder. This should not come as a surprise, for African American success resulted in a backlash of violence in antebellum Ohio and the Midwest many generations ago. I have written at length on the history of racial massacres and violence against people of African descent in the Midwest in my other publications, so I will only briefly note it here. Antebellum Ohio was certainly not exempt. Cincinnati's African Americans were repeatedly attacked, including a large riot sparked by the suggestion that a school be built for the African American children of the city. And African American churches, schools, barns, businesses, and homes were attacked and burned in many rural communities in Ohio before the Civil War.[16]

This violence was linked to the rising of these African Americans, their growing successes and entrepreneurship. In the early 1830s, around the same time that de Tocqueville was traveling around the United States, a young Oxford professor by the name of Edward Abdy was also making a tour of the new nation and writing about it. Abdy's focus, however, was on slavery and race relations in the United States, and he writes at length about a thriving African American farming settlement just outside Madison, Indiana, where African Americans settled on some of the best land in the region in the territorial days. He details their businesses and community, the delicious food he ate while being hosted by one of the wealthiest farmers, and of his hosts assisting freedom seekers who had just crossed the Ohio River. He also brings up the rising racism in the region: "While they [the African American farmers] were clearing their farms of the timber, they were unmolested; but now that they have got the land into a good state of cultivation, and are rising in the world, the avarice of the white man casts a greedy eye on their luxuriant crops; and his pride is offended at the decent appearance of their sons and daughters."[17]

Moving forward to the twentieth century and beyond, we see the destruction continue, but in ways that have erased the history of African American successes and accomplishments in Ohio. For years, most historians have assumed and argued that there were only a few communities that were home to successful African American propertied farmers in the antebellum Old Northwest states, including Ohio. While there has always been an acknowledgment of African Americans in this space, the assumption has been that African-descended people were rarely the earliest or most successful settlers on the midwestern frontier. As Leslie Schwalm states in her study of African American settlement in the post–Civil War Midwest, "Few antebellum black migrants chose settlement on the edge of newly opened frontier lands. . . . Those areas often presented greater dangers to free people of African descent than to whites."[18] Indeed, when I wrote my first book, I believed the myths surrounding Black settlement in the Midwest, stating in the introduction to *A Stronger Kinship* that people of African descent in the region "were rare and often hated with that odd midwestern racism that was not based on numbers, and could be touched off by the presence of only one black person, or none at all." This myth of low numbers or "none at all" has been asserted by historians for years, even as the descendants of these Black settlers tried to make their histories known.[19]

For too long the myth that African Americans came late to this region, were unsuccessful, and were primarily urban has allowed a collective blindness to grow. This blindness has resulted in real damage to the historical narrative of this region as well as hampered attempts to preserve and make known the historic sites and buildings that testify to the successes and accomplishments of early African American settlers and farmers.

One of the most notable examples in Ohio is the farmhouse that was home in 1855 to the young African American lawyer and activist John Langston. This home was attached to a large and thriving farm that Langston had hired a White English couple to manage. In 1855 Langston was the first known lawyer of African descent in that state and had just been elected to political office in Brownhelm Township, near the college of Oberlin. His election was of national significance because many at that fraught time thought he was the first African American to be elected to political office (although there were certainly others whose stories deserve researching). It was from this farmhouse that he wrote a letter to his friend Frederick Douglass, noting with wry irony, "They put up a colored man and he was elected clerk of Brownhelm, by a handsome majority indeed. Since I am the only colored man who lives in this township, you can easily guess the name of the man who was so fortunate as to secure this election."[20] Over time, however, this historically significant site of national heritage in which John Langston wrote that letter was allowed to decay and collapse.

Another lovely and historic home in Ohio that was lost was owned by Augustus West. West was a freeborn man of color who homesteaded in rural Ohio in the 1830s. He purchased multiple parcels of good farmland in both Fayette and Highland Counties, and in the early 1860s he built a home for his family so grand that locals called it the "Mansion." It must have been a sight—mill-sawn clapboards painted a gleaming white and beautiful, large plate-glass windows overlooking his cleared land. He used some of his land to rehome refugees from enslavement who had fled to Ohio during the Civil War. By the 1970s, however, a White farmer owned the land and the mansion. No attempts were made by local or state officials to preserve this important architectural and heritage site. The farmer decided to let his cows loose so they could use it as a barn, and it was quickly destroyed.[21] Unfortunately, such stories are common across Ohio. Within the last few decades, a graveyard of some of the most successful African American settlers in Columbus, Ohio, for example, was paved over for a parking lot.[22]

This refusal to preserve the monuments to successful midwestern and Ohio African Americans continues. Stephanie Ryberg-Webster's 2017 essay, "Beyond Rust and Rockefeller," noted this fact. She describes the frustrating denial of National Register of Historic Places acceptance for two buildings affiliated with Jesse Owens, the famous twentieth-century African American track star, in Cleveland, one of which had been his home for three years during a key period in his life, from 1927 to 1930. She notes that the homes were rejected for, among other reasons, a "lack of integrity and provenance." Ryberg-Webster adds, in defense of those rejecting the preservationists' efforts, that "a core struggle in African American preservation efforts [is] how to handle the high mobility and impermanence of African American residents, business operations, and other activities."[23] However, "high mobility" and "impermanence" are also "core" issues among an important population in America's past—the White pioneers who settled the midwestern American frontier. Indeed, one of the defining factors of White pioneers in the Midwest is their level of impermanence. As has been noted by many other historians, Manasseh Cutler, who was one of the men that David McCullough focused on in *The Pioneers,* only resided in the Ohio Territory for roughly a year in 1788. Yet his level of impermanence in Ohio did not affect how he is revered, celebrated, or remembered in Ohio. And there is no site affiliated with Laura Ingalls Wilder and the Ingalls family currently being used as a museum or preserved for posterity that has been faced with criticism or denial of recognition because her family was so "impermanent." Indeed, they and other White homesteaders are praised for their courage, heroism, and grit when they pulled up stakes and repeatedly left their settled homes to better their lives and live out the American dream. "Impermanence" only becomes a negative when it is affiliated with Blackness.

Admittedly, these issues of preservation and recognition facing the memorialization of high-achieving African Americans is not confined to Ohio or the Midwest. This is a national issue, affiliated with many sites that represent African American heritage. As Ryberg-Webster points out, only a small percentage of properties in the National Register of Historic Places are affiliated with any form of African American heritage.[24] The issue of preserving sites affiliated with African American success faces hurdles in many regions of the United States. A notable example concerns Jeremiah G. Hamilton, the African American Wall Street millionaire of New York City, who achieved huge success in that city in the 1830s and 1840s. Some have even credited him with inventing the concept of the "hedge fund." He challenged Cornelius Vanderbilt, almost succeeding in a hostile takeover of sections of Vanderbilt's shipping company. Hamilton also had numerous holdings and properties in and around New York City. In addition to his antebellum mansion in Manhattan, one of his homes was a luxurious ten-bedroom mansion with a ballroom on his 270-acre estate in New Jersey.[25] Yet not one of his properties has been recognized, acknowledged, or preserved, possibly because they break the myth that all African Americans throughout the history of the United States were poor, with properties and homes that would have had little architectural or heritage value.

The midwestern African American activist Eugene Hardy summed up this problem in 1883 in his speech to a large crowd gathered for an Emancipation Festival in Grand Rapids, Michigan: "Black is not a color despised by God or man. Four-fifths of the human race are black. Black appears to be the favorite color with the Lord for humanity, and is a favorite color with man everywhere else except in the human face. . . . But it is not the color that is despised, but it is despised in this country because it has become a badge of poverty and ignorance."[26]
The "badge" of "poverty and ignorance" was one that was created, a toxic myth and a reality often violently imposed on African Americans who dared to rise too high in Ohio and the North.

Yet even buildings that preservationists have managed to get designated as sites of historical importance at the state or federal level continue to be neglected and are at risk. John Langston's second home, in downtown Oberlin, Ohio, is one such example. For a while, the building was used to house students attending Oberlin College, and attempts to turn it into a museum have failed. The Clemens home, a grand brick and limestone mansion in Darke County, Ohio, continues to languish with little support from local or state officials, despite two generations of the Clemens family's assistance in funding and starting the Union Literary Institute, which was lauded by Frederick Douglass for its racially integrated precollegiate education. The school also educated Hiram Revels, who was the first African-descended person we know of to be elected to the United States Senate. The Clemens family were also active Underground Railroad operatives. Meanwhile, just a few miles from the Clemens home and the ruins of the Union Literary Institute, the home of the White Underground Railroad operative, Levi Coffin, is now a well-supported and publicized museum.

Benedict Anderson, in his book *Imagined Communities,* makes the argument that a shared sense of a nation's history held by that nation's citizens is one of the most crucial aspects of a postcolonial nation's sense of identity. And the United States is one of the first postcolonial nations. How that past is presented has very real power—the power to influence how many people feel about themselves, their region, and their nation.[27]

True, by suppressing and denying this history, some of the horrors of the past may be overlooked, but we also lose the hope these histories can offer us today. If the existence of these successful African American settlers, homesteaders, and farmers continues to be overlooked and underappreciated in Ohio, and the evidence of their existence destroyed, then we lose all that they accomplished—sometimes alongside their White and Indigenous allies. We lose the important stories of how Ohio's Black citizens advanced the causes of freedom, justice, and equality in this state.[28] To assist in helping make their stories better known, I have included a table of the African American propertied farmers in Ohio that have been found so far (see appendix). This table represents those who owned their own land before 1850. While far from complete, and only focusing on farmers, it stands as a rough roadmap for others who are willing to continue the work of making known, preserving, and celebrating all of Ohio's past.

Notes

1. David McCullough, *The Pioneers: The Heroic Story of the Settlers Who Brought the American Ideal West* (New York: Simon and Schuster, 2019), 144, italics mine.

2. Michael Schaub, *"The Pioneers* Dives Deep into Lives of Northwest Territory Settlers,"* review of *The Pioneers: The Heroic Story of the Settlers Who Brought the American Ideal West,* by David McCullough, NPR, May 8, 2019, Book Reviews, https://www.npr.org/2019/05/08/721352662/the -pioneers-dives-deep-into-lives-of-northwest-territory-settlers.

3. A few works have looked at African Americans in the frontier and rural antebellum Northwest Territory and states, although most have assumed that the settlements they covered were unusual or unique. There are a growing number of articles and dissertations on the subject, although most still focus on one county, city, or state. The books have been invaluable in laying the groundwork for this study. They include Alaina Roberts, *I've Been Here All the While: Black Freedom on Native Land* (Philadelphia: University of Pennsylvania Press, 2021); Cheryl Janifer LaRoche, *Free Black Communities and the Underground Railroad: The Geography of Resistance* (Champaign: University of Illinois Press, 2013); Stephen Vincent, *Southern Seed, Northern Soil: African-American Farm Communities in the Midwest, 1765–1900* (Bloomington: Indiana University Press, 1999); Juliet E. K. Walker, *Free Frank: A Black Pioneer on the Antebellum Frontier* (Lexington: University Press of Kentucky,

1983); Sundiata Keita Cha-Jua, *America's First Black Town: Brooklyn, Illinois, 1830–1915* (Champaign: University of Illinois Press, 2002); Leslie Schwalm, *Emancipation's Diaspora: Race and Reconstruction in the Upper Midwest* (Chapel Hill: University of North Carolina Press, 2009); Leon Litwack, *North of Slavery: The Negro in the Free States, 1790–1860* (Chicago: University of Chicago Press, 1970); Wilma Gibbs, *Indiana's African-American Heritage: Essays from Black History News and Notes* (Indianapolis: Indiana Historical Society Press, 2007); William Loren Katz, *Black Pioneers: An Untold Story* (New York: Atheneum Books for Young Readers, 1999); Emma Lou Thornbrough, *The Negro in Indiana: A Study of a Minority* (Indianapolis: Indiana Historical Bureau, 1957); David Gerber, *Black Ohio and the Color Line, 1860–1915* (Champaign: University of Illinois Press, 1991); Benjamin C. Wilson, *The Rural Black Heritage between Chicago and Detroit, 1850–1929: A Photograph Album and Random Thoughts* (Kalamazoo, MI: New Issues Press, Western Michigan University, 1985).

4. William R. Riddell, "A Negro Slave in Detroit When Detroit Was Canadian," *Michigan History Magazine* 18 (1934): 48, cited in Gene A. Smith, *The Slaves' Gamble: Choosing Sides in the War of 1812* (New York: Palgrave Macmillan, 2013).

5. John Brown to Henry L. Stearns, July 15, 1857, quoted in Louis Ruchames, *John Brown: The Making of a Revolutionary; The Story of John Brown in His Own Words and in the Words of Those Who Knew Him* (New York: Grosset & Dunlap, 1969), 46.

6. There is a growing body of work on slavery and racism in the Midwest, most recently Christopher Lehman, *Slavery's Reach: Southern Slaveholders in the North Star State* (St. Paul: Minnesota Historical Society, 2019); Christy Clark-Pujara, "Contested: Black Suffrage in Early Wisconsin," *Wisconsin Magazine of History* 100, no. 4 (2017): 21–27; M. Scott Heerman, *The Alchemy of Slavery: Human Bondage and Emancipation in the Illinois Country, 1730–1865* (Philadelphia: University of Pennsylvania Press, 2018).

7. J. H. Battle and William H. Lerner, *History of Morrow County and Ohio* (Chicago, 1880), 449; "Mark and Millie's Lightfoot Branch," Family Tree, Ancestry.com.

8. Carl Lightfoot et al., "Enoch 'Knuck' Harris: A Biography in Progress" (unpublished paper, 2009), in possession of Carl Lightfoot; "Black Pioneer 'Knuck' Harris Was a City Founder," *Mount Vernon News* (Mount Vernon, OH), February 21, 2008; Alexis A. Praus, "Enoch Harris: Negro Pioneer," *Michigan Heritage* 2, no. 11 (1960); "Enoch Harris," obituary, *Kalamazoo Telegraph* (Kalamazoo, MI), March 25, 1870; Battle and Lerner, *History of Morrow County and Ohio,* 449.

9. Tiya Miles, "Beyond a Boundary: Black Lives and the Settler-Native Divide," *William and Mary Quarterly* 76, no. 3 (2019): 417–26, https://

doi.org/10.5309/willmaryquar.76.3.0417; Roy E. Finkenbine, "The Underground Railroad in 'Indian Country,'" *Fugitive Slaves and Spaces of Freedom in North America* (Gainsville: University Press of Florida, 2018), 70–92; Diane Miller, "Wyandot, Shawnee, and African American Resistance to Slavery in Ohio and Kansas" (PhD diss., University of Nebraska, Lincoln, 2019).

10.   Silvana Siddali, "'Better to Kill Them Off at Once': Race, Violence, and Human Rights in Antebellum Western State Constitutional Conventions," *American Nineteenth Century History* 20, no. 1 (2019): 19–40, https://doi.org/10.1080/14664658.2019.1605756.

11.   These prejudiced Black laws hung over the heads of all Black settlers in antebellum Ohio. Indeed, newly arrived white pioneers could, and did, use the Black Code laws to force African American settlers who had been there before them to leave their land and homes. See Nikki Taylor, *Frontiers of Freedom: Cincinnati's Black Community, 1802–1868* (Athens: Ohio University Press, 2005); Ross Bagby, "The Randolph Slave Saga: Communities in Collision" (PhD diss., Ohio State University, 1998), 153; Stephen Middleton, *The Black Laws in the Old Northwest: A Document History* (Westport, CT: Greenwood Press, 1993). For more on attacks on teachers and schools, see Anna-Lisa Cox, *The Bone and Sinew of the Land: America's Forgotten Black Pioneers and the Struggle for Equality* (New York: Hachette, 2018).

12.   Smith, *The Slaves' Gamble*. Smith notes in his chapter on the Battle of Lake Erie that the numbers were between 8 and 20 percent and could be dependent on the ship.

13.   Lightfoot et al., "Enoch 'Knuck' Harris"; "Black Pioneer 'Knuck' Harris Was a City Founder"; Praus, "Enoch Harris: Negro Pioneer"; "Enoch Harris," obituary; Battle and Lerner, *History of Morrow County and Ohio*, 449.

14.   Olivette Otele, *African Europeans: An Untold History* (New York: Basic Books, 2021), 4–5.

15.   "Reckoning with Remembrance: History, Injustice and the Murder of Emmett Till," National Museum of American History, Washington, DC, https://americanhistory.si.edu/reckoning-with-remembrance.

16.   For a fuller list and descriptions of the racial massacres, attacks, and atrocities against African-descended people in Ohio and the Old Northwest Territories and states before the Civil War, see Leonard Richards, *Gentlemen of Property and Standing: Anti-abolition Mobs in Jacksonian America* (New York: Oxford University Press, 1971); Taylor, *Frontiers of Freedom;* Cox, *The Bone and Sinew of the Land*.

17.   E. S. Abdy, *Journal of a Residence and Tour in the United States of North America, from April, 1833, to October, 1834* (London: J. Murray, 1835), 366.

18. Leslie Schwalm, *Emancipation's Diaspora: Race and Reconstruction in the Upper Midwest* (Chapel Hill: University of North Carolina Press, 2009), 34.
19. Anna-Lisa Cox, *A Stronger Kinship: One Town's Extraordinary Story of Hope and Faith* (New York: Little, Brown, 2006), 6.
20. Quoted in Aimee Lee Cheek and William Cheek, *John Mercer Langston and the Fight for Black Freedom, 1829–1865* (Champaign: University of Illinois Press, 1996), 260.
21. Wayne L. Snider, *All in the Same Spaceship: Portions of American Negro History Illustrated in Highland County, Ohio, U.S.A.* (New York: Vantage Press, 1974), 35–36.
22. Suzanne Goldsmith, "The Story behind the Human Remains Found at Upper Arlington High School," *Columbus Monthly*, August 24, 2021, https://www.columbusmonthly.com/story/lifestyle/features/2021/08/24/human-remains-found-at-upper-arlington-high-school-pleasant-litchford-cemetery/8179013002/. For a fuller description of this history and events, see Diane K. Runyon and Kim S. Starr, *Secrets Under the Parking Lot: The True Story of Upper Arlington, Ohio, and the History of Perry Township in the Nineteenth Century* (self-pub., 2017).
23. Stephanie Ryberg Webster, "Beyond Rust and Rockefeller: Preserving Cleveland's African American Heritage," *Preservation Education and Research* 9 (2017): 7–23, https://engagedscholarship.csuohio.edu/urban_facpub/1510.
24. Webster, 7.
25. See Shane White, *Prince of Darkness: The Untold Story of Jeremiah G. Hamilton, Wall Street's First Black Millionaire* (Gordonsville, VA: Palgrave Macmillan, 2016).
26. "Colored Citizens Celebrate," *Grand Rapids Eagle* (Grand Rapids, MI), August 2, 1883, quoted in Randal Maurice Jelks, *African Americans in the Furniture City: The Struggle for Civil Rights in Grand Rapids* (Champaign: University of Illinois Press, 2006), 64.
27. Benedict Anderson, *Imagined Communities: Reflections on the Origin and Spread of Nationalism* (New York: Verso Press, 1991).
28. I use the term "citizen" deliberately to include people of African descent, despite their inability to vote for much of Ohio's history. For the reasonings behind this decision, please see Derrick Spires, *The Practice of Citizenship: Black Politics and Print Culture in the Early United States* (Philadelphia: University of Pennsylvania Press, 2019).

10

Federalist Failure

Conflict and Disorder in the Northwest Territory

JOSEPH THOMAS ROSS

July 4, 1788, was a day of celebration and optimism for the town of Marietta. Founded only three months prior by the Ohio Company of Associates, Marietta was to become the center of national governance in the newly erected Northwest Territory. The Ohio Company had recently received a million acres of land from the Confederation Congress, and the company's shareholders had secured for themselves the leading offices in the territorial government. Residents of the company town understood their role was to assert federal authority in the trans-Appalachian West, and they used the Fourth of July to voice their commitment to this national experiment. Festivities began with a salute of thirteen canons across the Muskingum River at Fort Harmar. A banquet quickly followed along the river's edge where US Army officers and company members feasted together on roasted fish, venison, bear, pork, and buffalo. Toasts were given to "the United States," "the Congress," "the new Federal Constitution," and "His Excellency General Washington." After the meal was finished, company member James Mitchell Varnum delivered an oration to the assembled crowd. Varnum rejoiced not only for American independence, but also for the relief offered by a new national government that would promote the union of the states and facilitate its westward expansion. The Articles of Confederation had failed to establish order, Varnum said. The constitution just recently ratified would be different. Under "the strongest and best of ties," American citizens would "find the reward of peace, plenty, and virtuous contentment." Varnum verbalized what many in the settlement already knew: it was the duty of the Ohio Company to support the ties of union and help bring order and stability to the American West.[1]

Historians have long recognized this special relationship between the Ohio Company and the United States. When the Confederation Congress set its eyes west after the Revolutionary War, it saw a region fraught with violence, disorganization, and unknown loyalties. If Congress wished to establish both its authority and its jurisdiction in the trans-Appalachian West, it would need loyal citizens to defend its territorial claims against imperial rivals, create amicable relations with Native Americans, and provide systematic settlement for White men. These necessities made a public-private partnership between the United States and the Ohio Company ideal. The Ohio Company was a joint-stock venture comprising mostly Continental Army veterans who had proved their loyalty to the United States during the recent war. Many members were also supportive of strengthening the national government and would soon become sympathetic to the fiscal-military program of Alexander Hamilton. Congress found these traits appealing. In 1787 the United States sold a million acres of expropriated Native American land to the Ohio Company and appointed company shareholders to four of the five offices created for the new Northwest Territory. Imbued with federal power and ownership over a significant portion of the western land market, the Ohio Company orchestrated what historian Andrew Cayton has called a "Federalist conquest" of the early American West. Company members acted in their federal capacity to bring an end to the violence that had plagued the region since the Revolution and did the work implementing the Northwest Ordinance's promises of religious freedom, public education, and orderly settlement. Their actions and their legacies transformed the Ohio Valley's dense woodlands into the agricultural, commercial, and cultural center it is today. James Mitchell Varnum's Fourth of July oration supposedly foreshadowed this larger process.[2]

Yet, if we only focus on the ceremonialism, officeholding, and legal authority of western Federalists like Varnum—as many historians have—we lose sight of the realities in the Northwest Territory. Throughout the 1790s, when western Federalists tried to control the territory, the Ohio Valley was not orderly and stable. It was dangerous and chaotic. Violence between Native Americans and White settlers intensified in the opening years of the decade, resulting in the new national government's first military conflicts. And when these settlers divided expropriated Indigenous land among themselves, the titles were often insecure and frequently disputed. Western Federalists were not just witness to this discord; they were responsible for it. They antagonized Indigenous peoples, who had their own claims to sovereignty, while also destabilizing the territory's budding land market. Their access to and command over federal resources exacerbated the situation. Governing power gave these western Federalists an inflated sense of authority that in turn led to the mismanagement and misuse of these federal resources. Rather than utilize the powers of the federal government to establish order and stability, western Federalists used it to further their own personal interests. The national project of a safe and stable northwestern frontier was thus jeopardized by western Federalists who failed to establish good relations with Native Americans and failed to provide secure land titles.[3]

This chapter explores these developments in greater detail by focusing on three key moments of Federalist failure. First, it explains how the millions of acres granted to western Federalists had an adverse effect on national policy by creating local interests within the territory. This is especially true of the Ohio Company, which decided to use its federal power to authorize military expeditions against Indigenous peoples who contested its land claims. The result was the Northwest Indian War, which depressed the western land market and threatened the establishment of federal jurisdiction in the region. Second, this chapter examines how Ohio Company agents in the territory were unable to administer the land claims of nonresident proprietors. Company shareholders who remained in New England placed great trust in the company members who moved west to manage their property and pay their taxes. These agents proved inadequate and unwilling to promote land sales or make tax payments. Their dereliction resulted in multiple seizures of nonresidents' lands by county sheriffs, which further destabilized the western land market and eroded the trust Congress had for the Ohio Company. Third, the chapter shifts focus away from the Ohio Company and toward John Cleves Symmes. Like the Ohio Company, Symmes also purchased a million acres from the Confederation Congress and received appointment to the territorial government. Symmes hoped to sell his grant between the Great and Little Miami Rivers in small parcels to make his fortune. However, the stabilization of public credit after the ratification of the Constitution combined with the escalating violence of the Northwest Indian War to depress his land sales. To make his payments to Congress, Symmes began to sell land outside his patent, leaving purchasers with insecure titles and nowhere to legally live. It took the federal government years to end the violence of the war and sort out the property disputes caused by these western Federalists.[4]

* * *

When the United States granted the Ohio Company of Associates a million acres of land, it thought it was gaining a western ally that would institute national policies on its behalf. Although company members did assume many of their duties as federal officials, they also devoted significant time, energy, and capital to developing their land. In the spring of 1788, company superintendent Rufus Putnam led the first thirty families to the confluence of the Muskingum and Ohio Rivers. Putnam directed the settlers to build cabins, erect fortifications, plant crops, and lay out the company town of Marietta. Once the initial settlement was secure, Putnam and a team of surveyors measured lines, marked trees, and mapped the lands they now claimed as their own. More settlers soon followed and new towns were established further up the Muskingum. A minister was hired by the company directors to ride the circuit and offer religious instruction to settlers. The directors also instituted strict property regulations for town lots and farmlands. Settlers were required to maintain good fences, build sturdy houses, and engage in commercial farming. Mill sites and iron works were encouraged and standardized. Company directors used their appointment to territorial and county offices to enforce these regulations. There was little doubt in these New Englanders' minds that disciplined towns with religious instruction, budding industry, and thriving farmsteads would entice White settlers to venture into the Ohio Company's grant. This hierarchical system of settlement served to both secure the property claims of company shareholders and enhance that property's value.[5]

The company's work developing Marietta was threatened almost as soon as it began. Violence between the Shawnee and Kentuckians persisted downriver, and company shareholders feared it would creep into their settlement. Members of the Lenape and Wyandot had also grown uneasy and complained about the Ohio Company's push up the Muskingum. Some tribal members had signed a treaty with the United States in 1785 that—on paper—ceded their tribes' claims to most of present-day Ohio, only after being threatened with death by the American commissioners. It is worth noting that none of the Indigenous speeches given at the treaty conference acknowledged cession, a tradition long understood by Native Americans to be just as binding as ink. Most of the Lenape and Wyandot rejected the land cession outright, proclaiming that a small handful of chiefs and warriors could not speak for an entire tribe. They denounced the White settlers as trespassers, threatened open warfare, and began the process of joining the growing Northwestern Confederacy centered around the Miami town of Kekionga. Their rejections not only discredited the United States' territorial claims, but also jeopardized the legitimacy of the Ohio Company's settlement. Arthur St. Clair, a company shareholder and recently appointed governor of the Northwest Territory, tried to accommodate the tribes while preserving his company's interests. He held what was supposed to be a general treaty with all the prominent chiefs and warriors of the Lenape, Miami, and Wyandot at Fort Harmar, but only a scattering of Native people desperate for food and supplies attended.[6]

With diplomacy stalled, the Ohio Company decided to employ the federal powers granted to it by the United States to foster a military solution. Such a move was contrary to the Washington administration's preferred policy of amity between the United States and Indigenous peoples. Secretary of War Henry Knox had instructed Governor St. Clair to continue diplomatic overtures and advised that military expeditions against the northern tribes should only be used as a last resort. St. Clair used the failed negotiations at Fort Harmar and the sporadic violence between the Shawnee and Kentuckians as an excuse to launch an offensive campaign against the tribes who were contesting the Ohio Company's land claims. He ordered Josiah Harmar, commander of US Army forces in the West and a fellow landholder in the Ohio Company grant, to organize the militias of Pennsylvania and Virginia and march them toward Kekionga. Harmar arrived with several hundred men in the fall of 1790 but was repulsed by a strong contingent of Native warriors led by the Miami chief Mihšihkinaahkwa (Little Turtle). Lenape and Wyandot warriors responded by attacking the Ohio Company settlement of Big Bottom. With the company's lands under siege, St. Clair led his own, larger expedition against the Confederacy. It was a disaster. Mihši-hkinaahkwa surprised St. Clair on the Wabash River, killing, wounding, and capturing over 95 percent of the American army. St. Clair himself barely escaped, having three different horses shot out from underneath him. As the remnants of St. Clair's expedition retreated south, the Miami stuffed the mouths of slain Americans with dirt, a symbol of White hunger for Indigenous land.[7]

The Ohio Company's defense of its local interests not only dragged the United States into its first military conflict after the Revolution, but it also created serious geopolitical concerns for the nascent federal government. Great Britain still occupied several forts along the Great Lakes—including Detroit—that had been ceded to the United States in the Treaty of Paris. At the same time, Spain was actively encouraging American settlers to cross the Mississippi River and settle around St. Louis and Cape Girardeau. If the United States could not defend its jurisdictional claims against Indigenous peoples, what was there to stop these European empires from further challenging American sovereignty? Such apprehensions necessitated a firm federal response to establish order and stability in the Northwest Territory. Peace negotiations were again attempted in 1792. Company member Rufus Putnam served as the American diplomat to the Wabash members of the Northwestern Confederacy but failed to produce a treaty acceptable for the US Senate. Likewise, Timothy Pickering was instructed to negotiate with the Lenape, Miami, Shawnee, and Wyandot at Fort Sandusky. The United States was serious about this negotiation, appropriating a significant sum for the treaty conference and inviting several British officials to attend. Prior to the conference, Pickering sent messengers to the Confederacy explaining that the United States would not surrender any of its land claims. Seeing no other point in talking with Pickering, the Confederacy refused to meet with him.[8]

In response to these failed negotiations, the United States authorized a third military expedition. General Anthony Wayne was appointed commander of the newly formed Legion of the United States and marched north to the Miami towns. By then the Northwestern Confederacy had grown in both confidence and strength. Wayne's army met the combined forces of Mihšihkinaahkwa and the Shawnee chief Weyapiersenwah (Blue Jacket) near the Maumee River. The ensuing Battle of Fallen Timbers was brief and had few casualties, but the display of American power broke the spirit of the Confederacy. The following year Wayne treated with the confederated tribes at Fort Greenville and secured the assent of the Confederacy's leading sachems and warriors to both the United States' territorial claims and the legitimacy of the Ohio Company's settlement.[9]

* * *

Anthony Wayne's victory at Fallen Timbers may have solved the Ohio Company's problems of legitimacy, but it also opened the floodgates for further contention. Euro-Americans swarmed north of the Ohio River following the Treaty of Greenville. Before the war, most White settlers made their way either to Marietta or to John Cleves Symmes's Miami Grant, where Forts Harmar and Washington provided immediate protection. Peace altered these settlement patterns. New federal land sales in the Seven Ranges and the opening of both the Virginia Military District and Connecticut's Western Reserve offered opportunities for settlers to claim land beyond the watchful gaze of Federalist proprietors. This was especially true of the Virginia Military District, where Virginian veterans of the Revolutionary War began to re-create many of the legal and social constructions of their native state. Their proclivities for land speculation and preference for county governance placed them in direct conflict with the federal authority and the national vision of Marietta's proprietors. Andrew Cayton has identified this cultural rift between the national interests of New Englanders and the local interests of Virginians as the central political issue of the Northwest Territory. Yet this explanation ignores the local interests of the Ohio Company. Western Federalists may have adopted a public discourse favoring the guiding hand of national governance, but they were every bit as interested in local governance as were their Republican adversaries. Local policy thus became a pressing issue for western Federalists who focused on the creation of a territorial legislature and the taxes it passed on the shareholders of the Ohio Company.[10]

The Northwest Ordinance at first authorized five federally appointed offices—the governor, secretary, and three judges—to administer the territory and pass laws to govern its citizens. Ohio Company shareholders and John Cleves Symmes held most of these positions and used their majority to enact legislation that benefited their landed interests. One of the principal functions of governance they sought to manage was taxation. For seven years, Governor Arthur St. Clair, Judge Symmes, and various Ohio Company members who served as justices did not pass a single tax on themselves. Even the first county levies instituted in 1795 only subjected "free persons dwelling, or residing" within the territory to taxation. Such language exempted many of the Ohio Company's share-holders in New England and John Cleves Symmes's associates in New Jersey and Kentucky. Nonresidents' property would not be assessed until 1798 when the governor and judges enacted a tax on all "unimproved" land within the territory. Yet, the tax rate was low. Every hundred acres would be assessed based on its quality as first-, second-, or third-rate land at thirty cents, twenty cents, and ten cents, respectively. An Ohio Company shareholder could pay as little as one dollar per year if their lands were assessed as third rate. And it would not be difficult to secure a third-rate assessment. County assessors were commissioned by the courts of general quarter sessions whose judges were appointed by the governor. Arthur St. Clair routinely appointed his fellow shareholders to the courts that presided over the Ohio Company grant, who in turn commissioned county officials from among Marietta's more notable inhabitants. From top to bottom, western Federalists with significant land claims in the territory used their authority to protect their property interests from outsiders.[11]

That authority eroded with the influx of new settlers. The Northwest Ordinance stipulated that once the territory's population reached "five thousand free male inhabitants of full age," the territorial government would transition to a second stage in which the legislature was separated from the governor and judges. This population threshold was met in 1798, and Arthur St. Clair authorized the creation of the bicameral legislature. The members of the upper chamber were appointed by the president of the United States, and the lower chamber members were elected by the freeholders of the territory. Elections were held in early 1799 and the new legislature met for the first time in Cincinnati the following winter. It was the lower chamber—the House of Representatives—that challenged the Ohio Company's monopoly over territorial governance. Most of the representatives were Republican in their politics, were not

210 | Joseph Thomas Ross

affiliated with the Ohio Company, and felt no obligation to protect the property interests of its shareholders. One of the legislature's first acts was to raise the territorial tax on all lands to eighty-five cents for first rate, sixty cents for second rate, and twenty-five cents for third rate. These assessments were nearly triple what the Ohio Company had taken a decade to place on themselves.[12]

The new taxes caused anxiety among the Ohio Company's shareholders. A flurry of letters passed between nonresident proprietors and their agents who had moved west. William Rufus Putnam—the son of Rufus Putnam—found himself inundated with dozens of requests from shareholders in New England asking him to pay their taxes. His father had concerned clients as well. Many were either confused or ignorant about the territorial tax system. One client hoped that the elder Putnam would give him "timely notice" of new taxes and promised "to keep [Putnam] in cash" so they could be paid. Another client sent Putnam ten dollars in the hope that it would be enough to pay the tax. But not everyone was able to forward money. Others ignored the taxes altogether. Although the Putnams were willing to pay their clients' taxes, they simply did not have enough cash on hand to do it. Those who became delinquent had to watch from afar as territorial sheriffs seized their lands for nonpayment. Jonathan Trumbull, the governor of Connecticut, was one such victim. He complained to Rufus Putnam that "if your rate of Taxes is to be continued I do not see but that the Lands must be swallowed up by them." Although agents like Putnam wanted to recover their clients' lands lost to delinquency, they were powerless to effect it. Western Federalists had lost their monopoly over territorial governance, and they were slowly losing control of the western land market as well.[13]

Land seizures were not what the federal government had in mind when it entrusted the territory to the Ohio Company. Members of Congress—who either owned shares in the Ohio Company or had influential constituents who did—lost confidence in their western agents. Manasseh Cutler, a Massachusetts representative who had personally secured the Ohio Company's grant from Congress, wrote to his son in Marietta about the "great complaint here about ye Law in your Territory." Rumors swirled in the nation's capital that forty thousand acres had been seized for delinquent taxes and sold for one cent per acre. Cutler recognized that "this has made a very unfavorable impression on members who would otherwise been disposed to do everything, consistently, for" the company's interest. Rather than confide in the company shareholders, some Federalist congressmen reached out to the Republican leaders of the new territorial legislature. Others toyed with the idea of dividing the Northwest Territory along the Scioto River. Such action would regress both halves to the first stage of territorial government and eliminate the territorial tax altogether. Paul Fearing, a company member who served as the territory's nonvoting delegate in Congress, suggested "there will be interest in such an arrangement" among eastern shareholders "as it will in some measure save a tax on their lands." Western Federalists were able to secure the assent of the territorial legislature to such a division in 1801, but their Republican opponents lobbied Congress to stop the scheme. Congress, disillusioned with the failures of the Ohio Company, wrested federal power away from its shareholders by allowing the western Republicans to form a state government.[14]

* * *

Ohio Company members were not the only western Federalists who failed to stabilize the territory. John Cleves Symmes caused problems as well. Symmes had contracted with Congress to buy one million acres of land stretching along the Ohio River between the Great and Little Miami Rivers. However, he did not have enough money to complete the purchase himself. He relied heavily upon public debt speculators in New York and New Jersey to invest in his western settlements. Such an arrangement seemed quite profitable in 1787 when the public debt crisis had sunk the value of public securities below what many considered western lands to be worth. Yet, the ratification of the new Constitution bolstered the securities market and made western land speculation less appealing. With his access to eastern credit dried up, Symmes had to sell large amounts of land to settlers to make his payments to Congress. The violence from the Northwest Indian War made these land sales almost impossible. Symmes quickly began defaulting on his payments. In response, Congress restructured his purchase to include only three hundred thousand acres.[15]

News of the restructure was slow to reach Symmes. Not only did it remove seven hundred thousand acres out of his grant, but it also limited his claims to only twenty miles along the Ohio River. This was a problem because Symmes had consistently advertised that he held claim to all the land along the Ohio between the Miami Rivers. Without knowing what the final grant looked like, Symmes sold to Benjamin Stites twenty thousand acres east of the new boundary line of the grant. Stites then began selling the land to other settlers. Federal officials were quick to recognize the error but were uncertain as to how to handle the problem. Arthur St. Clair chastised Symmes for his negligence, calling it an "Embarrassment." The governor feared that litigation over the conflicting claims would bring dishonor upon the United States, so he informed the Washington administration of the situation. Symmes responded by blaming his New Jersey investors for failing to properly inform him of the restructure in a timely manner. St. Clair also refused to assist the settlers who had obviously been defrauded. He even went so far as to issue a proclamation denouncing them as illegal squatters on federal land. It thus fell on Stites to try and remedy the matter. He and his purchasers petitioned Congress to alter the boundaries of the Miami Grant to include the land he had purchased from Symmes. Congress complied with the petition and altered the grant to extend along the entirety of the Ohio between the Miami Rivers.[16]

Despite the fiasco surrounding the Stites purchase and a scolding from Governor St. Clair, Symmes continued to engage in shady land deals. His personal papers at the Library of Congress reveal just how chaotic and disorderly these sales were. Folder after folder contains hundreds of different-colored parchment clippings and hastily written notes, a visual representation of how his land sales functioned. The clutter of warrants and receipts combined with improper and incomplete surveys would make it difficult for any person to effectively manage such a scheme. But this did not stop Symmes from being bold in his transactions. In 1795, he orchestrated one of the most fraudulent sales in the territory when he sold the land that would become the city of Dayton. Less than three weeks after the Treaty of Greenville was signed, Symmes contracted with a cadre of the American West's most prominent officials, including Governor St. Clair and Brigadier General James Wilkinson, for a tract of land along the Mad River. Jonathan Dayton, speaker of the House of Representatives and namesake of the town, was also a proprietor in the tract. However, the contract was completed before Symmes had finished surveying the northern reaches of his adjusted grant. When the proprietors laid Dayton out, it was located dozens of miles north of the Miami Grant. Those who purchased or received town lots—including several army officers and veterans of the Northwest Indian War—immediately became squatters on federal land without any claim to legal title.[17]

The public-private partnership between John Cleves Symmes and the United States resulted in mass disorder. Benjamin Stites and the Dayton proprietors were not the only ones defrauded by Symmes. Numerous settlers bought tracts from Symmes that he did not own and immediately found themselves residing illegally on federal land. Hoping to prevent a catastrophe, the United States sought to create a pathway toward legal title for Symmes's victims. Congress passed laws in 1799 and 1801 that required these settlers to enter their claims with federal land commissioners at Cincinnati. After the claims were entered, the settlers could receive a preemption right to repurchase the land first from the federal government. The laws said nothing about recovering their payments from Symmes; that would have to be worked out in the county or territorial courts. Hundreds of people registered their claims and received their preemptions. At the first federal land sale in Cincinnati, more people entered and paid for these preemption claims than those who bought land in the public auction. However, none of the Dayton proprietors took advantage of the preemption offer. Instead, one settler who had drawn a few town lots registered a claim and purchased most of the bustling town. The United States wanted John Cleves Symmes to bring order and regularity to territorial development, but Symmes failed to deliver.[18]

* * *

Western Federalists created violence, disorder, and political conflict throughout the Northwest Territory. Historians have largely ignored these negative exploits, choosing instead to portray the Federalists as harbingers of peace and stability in the West. As this chapter demonstrates, they were anything but. Federalists consistently failed in their self-professed duties, and in some ways left the Northwest Territory worse off than it was before they tried to claim it for themselves. This begs an obvious question: Who then is responsible for the stable economic and political development of the West? One need look no further than their adversaries and successors, the Republicans.

Western Republicans consistently advocated for a stronger federal presence in the West. They detested the blatant self-interest that was inherent in the public-private partnerships between the Ohio Company of Associates, John Cleves Symmes, and the United States. Instead, Republicans supported public institutions controlled by the federal government and staffed with less-interested officials. They created the first federal land offices where settlers could with regularity buy public land directly from the United States and not through the Ohio Company or middlemen like Symmes. They established more Indian factories and federal forts, making it easier for the United States to enforce its desired policies against Indigenous peoples. They erected multiple federal territories that expanded the political authority of the United States while giving settlers more access to representative government. And they secured multiple statehoods that brought law to bear more directly upon western citizens. Republican policies replaced the Federalist program of privatized expansion with an active and powerful national state. What emerged was an efficient imperial apparatus that often displaced and murdered large numbers of Native Americans and redistributed Indigenous land to White settlers for a nominal fee. The transformation of the Old Northwest from a cosmopolitan space of fur traders and subsistence farmers into an empire of commercial agriculture, market towns, and urban centers was not a Federalist conquest, but rather a Republican one.[19]

Notes

1. Samuel P. Hildreth, ed., *Pioneer History: Being an Account of the First Examinations of the Ohio Valley, and the Early Settlement of the Northwest Territory* (Cincinnati: H. W. Derby, 1848), 214, 504–9. For the Ohio Company's relationship with the federal government, see Andrew R. L. Cayton, *The Frontier Republic: Ideology and Politics in the Ohio Country, 1780–1825* (Kent, OH: Kent State University Press, 1986), 33–50.

2. Andrew R. L. Cayton, "Radicals in the 'Western World': The Federalist Conquest of Trans-Appalachian North America," in *Federalists Reconsidered,* ed. Doron Ben-Atar and Barbara B. Oberg (Charlottesville: University Press of Virginia, 1998), 77–96. The scholarship on western Federalists is becoming robust. See Andrew R. L. Cayton, "The Contours of Power in a Frontier Town: Marietta, Ohio, 1788–1803," *Journal of the Early Republic* 6, no. 2 (Summer 1986): 103–26; Cayton, *Frontier Republic;* Peter S. Onuf, *Statehood and Union: A History of the Northwest Ordinance* (Bloomington: Indiana University Press, 1987); Frederick D. Williams,

ed., *The Northwest Ordinance: Essays on Its Formulation, Provisions and Legacy* (East Lansing: Michigan State University Press, 1988); David Andrew Nichols, *Red Gentlemen and White Savages: Indians, Federalists, and the Search for Order on the American Frontier* (Charlottesville: University of Virginia Press, 2008); Bethel Saler, *The Settlers' Empire: Colonialism and State Formation in America's Old Northwest* (Philadelphia: University of Pennsylvania Press, 2014), esp. 41–81; John R. Van Atta, *Securing the West: Politics, Public Lands, and the Fate of the Old Republic, 1785–1850* (Baltimore: Johns Hopkins University Press, 2014), esp. 17–44; Paul Frymer, *Building an American Empire: The Era of Territorial and Political Expansion* (Princeton, NJ: Princeton University Press, 2017), esp. 32–71; Kristopher Maulden, *The Federalist Frontier: Settler Politics in the Old Northwest, 1783–1840* (Columbia: University of Missouri Press, 2019); David McCullough, *The Pioneers: The Heroic Story of the Settlers Who Brought the American Ideal West* (New York: Simon and Schuster, 2019); Gregory Ablavsky, *Federal Ground: Governing Property and Violence in the First U.S. Territories* (New York: Oxford University Press, 2021), esp. 57–73. A subtle critique of this view is Eric Hinderaker, *Elusive Empires: Constructing Colonialism in the Ohio Valley, 1673–1800* (New York: Cambridge University Press, 1997), 247–49.

3. The Northwest Indian War has received more attention than the chaos of the early western land market. For the war, see Wiley Sword, *President Washington's Indian War: The Struggle for the Old Northwest, 1790–1795* (Norman: University of Oklahoma Press, 1985); Alan D. Gaff, *Bayonets in the Wilderness: Anthony Wayne's Legion in the Old Northwest* (Norman: University of Oklahoma Press, 2004); and Colin G. Calloway, *The Victory with No Name: The Native American Defeat of the First American Army* (New York: Oxford University Press, 2014). The relationship between violence and access to government power existed in the areas south of the Ohio River prior to the establishment of the Northwest Territory. See Rob Harper, *Unsettling the West: Violence and State Building in the Ohio Valley* (Philadelphia: University of Pennsylvania Press, 2018).

4. For John Cleves Symmes, see R. Douglas Hurt, *The Ohio Frontier: Crucible of the Old Northwest, 1720–1830* (Bloomington: Indiana University Press, 1996), 160–64.

5. Archer Butler Hulbert, ed., *The Records of the Original Proceedings of the Ohio Company* (Marietta, OH: Marietta Historical Commission, 1917), 1:16, 20–23, 46–48, 2:1–10; "Journal of Executive Proceedings in the Territory Northwest of the River Ohio," in *The Territorial Papers of the United States,* ed. Clarence E. Carter et al. (Washington, DC: Government Printing Office, 1934–75), 3:278–93; see also Cayton, *Frontier Republic,* 39–40.

6. Arthur St. Clair to Henry Knox, January 27 and July 5, 1788, and Josiah Harmar to Henry Knox, March 9, 1788, in *The St. Clair Papers: The Life*

and *Public Services of Arthur St. Clair* [. . .], ed. William Henry Smith (Cincinnati: Robert Clarke, 1882), 2:43–46, 48–49; Arthur St. Clair to Henry Knox, July 13, 16, and 22, 1788, and Arthur St. Clair to the Indians in Council, July 13, 1788, in *Territorial Papers,* 2:125–32, 136–37. For the treaty conferences, see Nichols, *Red Gentlemen,* 32–35, 100–104.

7. Henry Knox to Arthur St. Clair, December 19, 1789, Arthur St. Clair to Winthrop Sargent, July 15 and November 27, 1790, Rufus Putnam to George Washington, July 24, 1790, and Arthur St. Clair to Henry Knox, September 19, 1790, in *Territorial Papers,* 2:224–25, 287, 293–94, 306–8, 313; Henry Knox to Arthur St. Clair, June 7 and September 14, 1790, and Arthur St. Clair to Henry Knox, September 19 and October 29, 1790, in *St. Clair Papers,* 2:147–48, 181–84, 188–89; Josiah Harmar to Henry Knox, March 24, 1790, Rufus Putnam to George Washington, January 8, 1791, and Arthur St. Clair to Henry Knox, November 1 and 9, 1791, in *American State Papers: Indian Affairs,* ed. Walter Lowrie et al. (Washington, DC: Gales and Seaton, 1832–34), 1:91, 121–22, 136–38. The best description of St. Clair's defeat is Calloway, *Victory with No Name,* 115–28. For the Washington administration's policy of amity, see Nichols, *Red Gentlemen,* 98–127.

8. For the geopolitical concerns of the United States in the West, see James E. Lewis Jr., *The American Union and the Problem of Neighborhood: The United States and the Collapse of the Spanish Empire* (Chapel Hill: University of North Carolina Press, 1998); Eliga H. Gould, *Among the Powers of the Earth: The American Revolution and the Making of a New World Empire* (Cambridge, MA: Harvard University Press, 2012). For American settlers crossing the Mississippi, see Stephen Aron, *American Confluence: The Missouri Frontier from Borderland to Border State* (Bloomington: Indiana University Press, 2006), 82–84. Putnam's and Pickering's diplomatic missions are discussed in Nichols, *Red Gentlemen,* 142–51.

9. For the Battle of Fallen Timbers and the Treaty of Greenville, see Gaff, *Bayonets,* 301–13; Andrew R. L. Cayton, "'Noble Actors' upon 'the Theatre of Honour': Power and Civility in the Treaty of Greenville," in *Contact Points: American Frontiers from the Mohawk Valley to the Mississippi, 1750–1830,* ed. Andrew R. L. Cayton and Fredrika J. Teute (Chapel Hill: University of North Carolina Press, 1998), 235–69.

10. For the rush of settlement, see Hurt, *Ohio Frontier,* 164–68. For the cultural conflict, see Andrew R. L. Cayton, "Land, Power, and Reputation: The Cultural Dimension of Politics in the Ohio Country," *William and Mary Quarterly* 47, no. 2 (April 1990): 266–86.

11. Salmon P. Chase, ed., *The Statutes of Ohio and of the Northwestern Territory, Adopted or Enacted from 1788 to 1833 Inclusive* (Cincinnati: Corey & Fairbank, 1833), 168–74, 208–9. For the Northwest Ordinance, see "Ordinance of 1787," in *Territorial Papers,* 2:41–44. St. Clair's appointments are discussed in Cayton, *Frontier Republic,* 27.

12. "Ordinance of 1787," in *Territorial Papers,* 44–45; Chase, *Statutes of Ohio,* 267–72. For the territorial election, see Cayton, *Frontier Republic,* 70.

13. Samuel Hershaw to Rufus Putnam, May 30, 1800, Jonathan Trumbull to Rufus Putnam, August 5, 1802, and Thomas Hawthorne and Jonathan Peele to Rufus Putnam, December 2, 1800, Rufus Putnam Papers, Marietta College Library, Marietta, OH; Tax Account Book, 1800, William Rufus Putnam Collection, Marietta College Library; William Rufus Putnam to John May, July 24 and June 12, 1801, and John May to William Rufus Putnam, October 19, 1802, and November 14, 1804, May Family Papers, MS 0401, Western Reserve Historical Society, Cleveland, OH; Return J. Meigs to Ephraim Cutler, December 8, 1801, and Paul Fearing to Ephraim Cutler, December 9, 1801, Ephraim Cutler Family Collection, Marietta College Library.

14. Manasseh Cutler to Ephraim Cutler, January 12, 1802, Paul Fearing to Ephraim Cutler, January 18, 1802, Ephraim Cutler Family Collection, Marietta College Library, Marietta, OH; James Ross to Thomas Worthington, January 15, 1802, Thomas Worthington Papers, MIC 96, Ohio History Connection, Columbus, OH; Cayton, *Frontier Republic,* 76.

15. Symmes's credit network has been hard to piece together. See John Cleves Symmes, *To the Respectable Public* (Trenton, 1787), esp. 7–8; John Cleves Symmes, "The Subscriber Begs Leave," and "To the Public," *New-Jersey Journal* (Elizabethtown, NJ), September 5, 1787, March 19, 1788; John Cleves Symmes to Elias Boudinot, July 18, 1788, in *The Correspondence of John Cleves Symmes: Founder of the Miami Purchase,* ed. Beverley W. Bond Jr. (New York: Macmillan, 1926), 25–29; Joseph Lewis to Jonathan Dayton, August 21, 1788, Jonathan Dayton Family Papers, William L. Clements Library, Ann Arbor, MI. For the reduction of the grant, see Jacob Burnet, *Notes on the Early Settlement of the North-Western Territory* (New York: D. Appleton, 1847), 490–91.

16. Arthur St. Clair to John Cleves Symmes, May 23, 1791, John Cleves Symmes to Arthur St. Clair, May 23, 1791, Arthur St. Clair to Alexander Hamilton, May 25, 1791, "An Act to Ascertain the Boundaries of the Purchase of John Cleves Symmes," Arthur St. Clair to John Cleves Symmes, July 12, 1791, Arthur St. Clair, "Proclamation," July 19, 1791, in *Territorial Papers,* 2:342–48, 388–89, 3:349–51, 354–55; *Annals of Congress,* 2nd Cong., 1st Sess., 480.

17. Benjamin Van Cleve, *Memoirs of Benjamin Van Cleve,* ed. Beverley W. Bond (Cincinnati: Abingdon Press, 1922), 56, 58; John F. Edgar, *Pioneer Life in Dayton and Vicinity, 1796–1840* (Dayton, OH: H. B. Publishing, 1896), 20–21.

18. *Territorial Papers,* 3:16–18, 29–45, 57–58, 189–96; Act of March 3, 1801, ch. 23, 2nd *Stat.,* 112–114; "Benjamin Van Cleve, Patent, October 12, 1805, CV-0074-020," General Land Office Records, Bureau of Land Management, US Department of the Interior, https://glorecords.blm.gov/details

/patent/default.aspx?accession=0074-020&docClass=CV&sid=0xgv3r1k
.cms; Van Cleve, *Benjamin Van Cleve,* 64.

19.　The literature on the early American state is vast but it often leaves partisanship out of its analysis. For a summation, see Gautham Rao, "The New Historiography of the Early Federal Government: Institutions, Contexts, and the Imperial State," *William and Mary Quarterly* 77, no. 1 (January 2020): 97–128. For the Republicans as supporters of strong federal government, see Joseph Thomas Ross, "'Strange Doings with Respect to Preemptions': Federal Power and Political Interests at the Chillicothe Land Office, 1800–1802," *Ohio Valley History* 20, no. 3 (Fall 2020): 3–25.

11

Public Education in the Old Northwest

Legacies of Ohio's First Land Grant

ADAM R. NELSON

In his book *The Pioneers,* David McCullough devotes a whole chapter to the Northwest Ordinance's provisions for public schools and Manasseh Cutler's hopes for republican education on the frontier. He suggests that Ohioans embraced the idea of schools funded by public land and, later, by taxes on their landed property—mostly, he says, because they recognized the social and economic benefits of a well-educated society.[1]

In general, McCullough repeats the conventional narrative of the common-school crusade, the one where Horace Mann in Massachusetts and Henry Barnard in Connecticut forged a bold political consensus in which reluctant Democrats joined reformist Whigs across the country to support new statewide systems of tax-supported public schools. But what if this narrative is, at best, only half-true?

What if the story was not so simple, not so straightforward? What if the story of common schools was not only a story of eventual consensus but also a story of enduring *contentiousness*? What if the story was not only a story of Whig success but, rather, of Whig *struggle*? History is rarely simple or straightforward, and the appropriate categories for historical narrative may not be "fiction" and "truth" but rather "fiction" and, well, "*nonfiction.*"

This chapter documents the challenges that Federalists like Manasseh Cutler and Whigs like Ephraim Cutler faced in their efforts to establish public schools on the northwest frontier—not only in Ohio but also in Indiana, Illinois, Michigan, and Wisconsin, where neither Federalists nor Republicans, Whigs nor Democrats, had a clear political majority, and voters did not always welcome the plans of school reformers.

The idea that republican government hinged on publicly funded education was hardly new. Thomas Jefferson had made this case as early as 1779 in his Bill for the More General Diffusion of Knowledge, which assumed that voters would accept property taxes for public schools as soon as they understood how education helped each and every citizen: rich and poor, urban and rural. In the end, though, Jefferson's bill went down in defeat.[2]

Many parents in Virginia—rich and poor, rural and urban—said their children should not have to attend tax-supported schools, because (a) the schools were far away from their home, (b) they preferred to pay for private tutors, or (c) they did not have children of their own to send to school. A great many Virginians asked why they should have to subsidize the education of their neighbors. Instead, they considered education primarily a *private good.*[3]

Of course, when it came to school funds in the Early Republic, there was a potential alternative to property taxes—namely, the proceeds from the sale of public lands. Connecticut, for example, had used its vast western reserve to set up a school fund that yielded a yearly income and relieved citizens of personal taxes. Similar financial strategies had been used to fund district schools in England, and many thought it might work in the American West.[4]

Hence the provision in the Northwest Ordinance of 1785 that revenue from the sale of federally owned lands was to be set aside to support education. Specifically, one thirty-sixth of the land in each six-square-mile township was to be rented or sold, with the proceeds used to pay for a school building and teacher. When the Northwest Ordinance of 1787 outlined the process by which a frontier territory could apply for statehood, it *required* the designation of school lands.

The rhetoric was classically republican. The ordinance stated that "religion, morality, and knowledge being necessary to good government and the happiness of mankind, schools and the means of education shall forever be encouraged." So, did it work? Did the Northwest Ordinances ensure the creation of public schools in the West? Perhaps, but there were lots of problems with the proposed system of public land revenues for public schools.[5]

The late historian of education Carl Kaestle (my doctoral mentor) examined these problems in his book *Pillars of the Republic: Common Schools and American Society, 1780–1860* (1983) and, later, in his article "Public Education in the Old Northwest: 'Necessary to Good Government and the Happiness of Mankind,'" both of which identified the problems that faced public school and, in turn, have informed this essay.[6]

Any historian in the 1780s could have predicted these problems, for the same ones had occurred a century and a half before, in the early colonies. In territories with a large supply of appropriated land, the price of land was low, so the revenue that could be collected from this land was limited. In fact, at the outset, when the land was "unimproved," it was often given away free of charge to entice settlers who might otherwise be risk averse.

Obviously, if land was given away free, then it would take a while for a state's so-called school fund to accumulate ... funds. Even where school lands were rented at rock-bottom rates, these revenues were vulnerable to fraud, embezzlement, and bad investments. State governments were small (which is how residents liked them), but smallness made financial oversight practically impossible, and people took advantage of this situation.

One frustrated state auditor declared as late as 1843 that "there seems to be no end to the plunder upon this fund." Some might even say the story of the Northwest Ordinances' policy of public land revenue for public schools was, at best, a story of public neglect. Moreover, one must remember the longer history of these lands. They were federally "owned" because they had been appropriated from their Native inhabitants.[7]

One must not forget that western lands that were later taxed for the support of public education had *prior* occupants, and the public schools that provided this education cannot be disconnected from a long history of Indian dispossession. The Northwest Ordinances of 1785 and 1787 initiated a narrative that linked the idea of "public" lands with "public" schools, but how did this conception of "the public" shape the actual function of schools in this region?

To answer this question, this chapter offers a few thoughts about the efforts of Manasseh Cutler in the 1790s and 1800s and Ephraim Cutler in the 1810s and 1820s, as well as the efforts of their Indiana counterpart and successor Caleb Mills in the 1830s and 1840s. Each figure had something to say about the gap between rhetoric and reality in the creation of publicly funded schools.

Let us begin with Cutler the elder, an agent of the Ohio Company and the architect of the Northwest Ordinance's educational provisions. By the mid-1790s, after the Battle of Fallen Timbers and the Treaty of Greenville with the Miami Confederacy, the Ohio Territory had begun to swell with settlers from the East. By the end of the decade, some have estimated that up to 5 percent of New England's White population migrated west every year.[8]

Cutler and his colleagues in the Ohio Company encouraged settlers to write to relatives in Cambridge, Massachusetts; New Haven, Connecticut; Hanover, New Hampshire; Brunswick, Maine; and other college towns with descriptions of the West's fertile soil and potential for population growth. They hoped to attract settlers who were "intelligent" and "industrious"—just the sort of people they hoped would enroll their children in public schools.

Cutler famously put it this way: "An early attention to the instruction of youth is of the greatest importance to a new settlement. It will lay the foundations for a well-regulated society. It is the only way to make subjects conform to its laws and regulations from principles of reason and custom rather than the fear of punishment." The emphasis on education for republican self-government could not have been clearer.[9]

Of course, Cutler also saw a connection between public order and his own private gain: if schools attracted virtuous settlers and boosted land values, then Cutler and his colleagues in the Ohio Company would get richer, faster. But never mind these subtleties about whether education was a public or private good. Did the plan work? Did the settlers actually establish schools to ensure a virtuous society?[10]

Not exactly. Unfortunately for Cutler, his worst fears came true when he discovered that, in the earliest stages of settlement, most newcomers could not be bothered to build schools. And he was not the only founder of the Ohio Company to notice. Another founder complained in 1800, there was "no public spirit to be found [on behalf of education] . . . except only in the proprietors of the Ohio Company."[11]

One problem was that settlements were dispersed, so it was not easy to decide where to put a school. Settlers did not want to fund schools that seemed far away or, God forbid, seemed closer to a neighbor's house. If one's sons or daughters could not attend conveniently, then why build a school in the first place? Most early settlers had other priorities, and there was little that Cutler's generation could do to change their minds.

Eventually, as McCullough notes, Cutler got help with education from his son Ephraim, whose efforts illustrate both the achievements and the aggravations of early school advocates. As early as 1802, when Ephraim helped draft a state constitution for Ohio, he seized the opportunity to insert a clause about the role of education in a republic—a sentiment expressed repeatedly in his personal diary.[12]

Three years later, in 1805, Ephraim settled in Ames Township, just up the road, and one of his first projects was to set up a town library. Shortly thereafter, one of his cousins established a school in his house. A bit later, a group of teachers in Ames set up a series of local subscription schools, which asked parents to pay as much as they could for the education of their children—a dubious system, because many said they could pay very little indeed.[13]

To reach nearby settlements, some other teachers set up a so-called moving school, with teachers who traveled from place to place and spent a few weeks in each of several rural schools in a given area. Here, too, parents contributed what they felt they could afford. Granted, it was a charitable age, when in-kind offerings were not uncommon, and this system laid the groundwork for later developments, but school budgets remained slim.

The *quality* of the schools usually reflected the *quantity* of contributions. Ephraim nonetheless declared that "schools of an elevated character" had been established throughout southeastern Ohio: indeed, he said, the students who attended these schools had become very "useful and respectable citizens"—respectable enough in 1804 to supply the newly opened Ohio University with a total of *two* students.[14]

By 1809, Ohio had two universities, one in Athens, the other in Oxford, and both had grand plans for the future as eastern migrants continued to flood into the region in pursuit of low-priced land. The promise of public schools only increased their numbers—even if many of them did not actually send their children to school (or, if they did, they sent them for only a few weeks a year).

In fact, Ephraim, like his father, was prone to exaggeration (as land boosters often were). He ran into an endless string of difficulties as he pushed for the establishment of public schools. For example, despite the rules he wrote into the state's constitution, he found that revenue from the rent or sale of federal lands was still woefully inadequate to build schools, let alone pay teachers.

As one of Ephraim's own brothers noted after 1810, it had "been said again and again that these public [school] lands were of no real value, [and] the time expended in legislating upon them costs the state more than they are worth." Ephraim therefore joined a legislative commission to devise a new system. In 1818, he proposed a property tax, not unlike the one Thomas Jefferson had proposed three decades earlier.[15]

It met a similar fate. In 1821, after three years of hard negotiation and compromise, all the committee was able to show for its effort was a bill for property taxes that could be paid on a *voluntary* basis. One frustrated Ohioan complained that, under this system of taxpayer philanthropy, "scarcely a dollar" was generated for public schools. But it was the only system voters would approve. It was not until 1824 that legislators passed a *mandatory* property tax for schools.[16]

Ephraim was elated, but he celebrated too soon. The law had giant loopholes and was poorly enforced, so very few property owners actually paid any tax. Here, then, was the dilemma: the Cutlers believed that republican government—as well as economic development—required broad access to public education, but settlers refused to tax themselves for the support of schools. What to do?

This question applied not only to public schools but also to public universities, neither of which found sure footing in Ohio in this period. Instead, higher education, like primary education, remained a mostly private—typically denominational—enterprise, as the examples of Kenyon in 1824, Western Reserve in 1826, Denison in 1831, and Oberlin in 1833 all demonstrated. How could states offer public education if few wanted to pay for it?[17]

Of course, as Oberlin's turbulent origins made clear, the *financial* question was equally a *political* question. In a border region increasingly divided over the issue of slavery and the abolitionist movement, it was not clear that "common" schools and colleges would be able to satisfy a polarized electorate. So contentious was this debate that even Horace Mann in Massachusetts declined to support racially integrated public schools.[18]

By the 1830s, the issue of integrated schools had become increasingly fraught in New England, where, in 1831, a woman named Prudence Crandall started admitting Black students to her private girls' seminary in Canterbury, Connecticut, which led White parents to withdraw their daughters (on grounds that Nat Turner's rebellion that year had illustrated the violent tendencies of Black people).[19]

Two years later, in 1833, with no Whites left, Crandall made her school into an all-Black academy for students from Connecticut as well as other states. Even in an era that saw the rapid expansion of female seminaries for Whites (notably Emma Willard's seminary in Troy, New York, and soon, Mary Lyon's innovative Mount Holyoke Female Seminary in South Hadley, Massachusetts), it was a novel idea to offer such a school entirely to Black girls.[20]

She had the help of William Lloyd Garrison and other abolitionists, but local Whites said her school would draw more Blacks to Connecticut, where they would glut the labor market and steal jobs. Crandall's students faced constant harassment. They were insulted, the stores in town refused to sell them anything, and the local doctor refused to care for them. On one occasion, racist hoodlums filled every classroom in her school with manure.[21]

Finally, the state legislature took action. In an era of widespread calls for common schools funded by the state, when reformers like Henry Barnard argued that republican government itself depended on broad access to education, the legislature passed a law to *prohibit* the establishment of schools for Blacks who were not state residents. For a while, Crandall defied the law, but she was soon arrested and thrown in jail. She eventually had to close her school.[22]

The debate over integrated schools was not limited to primary education. The same year Crandall opened her all-Black academy, William Lloyd Garrison had suggested the creation of a college for Black students in New Haven, where Yale professors and townspeople met to discuss the idea. In the end, they rejected the proposal by a vote of seven hundred to four on grounds that a college might distract attention from their primary goal: recolonizing Black people in America to Liberia.[23]

One opponent of the college asked, "What good can arise from giving them a collegiate education of the highest classical honors and attainments? Will it give them that equality which exists among White men? Certainly not. The very leaders who [demand a common-school education for Black children and] open their purses for such objects will not allow a learned [Black collegian] to sit at their table or marry their daughter."[24]

Was the situation any different in the West? No. By the 1830s, Black property owners in Ohio were taxed for schools their own children were not allowed to attend. Even worse, in 1829, 1836, and 1841, a series of antiabolitionist riots broke out, first in Cincinnati and later in Zanesville and other towns. Black churches and businesses were burned, as was the printing press of the Ohio Anti-Slavery Society. Many Black residents were killed.[25]

And what about schools? Mary Cheney, an Oberlin graduate who led a school in Pike County, wrote in the middle of the crisis: "It is now four weeks since my school house was torn down. . . . Repeatedly has word been sent to me that, if I was not sent away, they would come and take me out of the house, give me a dress of tar and feathers, and treat me in a manner too inhuman to mention."[26]

Cheney tried to be brave. "I have not been alarmed," she wrote, "until recently, when I am told that the number is increased to twenty, who have engaged to mob me, [and have signed a pledge to do so,] being backed up in it by rich men. They are all drinkers, armed with guns and pistols and each a bottle of whiskey." Under these circumstances, one might ask, If Black students could not have schools at all, then what kind of schools could White students have?[27]

To address this question, one might shift from Ohio to Indiana, where education advocate Caleb Mills led his state's common-school crusade. Like the Cutlers, he was a New Englander—a New Hampshire native. He graduated from Dartmouth in the class of 1828 and then from Andover Theological Seminary in 1833, whereafter he moved to Indiana as a missionary teacher for the American Sunday School Union and, later, became a professor at Wabash College.[28]

He taught until 1846, when, frustrated by Indiana's continued low rates of literacy, he wrote an open letter to legislators in which he noted that systems of tax-funded schools were already in place in Ohio and Michigan, as well as most eastern states. Appealing to Indianans' competitive instincts—after all, every state wanted to attract more settlers than its neighbors—he argued that Indiana could not afford to fall behind.[29]

By the 1840s, literacy was on the rise. William Holmes McGuffey had published his first *Reader* in the mid-1830s while he taught at Miami University, and by 1836, when he became president of Cincinnati College, and 1839, when he became president of Ohio University, sales had sky-rocketed. Yet, even as he left Athens in 1843 to lead a new public high school in Cincinnati, many public schools did not have the money to buy his *Reader*, as Mills in Indiana well knew.[30]

Mills said the way to win settlers was not to exempt them from taxes but, rather, to show them how tax revenues could be spent to improve public services: roads, bridges, and schools. How much had Indiana taxed its citizens for schools since it became a state in 1816, he asked? "I will state it in *round* numbers: $0.000.00." It seemed a persuasive argument, but, evidently, Indianans were hard to persuade.[31]

Mills's campaign for schools went nowhere in 1846—the year Black migrants from Ohio and elsewhere founded the Union Literary Institute in Randolph County, Indiana, a school notable for its integration of Black and White students (its headmaster was an Oberlin graduate). Of course, since Indiana had outlawed racially integrated schools three years earlier, the institute relied on private donations and its students' manual labor to make ends meet.[32]

Men like Mills, however, wanted Indianans to support *publicly* funded schools. In 1847, he tried again, with slightly more success. The legislature agreed to put the question of a school tax before the voters in a referendum. Over half the voters favored a system of common schools, but almost none felt their property should be taxed to fund it. Apparently, they believed schools would build themselves and teachers would teach for nothing. Mills was flabbergasted.

Echoing Thomas Jefferson, he said anyone who voted *for* schools but *against* taxes was obviously too uneducated to understand the issue and thus needed the very schools they voted not to fund. Such observations were typical of Whig school reformers in this period, who often saw themselves as enlightened leaders and their political opponents as simple-minded farmers too ignorant to see the benefits of public institutions that Whigs usually ran.[33]

At the heart of such criticisms was a question about the role of public schools in relation to democratic self-government. If farmers opposed taxes for schools, was it because they needed to be educated differently in order to support them? Or was it that some feared the schools would not share their social values and would use public resources to lure their children off the farm? What if they wanted nothing to do with an education system they felt did not respect their folkways?

Caleb Mills did not dwell on these questions. Like any good Whig, he trusted himself to know the public interest—and it seemed to work. In 1849, the Indiana state legislature finally passed a law for tax-supported schools, then expanded this law three years later. Mills himself served as superintendent of schools from 1854 to 1857 and was sure that, under his leadership, popular enthusiasm for tax-supported common schools had taken hold.[34]

But, like the Cutlers in Ohio, he was over-confident. The very year Mills became superintendent, the state's supreme court said the school tax was unconstitutional—a decision that sent legal shock waves across the region, since public aid to schools had been written into every state constitution to comply with the requirements of the second Northwest Ordinance. Some feared the entire substructure of public schools was at risk.[35]

It was not just public schools that suffered from the court's intervention; it was Indiana's public university as well. In 1816, the state had created a university through a seizure of federal lands that had been given to Vincennes University a decade earlier. But in the case of the *Board of Trustees of Vincennes University v. the State of Indiana,* the US Supreme Court ruled in 1853 that Indiana had to compensate the original holder of this land.[36]

Clearly, there were huge obstacles to funding public education in this period—a period when large numbers of voters did not believe that they should be taxed to pay for schools. In such a situation, what kind of schools did citizens actually get? Well, of course, school quality varied, but mostly they got the schools they wanted—that is, privately funded schools they could oversee themselves.

Let us close with an example of public education in a town that chose to maintain "local control" over its schools. This example comes from author Edward Eggleston's fictional account, *The Hoosier School-Master,* published in the 1870s but set in rural Indiana in the 1850s. In this story, the hero is a young and enthusiastic teacher named Ralph who hears that a schoolmaster's post has become available in the so-called Flat Crick District of Hoopole County.[37]

Ralph goes to Flat Crick, and the first person he meets is Old Jack Means, a trustee of the local school who nearly scares him away from the job. Means's words are written in dialect, and it is not difficult to detect Eggleston's caricature of the rural midwesterners who opposed common schools. Eggleston was a political ally of Caleb Mills and shared his disdain for the allegedly unenlightened.

"Want to be a school-master, do you?" asks Old Jack Means. "Well, what would *you* do in Flat Crick deestrick, *I'd* like to know? Why, the boys driv off the last two, and licked the one afore them like blazes. You might teach a summer school, when nothin' but [the younger] children come. But I 'low it takes a right smart man to be schoolmaster in Flat Crick in the winter [when the older boys attend]. They'd pitch you out of doors, sonny, neck and heels, afore Christmas."[38]

Mr. Means's comments reflect a few important features of public schooling in the early nineteenth century. First was the idea of a summer school attended by younger children and girls and a winter school attended by older boys (who spent their summer days working on the farm). Also, one can hear in Mr. Means's description the supposed resistance to authority, or rebellious insubordination, that Whigs hoped schools would get under control.

Like their Federalist predecessors, the Whigs sometimes worried that perhaps the spirit of self-government had let a disciplinary genie out of the bottle. What if Americans misunderstood the meaning of self-government or took individual freedom too far? Was it not a teacher's job to get children into line by teaching moral order? Was it not the schools' example of authority that ensured obedience to the rule of law?

Well, in *The Hoosier School-Master,* Ralph himself was no rebel; he was a very polite young man. He asks Mr. Means if he should talk with any other trustees about getting the job of teacher in Flat Crick, but Means says no, for two reasons. First, he notes that no one else has applied for the job. Second, he explains that, since he pays the most for the school, all the other residents simply let him run it as he pleases.

Ralph spends his first month in Flat Crick boarding with Mr. Means, then moves on to other families, who soon decide he is too gentle with their children. "Don't believe he'll do" is the remark of a Mr. Jones. "Don't thrash enough. Boys won't larn 'less you thrash 'em, says I. Leastways, mine won't. Lay it on good, is what I says to a master. Lay it on good. Don't do no harm. Lickin' and larnin' goes together. No lickin', no larnin', says I."[39]

As if the problem of discipline were not serious enough, Ralph eventually realizes that he faces an even greater challenge in Flat Crick, namely, the problem of anti-intellectualism. In an age when practical skills were more highly valued than literary refinement, local residents *said* they valued scholastic achievement but did not support Ralph's efforts to actually *produce* such achievement with his students.

In fact, Ralph has trouble getting past basic spelling in his school. The climax of Eggleston's book comes with the annual spelling bee, when students have an opportunity to show off what they had learned during the year—basically, how many words they have memorized. As Mr. Means remarks, "What do you want to know the *meaning* of a word for? Words were made to be spelled, and men were created that they might spell them."[40]

In the end, Ralph's experience as a young teacher comes to an illustrative conclusion—literally. After several chapters on Ralph's attempts to paint a picture of the life of the mind, to portray the glories of civilization, both ancient and modern, in literature and the fine arts, the story closes when he loses the spelling bee to a young girl in the last round by failing to spell the word "daguerreotype."[41]

So, what does Ralph's experience in Flat Crick say about schools on the western frontier? First, it suggests that schools in this period were still mostly local, private, unregulated, and, consequently, very uneven in their quality. This was *not* the system the Cutlers or common-school reformers had envisioned, but it *was* the system that a majority of residents seemed to want—not only in Ohio and Indiana but across the region.

Of course, school reformers usually perceived local control as local resistance, and they did what they could to counteract it. Take, for example, the work of teacher Mary Roper, a young woman from Connecticut who had joined the National Popular Education Board, established in 1847 by the famed women's reformer Catharine Beecher to improve the quality of education on the frontier.[42]

Beecher had moved to Cincinnati with her father Lyman Beecher in 1832 and had founded a female seminary, but poor health led her to close that school after just a few years. Thereafter, she dedicated herself to identifying and training hardy women from the East to lead schools in the West. First came the Ladies' Society for Promoting Education in the West, followed by the National Popular Education Board.[43]

Among the women who signed up was Roper, sent in 1852 to a small school in Mill Point, Michigan, a community of four hundred residents, mostly immigrants working in a local textile mill. At first, Roper put a brave face on her work, but after just a few weeks in Mill Point, she wrote to Beecher that, unfortunately, "there are only four families in the whole place of any intelligence. A few other families possess influence but are bad men."[44]

In spite of Roper's four weeks of pedagogical training with Beecher and her motherly approach, the parents of Mill Point disagreed about her effectiveness as a teacher. Like the parents in Flat Crick in the same period, the parents in Mill Point thought Roper was too gentle with their children. They said they were tired of "pious Easterners" sent to educate their children, and some of the angriest parents decided to open a rival school on the other side of town.[45]

Public school advocates had not anticipated the possibility of institutional competition. They had assumed that public schools would crowd out private and parochial ones and eventually hold a monopoly on public funds in each district. They worked hard to professionalize instruction and standardize curriculum across schools, and they never imagined that public funds would be used to create a legally protected marketplace of parental choice.

Roper was offended. In her view, the rival schoolteacher was clearly sub-par. As she put it, the other woman had no education and was "[hardly] a lady, destitute of religious principles . . . [and only] hired to teach the children of the dissatisfied." She added: "No effort was left untried to injure my school." First, she reported, "They . . . circulated suspicions of my good character." Then, she noted, they began to spread "the most indecent stories" about her private life.[46]

By the start of Roper's second year as a teacher in Mill Point, her enrollment had fallen to half its original size, and her critics had become so "violent" that Mill Point's school committee decided not to hire her back. To top it all off, Roper had contracted malaria, and Beecher insisted that she return to Connecticut. Ironically, the main objection to Roper's teaching was that she, like Ralph in Flat Crick, loved her students too much and beat them too little.[47]

Roper's experience raised two key questions about the prospects for publicly funded common schools in this period. First, was it wise for teachers to risk offending local parents if they might simply pull their students out of school or fire any instructors they did not like? Second, if public schools had to compete for students in towns where anti-intellectualism reigned, then what kind of curricula or pedagogy should they adopt if they wanted to stay open?[48]

How should public schools in a republic respond to popular demand or market competition? This question applied not only to primary education but also to higher education, as institutions like Ohio University had to contend by the 1850s with a growing demand for more "practical" studies in agricultural or industrial sciences. With a proposal for a new Farmer's College outside Cincinnati (in Hamilton County) arose new appeals for curricular modernization.

Space is too limited to follow all these debates to resolution, but suffice it to say that early calls for publicly supported education required constant political negotiation. If this story, which began over two centuries ago, resonates with public school debates today, it only confirms the ways in which the story of Ohio settlement—and the contentious political culture it engendered around education—continues to shape the history of the nation and its schools.

Notes

1. David McCullough, *The Pioneers: The Heroic Story of the Settlers Who Brought the American Ideal West* (New York: Simon and Schuster, 2019).
2. See Alan Taylor, *Thomas Jefferson's Education* (New York: W. W. Norton, 2019); Jennings Wagoner, *Jefferson and Education* (Charlottesville, VA: Thomas Jefferson Foundation; Chapel Hill: University of North Carolina Press, 2004).
3. See, for example, Mark Boonshoft, *Aristocratic Education and the Making of the American Republic* (Chapel Hill: University of North Carolina Press, 2020); see also Lawrence Cremin, *American Education: The National Experience, 1783–1876* (New York: Harper Collins, 1980); Paul H. Mattingly and Edward W. Stephens, *"Schools and the Means of Education Shall Forever Be Encouraged": A History of Education in the Old Northwest, 1787–1880* (Athens: Ohio University Libraries, 1987); and Johann Neem, *Democracy's Schools: The Rise of Public Education in America* (Baltimore: Johns Hopkins University Press, 2017).
4. See, for example, Kenneth Lottich, *New England Transplanted: A Study of the Development of Educational and Other Cultural Agencies in the Connecticut Western Reserve in Their National and Philosophical Setting* (Dallas, TX: Royal Publishing, 1964); Robert Wheeler, *Visions of the Western Reserve: Public and Private Documents of Northeastern Ohio, 1750–1860* (Columbus: Ohio State University Press, 2000); Harlan Hatcher, *The Western Reserve: The Story of New Connecticut in Ohio* (Indianapolis: Bobbs-Merrill, 1949); James Beasley, "Emerging Republicanism and the

Standing Order: The Appropriation Act Controversy in Connecticut, 1793 to 1795," *William and Mary Quarterly* 29, no. 4 (1972): 587–610; and James R. Rohrer, "The Connecticut Missionary Society and Book Distribution in the Early Republic," *Libraries and Culture* 34, no. 1 (1999): 17–26.

5. See, for example, Peter Onuf, *Statehood and Union: A History of the Northwest Ordinance* (Bloomington: Indiana University Press, 1987); Frederick Williams, *The Northwest Ordinance: Essays on Its Formulation, Provisions, and Legacy* (East Lansing: Michigan State University Press, 1989); and Robert Alexander, *The Northwest Ordinance: Constitutional Politics and the Theft of Native Land* (Jefferson, NC: McFarland, 2017); see also Howard C. Taylor, *The Educational Significance of the Early Federal Land Ordinances,* Teachers College Contributions to Education No. 118 (New York: Columbia University, 1922).

6. Carl F. Kaestle, *Pillars of the Republic: Common Schools and American Society* (New York: Hill and Wang, 1983); and "Public Education in the Old Northwest: Necessary to Good Government and the Happiness of Mankind," *Indiana Magazine of History* 84, no. 1 (1988): 60–74.

7. *Annual Report of the Auditor of State to the Forty-Second General Assembly, December 5, 1843* (Columbus, OH: Samuel Medary, State Printer, 1843), 19.

8. For a history of Indian education during the Early National period, see Christina Snyder, *Great Crossings: Indians, Settlers, and Slaves in the Age of Jackson* (New York: Oxford University Press, 2017); see also John Demos, *The Heathen School: A Story of Hope and Betrayal in the Age of the Early Republic* (New York: Vintage Books, 2014).

9. Kaestle, "Public Education in the Old Northwest," 64, quotation from William Parker Cutler and Julia Perkins Cutler, *Life, Journals, and Correspondence of Rev. Manasseh Cutler, LLD, by His Grandchildren* (Cincinnati: Robert Clarke, 1888), 2:449.

10. Kaestle, 64.

11. Kaestle, 65, quotation from Andrew R. L. Clayton, *The Frontier Republic: Ideology and Politics in the Ohio Country, 1780–1825* (Kent, OH: Kent State University Press, 1986), 142.

12. See Julia Perkins Cutler, *Life and Times of Ephraim Cutler: Prepared from His Journals and Correspondence* (Cincinnati: R. Clarke, 1890).

13. Kaestle, "Public Education in the Old Northwest," 65.

14. Kaestle, 65; see also Thomas N. Hoover, *The History of Ohio University* (Athens: Ohio University Press, 1954); and Ohio University Board of Trustees, *A Legal History of the Ohio University, Athens, Ohio: Including Resolutions of Congress, Contracts, Territorial and State Enactments, Judicial Decisions, etc.* (Columbus, OH: Cott and Hann, 1881).

15. Kaestle, "Public Education in the Old Northwest," 66.

16. Kaestle, 66.

17. In 1828, Kenyon College petitioned for support from the federal government, but this request was refused. See United States Congress, *Debates in Congress, Comprising the Leading Debates and Incidents of the First Session of the Twentieth Congress: Together with an Appendix, Containing Important State Papers and Public Documents and the Laws Enacted during the Session, with a Copious Index to the Whole* (Washington, DC: Gales and Seaton, 1828), 4:533–46.

18. See John Bell, *The Abolitionist College: Dreams of Racial Equality Deferred* (Baton Rouge: Louisiana State University Press, 2021); Gary Kornblith and Carol Lasser, *Elusive Utopia: The Struggle for Racial Equality in Oberlin, Ohio* (Baton Rouge: Louisiana State University Press, 2018); J. Brent Morris, *Oberlin, Hotbed of Abolitionism: College, Community, and the Fight for Freedom and Equality in Antebellum America* (Chapel Hill: University of North Carolina Press, 2014); and Carol Lasser, "Enacting Emancipation: African-American Women Abolitionists at Oberlin College and the Quest for Empowerment, Equality, and Respectability," in *Women's Rights and Transatlantic Antislavery in the Era of Emancipation,* ed. Kathryn Kish Sklar and James Brewer Stewart (New Haven, CT: Yale University Press, 2007).

19. See, for example, Susan Strane, *A Whole-Souled Woman: Prudence Crandall and the Education of Black Women* (New York: W. W. Norton, 1990); Edmund Fuller, *Prudence Crandall: An Incident of Racism in Nineteenth-Century Connecticut* (Middletown, CT: Wesleyan University Press, 1971); Marvis O. Welch, *Prudence Crandall: A Biography* (Manchester, CT: Jason, 1983); and Philip S. Foner and Josephine F. Pacheco, *Three Who Dared: Prudence Crandall, Margaret Douglass, Myrtilla Miner: Champions of Antebellum Black Education* (Westport, CT: Greenwood Press, 1985).

20. See, for example, Margaret Nash, *Women's Education in the United States, 1780–1840* (New York: Palgrave Macmillan, 2005); Anne Firor Scott, "The Ever Widening Circle: The Diffusion of Feminist Values from the Troy Female Seminary 1822–1872," *History of Education Quarterly* 19, no. 1 (1979): 3–25; Leonard I. Sweet, "The Female Seminary Movement and Woman's Mission in Antebellum America," *Church History* 54, no. 1 (1985): 41–55; Linda Perkins, "The Impact of the 'Cult of True Womanhood' on the Education of Black Women," *Journal of Social Issues* 39, no. 3 (1983): 17–28; Jacqueline Jones Royster, *Traces of a Stream: Literacy and Social Change among African American Women* (Pittsburgh: University of Pittsburgh Press, 2000); and Kabria Baumgartner, *In Pursuit of Knowledge: Black Women and Educational Activism in Antebellum America* (New York: New York University Press, 2019), which deals extensively with Hiram Huntington Kellogg's Young Ladies' Domestic Seminary in Clinton, New York.

21. For more on William Lloyd Garrison and education for abolition, see John L. Thomas, *The Liberator, William Lloyd Garrison: A Biography*

(Boston: Little, Brown, 1963); and Henry Mayer, *All on Fire: William Lloyd Garrison and the Abolition of Slavery* (New York: W. W. Norton, 2008).

22. See Hilary J. Moss, "Education's Inequity: Opposition to Black Higher Education in Antebellum Connecticut," *History of Education Quarterly* 46, no. 1 (2006): 16–35.

23. See James Brewer Stewart, "The New Haven Negro College and the Meanings of Race in New England, 1776–1870," *New England Quarterly* 76, no. 3 (2003): 323–55.

24. "A Useful Blast," *The Liberator* (Boston), December 3, 1831.

25. Hilary J. Moss, *Schooling Citizens: The Struggle for African-American Education in Antebellum America* (Chicago: University of Chicago Press, 2009); and Stacey M. Robertson, *Hearts Beating for Liberty: Women Abolitionists in the Old Northwest* (Chapel Hill: University of North Carolina Press, 2010); see also Joan E. Cashin, "Black Families in the Old Northwest," *Journal of the Early Republic* 15, no. 2 (1995): 449–75.

26. Quoted in Leonard Erickson, "The Color Line in Ohio Public Schools, 1829–1890" (PhD diss., Ohio State University, 1959), 107–8.

27. Quoted in Erickson, 107–8.

28. Kaestle, "Public Education in the Old Northwest," 67; see also William J. Reese, "Indiana's Public School Traditions: Themes and Research Opportunities," *Indiana Magazine of History* 89, no. 4 (1993): 289–334.

29. For more on the history of literacy, see Carl F. Kaestle, *Literacy in the United States: Readers and Reading since 1880* (New Haven, CT: Yale University Press, 1991).

30. See, for example, Dolores Sullivan, *William Holmes McGuffey: Schoolmaster to the Nation* (Rutherford, NJ: Farleigh Dickinson University Press, 1994); and John H. Westerhoff, *McGuffey and His Readers: Piety, Morality, and Education in Nineteenth-Century America* (Nashville, TN: Abingdon Press, 1978)

31. Quoted in Kaestle, "Public Education in the Old Northwest," 67.

32. Anna-Lisa Cox, *The Bone and Sinew of the Land: America's Forgotten Black Pioneers and the Struggle for Equality* (New York: Public Affairs, 2018); see also J. C. Carroll, "The Beginnings of Public Education for Negroes in Indiana," *Journal of Negro Education* 8, no. 4 (October 1939): 649–58.

33. Kaestle, "Public Education in the Old Northwest," 67–68.

34. Kaestle, 68.

35. The idea of taxing private land to pay for public schools did not reemerge in Indiana until the 1870s, and, even then, it was subject to legal action. The issue eventually went before the US Supreme Court in Davis v. Indiana, 94 U.S. 792 (1876).

36. Trustees for Vincennes University v. Indiana, 55 U.S. 268 (1852). See Matthew E. Welsh, "An Old Wound Finally Healed: Vincennes University's

Struggle for Survival," *Indiana Magazine of History* 84, no. 3 (1988): 217–36.

37. Edward Eggleston, *Hoosier School-Master: A Novel* (New York: O. Judd, 1871); see also William P. Randel, *Edward Eggleston, Author of "The Hoosier School-Master"* (New York: King's Crown, 1946).
38. Eggleston, *Hoosier School-Master*, 11.
39. Eggleston, 24.
40. Eggleston, 25.
41. Eggleston, 55.
42. See Kathryn Kish Sklar, *Catharine Beecher: A Study in American Domesticity* (New Haven, CT: Yale University Press, 1973); Jeane Boydston, *The Limits of Sisterhood: The Beecher Sisters on Women's Rights and Woman's Sphere* (Chapel Hill: University of North Carolina Press, 1988); Mae Harveson, *Catharine Esther Beecher, Pioneer Educator* (New York: Arno Press, 1969); and Andrea Turpin, *A New Moral Vision: Gender, Religion, and the Changing Purposes of American Higher Education, 1837–1917* (Ithaca, NY: Cornell University Press, 2016).
43. See Mary Kelley, *Learning to Stand and Speak: Women, Education, and Public Life in America's Republic* (Chapel Hill: University of North Carolina Press, 2006).
44. Kaestle, "Public Education in the Old Northwest," 70. For more on Mary Roper, see Polly Welts Kaufman, *Women Teachers on the Frontier* (New Haven, CT: Yale University Press, 1984); and Jacqueline Jones, "Piety and Politics on the Frontier—or, the Short, Unhappy Life of Arozina Perkins," *Reviews in American History* 12, no. 4 (1984): 502–6.
45. Kaestle, "Public Education in the Old Northwest," 71.
46. Kaestle, 70.
47. Kaestle, 71.
48. For more on these questions, see, for example, Benjamin Justice, *The War That Wasn't: Religious Conflict and Compromise in the Common Schools of New York State, 1865–1900* (Albany: State University of New York Press, 2005); and Robert N. Gross, *Public vs. Private: The Early History of School Choice in America* (New York: Oxford University Press, 2017).

Conclusion

TIMOTHY G. ANDERSON

The genesis of this collection of essays can undoubtedly be traced to the publication of David McCullough's *The Pioneers* in 2019 and the interest it generated—both in academic circles and among the general public—in the history of Ohio's settlement during the formative years of the Early Republic. That the book is cited dozens of times herein reflects this. But as Brian Schoen notes in the introduction, as coeditors we did not set out to assemble a volume that would serve as a rejoinder to McCullough's monograph. McCullough was a Pulitzer Prize–winning historian and consummate storyteller, and *The Pioneers* stands on its own as a work of remarkable scope. Rather, we began from the position that McCullough's history of the Ohio Company, its organizers, and its activities in the incipient Old Northwest—as well told as that history is—focuses on the influences of but one group of people: White settlers of European ancestry. From the outset, our idea was to bring together a group of scholars who could provide critical insight into the contributions of other groups of settlers who, although fewer in number, nevertheless played foundational roles in the story of Ohio's early settlement.

McCullough credits people like Rufus Putnam and Manasseh Cutler with introducing the "American ideal"—freedom of religion, free universal education, and prohibition of slavery—to the Northwest Territory and beyond. But while these idea(l)s were codified in the Northwest Ordinance of 1787 (and elsewhere), the essays in this volume illustrate that in practice the implementation of such notions "on the ground" was complex, problematic, and often highly contested. Freedom of religion was certainly not bestowed upon Indigenous populations, most of whom made no distinction between their "culture" and their "religion." The processes of settler colonialism dispossessed first peoples of not only their ancestral territories but often their cultures and religions as well. Free education was anything but "universal," given that it was not granted to either Native Americans or African Americans, many of whom, Anna-Lisa Cox reminds us, were some of Ohio's earliest landowners and successful farmers. And while chattel slavery was indeed proscribed in the Northwest Territory, the implementation of Ohio's notorious Black Laws (1807) prohibited the full participation of African Americans in the state's economic and political arenas.

One need look no further than early newspaper clippings for evidence of the racial tropes and attitudes that remained deeply ensconced despite the legal prohibition of slavery. A column from 1836 in the *Hamilton Intelligencer,* a Whig-supporting newspaper, provides an example. Responding to Democratic accusations that William Henry Harrison's voting record in the Ohio legislature was too weak with regard to racial issues, the piece attacks Democratic vice presidential candidate and Kentuckian Richard Mentor Johnson's public relationship with Julia Chinn, one of his slaves:

> The "black arts" prints, throughout the Union, are railing against what they term Gen. Harrison's *"white slavery vote,"* while in the Ohio Legislature, and detailing *imaginary* instances of "poor white men" being sold to *"rich negroes."* Now there exists a *real* and not *imaginary* exemplification of a fact somewhat similar to the circumstance alluded to; an instance of a *"rich white man"* being married to and living with a NEGRESS, a man, who in open violation of the laws of decency and the outraged feelings of community, acknowledged her as his wife, and endeavored to introduce his colored offspring within the pale of civilized and enlightened society. . . . In the above occurrence we have a sight which might please the amalgamationist; but what would every man, who has any regard for decency say? Would he not rather spill his last drop of blood, than see his FRIENDS OR BROTHERS associating themselves with the degraded sons of Africa, and living in open union with a *wooly headed* and *thick lipped* negress? . . . Can any man who loves his country—who has any regard for decency and the laws of civilization, be found supporting a man who publicly attempts to justify such a measure?[1]

Regardless of political party, few White Ohioans could envision non-Whites as members of a "civilization" they defined in exclusionary ways.

Two years later, accompanied by an illustration of an African American slave "escaping" to the North, the same newspaper published two sections of one of the Black Laws passed by the Ohio General Assembly in 1804 and 1807, including the section describing the penalties for offenders and for those harboring or abetting such offenders.[2] These laws required Black and mulatto people to prove they were not slaves and to find at least two people who could provide a surety of five hundred dollars for their "good behavior" and who could provide for them if they could not support themselves. Among other provisions, these laws also prohibited gun ownership and restricted rights to marry Whites.[3]

* * *

Many Americans tend to perceive the history of western expansion as a rather one-dimensional process in which a wave of White settlers from the East slowly but surely conquered an uncivilized, disordered series of frontiers, bringing democracy, free-market capitalism, and social and political order in the process. Over time a binary conceptualization of the frontier emerged: a place in which order displaced chaos and civilization replaced "savagery." Such notions became deeply engrained in the nation's popular culture, engendering a deep, romanticized nostalgia for our frontier, western past. Discourses associated with these powerful tropes permeate our popular music (country western and bluegrass), film (John Wayne westerns), television (*Rawhide, Bonanza*), and literature (James Fenimore Cooper, Willa Cather, Laura Ingalls Wilder).

But the Ohio frontier in the late eighteenth and nineteenth centuries was anything but one dimensional, binary, or romantic. Rather, it was a place shaped from the very beginning by complicated interactions among diverse groups of people. Ohio was in many ways a proving ground for ideas and policies that would later be codified in law and in practice throughout the country farther west, a place in which such ideas and policies were "worked out." Experimentations regarding public education, public land policy, and the disposition of Native American territories are but three examples. The "working out" of such policies was often messy and contentious, with the ultimate outcome anything but certain at the time, and often violent.

The idea of Ohio as a kind of palimpsest of the country with respect to its social and political history and its ethnic pluralism is not new. The noted historian R. Douglas Hurt contextualized early Ohio as a "crucible" for ideas and policies that were subsequently put into practice throughout the Old Northwest in the nineteenth century.[4] Likewise, previous scholars have described how the geographical clustering of Yankee, mid-Atlantic, and Upland Southern settlers along roughly latitudinal zones in Ohio was repeated in Indiana and Illinois, and how the pattern of African Americans and European immigrants settling in "ethnic islands" in southern and western Ohio recurred in the incipient Midwest and elsewhere.[5]

Collectively, the essays in this book add to our understanding of how Ohio was from the outset not only a meeting place of diverse groups of people, but also a place where diverse idea(l)s and discourses were contested. So, too, they reveal that the settlement of Ohio was accomplished by multiple groups, and that this process began long before Anglo-Europeans and Anglo-Americans set foot in the region. Each group made distinctive contributions to this process, revealed in the state's cultural landscapes and historical chronicle. And while the Anglo-European/American narrative of this settlement became dominant over time, other narratives—including several presented here—are there to be discovered if we only lift the curtains behind which they are shrouded. Adding those narratives makes not only for a far more inclusive and dramatic history, but also a more accurate one.

Notes

1. *Hamilton Intelligencer* 5, no. 51 (October 27, 1836): 2. Johnson was Andrew Jackson's running mate in the 1836 presidential election and became the nation's ninth vice president in 1837.
2. *Hamilton Intelligencer* 6, no. 18 (March 29, 1838): 3.
3. For a detailed analysis of Ohio's Black Laws, see Stephen Middleton, *The Black Laws: Race and the Legal Process in Early Ohio* (Athens: Ohio University Press, 2005).
4. R. Douglas Hurt, *The Ohio Frontier: Crucible of the Old Northwest, 1720–1830* (Bloomington: Indiana University Press, 1996).
5. John Hudson, "North American Origins of Middlewestern Frontier Populations," *Annals of the American Association of Geographers* 78, no. 3 (1988): 395–413; Robert P. Swierenga, "The Settlement of the Old

Northwest: Ethnic Pluralism in a Featureless Plain," *Journal of the Early Republic* 9, no. 1 (1989): 73–105; and Michael P. Conzen, "Culture Regions, Homelands, and Ethnic Archipelagos in the United States: Methodological Considerations," *Journal of Cultural Geography* 13, no. 2 (1993): 13–29.

Afterword

History vs. Legacy

CHIEF GLENNA J. WALLACE

This collection of essays is an outgrowth of a conference entitled "Settling Ohio: First Nations and Beyond" held in February 2020 at Ohio University. David McCullough's 2019 book, *The Pioneers: The Heroic Story of the Settlers Who Brought the American Ideal West,* figured prominently and was a central reference point. The dozen or so presentations at the conference focused on the history and legacy of the numerous population groups that contributed to the history and landscapes of what is now Ohio, including Indigenous groups, Anglo-Americans, African Americans, and European immigrants. As the final presenter, I was asked to comment on these sometimes disparate histories and legacies together from the point of view of the very first Ohioans.

Let's begin with history. The year was 1830. The Indian Removal Act was passed that year and we, the Mixed Band of Seneca and Shawnee living on a small reservation known as the Lewistown Reserve near Wapakoneta, Ohio, were chosen for removal. We were the biblical "chosen few." We were the first to be forcibly removed from the Ohio Valley to a land far away known as Indian Territory, a distance of some seven hundred to eight hundred miles in a land that almost eighty years later became the state of Oklahoma. The treaty was signed in 1831, and its terms painted Indian Territory as a land of milk and honey. We could live our lifestyle. We could be free, unrestrained. We could be where only Indians would be. We would have sixty thousand acres to roam, to hunt, to plant as we wanted. We would never have to move again. We were told it was for "perpetuity," unending. And so it was that in September of 1832 we were forced to leave Ohio. We left on our own terms, however. They told us we would be leaving on watercraft. We refused. My ancestors had no trust in the United States. We were afraid of the possibility that, because of constant smoke, the watercraft might catch fire. We were afraid there would be no way to escape, to survive. And we were afraid that the fire might be deliberate. Then there was the issue of fear of incidents like cholera-infested blankets. Again, there was no trust in this "Great White Father" who was making us leave our homelands. And so, we said, "No. No, we will not go by watercraft. We will leave this Ohio Valley the same way we came to this land, the same way we had traveled to and lived in at least twenty-six states. We will go on foot. We will walk. We will take our horses. Some may ride on them. We will take wagons, and some may ride in them. But we will not go on your watercraft."

And so it was that the Seneca and Shawnee Mixed Band left in September of 1832 and walked, and walked, and walked. For four long months they walked. More than one in five died along the way. They left the bones of their people, their families, their loved ones wherever they happened to be. No time to set aside days for mourning, no time for ceremonials, no time for feasts. No rites, no rituals. Instead, they walked in sorrow, unsure of what the future held for them. The Great White Father had planned poorly for this expedition. There was insufficient money, insufficient food, insufficient information. The US government ran out of money and had to take money from us. Food was scarce. My people consumed more squash and pumpkin than anyone conceived possible. Eat or die, without questioning. That was the choice. Many did die. And then they were taken to the wrong land. My people were Woodland Indians. They lived where there were trees, water, game. My people were taken beyond the land designated for the Mixed Band on into Cherokee lands. Once again, my people said, "No. No, we will not stay here. There are no trees. There is no game. We are hunters. We are planters. We need water." So, they retraced their footsteps. Recrossed the Neosho River. Recrossed the Spring River and settled on lands where the Elk River flows today south of the Spring River. The Seneca settled on the southern portion of the sixty thousand acres, with the Shawnee occupying the north end. The Mixed Band was home at last with sixty thousand acres in perpetuity, or so they were told.

It was the month of December when my people finally arrived at what would become their home forever. December in Indian Territory is a cruel month. The weather is unpredictable. Temperatures are cold, often below freezing, at times plunging below zero, sometimes remaining there for days. There are no crops to harvest, no berries, no fruits, no three sisters of corn, beans, and squash. Nor is December a time to plant. They did have rabbits, squirrels, deer, fish. They lived off the harsh land during these winter months.

The land was not the only thing that was harsh. Indian Territory for the Mixed Band meant being located next to the state of Missouri, a state like Ohio that was not friendly to Indians, preferred they live elsewhere, and also removed them. Even today, both states have no federally recognized tribes. Protection for the Indians was limited at best, and it was worse for the Shawnees because of their location in what would one day become the extreme northeast county in Oklahoma, bordering the states of Missouri and Kansas. The little town of Seneca, Missouri, became known as "Hell on the Border."

Protection was basically nonexistent in the initial year of 1832 but became even less as the Civil War approached. The Great White Father's attention focused less and less upon Native Americans in Indian Territory and more and more upon issues involving civil unrest and slavery dividing the North and South. Stealing, destruction of property, and physical violence became the norm, and many of the Shawnees fled from the Missouri border to seek safety in Kansas with the Ottawa Tribe, who offered to "share their blanket" with the Shawnees. They remained there until the Civil War was over, returning to find little if any improvements they had made to the land. Fences were destroyed, livestock of cattle and horses nonexistent, and homes made unfit to live in. It was 1832 all over—begin from nothing.

Indian Territory in what is now Ottawa County in Oklahoma began with the Mixed Band in 1832 who were then joined by the Quapaw Tribe in 1833 from the Red River in Arkansas. More tribes were later added. Following on the heels of the Civil War, in 1867 the United States signed an omnibus treaty with several of the tribes relocating them from Kansas to Indian Territory, taking most of the sixty thousand acres promised to the Mixed Band. What happened to perpetuity? Yes, we were paid for the land, but it amounted to pennies on the dollar with no choice to sell or not to sell. In essence, Indian Territory tribes were penalized for supporting the Confederacy rather than the Union. In that omnibus treaty, the Mixed Band officially separated and became two tribes—the Senecas becoming the Seneca-Cayuga and the Shawnees becoming the

Eastern Shawnees. This part of Indian Territory was now home to the Eastern Shawnee, Seneca-Cayuga, Quapaw, Miami, Ottawa, Peoria, and Wyandotte. Within five or six years, the Modoc Tribe was removed from Oregon and California, making eight tribes in this small area. Finally, in 2000 the Shawnee Tribe—located in Miami, Oklahoma, and formerly known as the Cherokee-Shawnee—became federally recognized when it separated from the Cherokee, making nine federally recognized tribes in Ottawa County, the most of any place in the United States.

Life for these tribes was not easy. Few spoke English. Financial means were severely limited. And the death rate remained high. Just before 1900, my tribe, the Eastern Shawnee Tribe, was down to only sixty-nine people. It truly was a case of an almost successful mass genocide, both physically and culturally. With only sixty-nine people and only five or six of them being adult males, we were unable to conduct our ceremonies. We became assimilated into the non-Indian world. We lost our language, our ceremonies, our traditional way of life. Our grandmothers and grandfathers thought they were doing the right thing, making the right choices when they told us that the past is the past. If we are going to live in this world, they said, then we must be of this world. We must live, act, breathe as if our traditional world never existed, and for us, the Eastern Shawnee, that is basically the way it was. We were assimilated.

Assimilation was further attained with the Dawes Allotment Act, passed in 1887. An act to provide for the allotment of lands in severalty to Indians on the various reservations, this act made each Native American an individual landowner rather than collective landowners as members of tribes. It is estimated that Native Americans lost control of about one hundred million acres of land, or about two-thirds of the land base they held in 1887. For my tribe, the Eastern Shawnee Tribe, by 1937 we had gone from partners in a treaty specifying 60,000 acres down to a mere 58.19 acres. And we were fortunate to even have that. A tribal member who was originally allotted this parcel of land asked the US government if she could trade it for land near Colony, Oklahoma, where her husband's tribe was. The US government agreed and gave title to the Eastern Shawnee Tribe when it adopted its first constitution in 1939. This was the only land the Eastern Shawnee owned until the late 1980s.

And this land, this land we were led to believe was the land of milk and honey, the land that would be so good for us, how do we describe this land where we live? We live in Ottawa County, a small county with nine federally recognized tribes, seven of which were forcibly removed from the Ohio Valley, with a total county population of about thirty-two thousand. We live in a county that is classified as a "StrikeForce" county, one in which the median income has been below the national poverty level for twenty or more consecutive years. For us, it has been more than thirty. We live in a county that according to the federal government contains the most polluted Superfund site in the United States. We live in a county where the waters run red when it rains because of the numerous lead and zinc mines that were not regulated, and when closed left numerous chat pile tailings that pollute the air and the environment daily. We live in a county where statistics for cancer, tuberculosis, lead poisoning, diabetes, and other diseases are significantly higher than the norm.

My father was one of those lead and zinc miners. He chose to try to take his family elsewhere, to find better living conditions, less pollution, more money. And so it was that at the end of my fourth grade of education, he cashed in his miner's settlement, purchased a flatbed truck, added trusses, pitched a tarpaulin on top, and set off for the West Coast with eleven of us, becoming some of the first RVers in the United States. My father, mother, and their five children and my mother's brother, his wife, and their two children looked like the Beverly Hillbillies taking off to what we hoped were greener pastures. We became migrant workers, going from one farm to another, one state to another, one crop to another, one school to another. We left Oklahoma as youngsters, but we became adults very quickly. We each had a role in helping to support the family. We had our daily assignments, our daily quotas for whatever crop or product it was. Exceeding that quota meant we were generously rewarded. Yes, our living quarters were not always the best—sometimes a migrant cabin, sometimes an abandoned barn, sometimes staying in the truck, one time even living in an actual pigsty, for anyone who wanted to clean it out. I chose the pigsty and swept it until the dirt floor glistened. These experiences taught us to set goals, accomplish those goals, and in most cases, to exceed those goals, resulting in inner satisfaction far beyond any monetary reward. Unfortunately, my father's years in the lead and zinc mines, followed by working in the tunnels in California, resulted in his having tuberculosis of the spine. We returned to Oklahoma just as poor as we left, and Dad entered the Veterans Hospital in Muskogee, Oklahoma, where the surgery was successful; but he was disabled, never able to work again. It was there, when seeing my father helpless on a hospital bed and knowing that my mother, who had never finished high school and would never be able to have a good-paying job, knowing we were going to be on welfare, that one word became my mantra for life—options. I wanted options, and the only way I knew to have those options was to get an advanced education.

* * *

Education changed my life. I married while still in high school, graduated (the first female ever in my family to do so), went to business college, and took a bookkeeping job, and my husband and I became parents to three children. That word "options" kept nagging me. What if my husband became disabled like my father had and I had to support those three children? When our youngest child was one year old, that fear motivated me to enter college. My pastor's wife had a few college hours at another institution, and she wanted to continue her education but needed moral support. I became her support just as she became mine. Five years later, after commuting 110 miles daily and having early morning classes, I graduated with a master's degree in hand. I landed a communications teaching position at our local community college in Missouri, which had just been established and was less than fifteen miles from my home and the Oklahoma border.

Blessed with progressive administrators and since childhood having been schooled in surpassing established goals, I thrived in that atmosphere. I became accustomed to wearing several hats, always a full-time, year-round instructor. I also sponsored college cheerleaders and moved on to help establish and direct adult basic education programs and classes for those who had been unable to complete their high school diploma. Within five years I was named director of the Communications Department. Later, the administration made the decision to combine some departments into divisions and I was then named chair of the Communications / Fine Arts and Design Division. That division included written and oral communications, literature, grammar, journalism, foreign languages, theater, music, and the arts. I was ill prepared for the latter part of that assignment. What did this Native American-who-never-lived-as-a-Native American, Okie migrant worker know about fine arts and design? I knew how to curl up and sleep on a hay bale; was skilled in living in and sweeping pigsties; had ample experience in picking strawberries, loganberries, raspberries, apples, and cherries and chopping lettuce; and was an adaptable person as a result of having relocated to several locations. None of those skills, however, were remotely related to theater, music, and the arts.

Although I felt ill-equipped to teach these subjects, most of the people living in our two-county college jurisdiction area, made up of McDonald and Newton Counties, did not know much about fine arts and design either. McDonald County was the second poorest of 114 Missouri counties, and only 10 percent of high school graduates went on to college. Those were hardly statistics that indicate a thriving interest in the fine arts. We tried bringing some noteworthy events to the college, but attendance was disappointing. The answer, as has been said, was "If the mountain won't go to Mohammed, then Mohammed must come to the mountain." I designed a series of travel adventures, for which we provided partial scholarships to our college students and low-cost fares to community members. These trips were always to places where students and community members were exposed to the finest musical performances and theatrical productions, important historical sites, and prestigious museum collections. These trips were so popular, we organized three per year, one in the United States and two in foreign countries. We walked the Great Wall of China, explored the Acropolis ruins, meditated at Stonehenge, rubbed the foot of St. Peter's statue in Rome, had an audience with the Pope, climbed the Eiffel Tower, went to Stratford-on-Avon, then on to the Great Barrier Reef in Australia, and breathlessly viewed the Great Pyramids, with several trips to Broadway interspersed through the years, ultimately traveling to more than seventy countries and throughout the United States. Combining these adventures with the experiences of student exchanges from Russia and other countries, along with faculty teaching exchanges with the Aussies and the Brits, I came to know about fine arts and design. I also came to know about World Heritage designations.

In 2000 I had just returned from a nine-month teaching faculty exchange program in Melbourne, Australia, when another life-changing event came my way. Michael Bouman, executive director of the Missouri Humanities Council, appeared unannounced at my office door. Always an organized visionary, he was anticipating and planning for the 2003 bicentennial of Lewis and Clark's Corps of Discovery, which began in

Missouri. He wanted to honor all the Indian tribes living in Missouri that had been mentioned in the Lewis and Clark journals. Furthermore, he wanted tribal representatives to present Chautauqua performances across Missouri over a two-year period. My college president, who was on the board of the Missouri Humanities Council, had given him my name, saying I was Shawnee, lived in Missouri, and was capable of doing this. I told Michael that I could not do this, that I did not know the history of my tribe and neither did anyone else because we had always been so poor, had always had to concentrate on just making a living and exist-ing, and had never had any resources until gaming came to our tribe in 1984. No one has ever had the time, nor the interest or information, to record our history. Researching my tribe was on my bucket list after I retired, not now. Not one to take no for an answer, Michael looked at my office wall where several credentials were hanging and replied, "Those degrees indicate you know how to research, you have had to have written numerous research papers, and you teach speech. This is 2000 and we don't begin these Chautauqua presentations until 2003. That's three years from now. You have time to research, write that script, and rehearse that presentation." Three years later I was a Chautauqua performer presenting the history and culture of my tribe.

In those three years, I read every book, every article, every interview I could find. I learned much about Ohio, our homeland, traveling to several places and talking with various people. It was that three-year research project—two years teaching and performing as Kokumthena, the Shawnee female deity, plus two additional years on the Chautauqua circuit as the fiery female Kansas political figure Mary Elizabeth Lease, along with all my travels—that prepared me to run for the position of chief of the Eastern Shawnee Tribe in 2006. That election ended with my being the first female principal chief elected by Shawnees.

* * *

The following year, in 2007, another event happened that also shaped much of my life. Ohio State University was sponsoring a lecture series of prominent authors and activists in the Native American world. One of the speakers was John Sugden, a renowned British author who had penned a biography of Tecumseh, the most famous Shawnee. I traveled to Ohio to hear that speech. I was not disappointed. An additional requirement of the speaker series was for the lecturer to visit Newark Earthwork Mounds, some thirty miles east of Columbus, the following day. I joined the group, never having heard of the town of Newark, Ohio, never having heard of the Newark Earthworks, but wanting to hear more from John Sugden. That trip changed my life. I was directed to walk along a path to a wooden viewing platform where I could see the mounds. The path was crowded with visitors, golf carts, golfers, and our group. There was a golf tournament underway. Not knowing that there was a golf course—an active golf course—at the mounds, I proceeded to walk the path, only to hear loud voices chastising us, yelling, "You've got to get back. You're in the way. You're blocking the carts. You've got to get back. We have a tournament today. You don't belong here. Leave and come back some other time." Stepping back as far as I could, I hesitantly moved toward the viewing platform, climbed the steps, and looked out. There before me was a scene as impressive as any World Heritage site I had ever seen, and I had experienced numerous ones. There were the unending lines of curves, heights, and breadths of basket after basket of Mother Earth molded and shaped into what was originally—and still should be—a living, revered natural sanctuary. Inhaling deeply, I tried to take in what I was seeing, what I was feeling. At first, I was so proud. This is magnificent. This place, this structure, was built by my ancestors—that is, Native Americans in general. They loved this place, repeatedly returned to this place on pilgrimages bringing valuables from throughout the United States, worshipped at this place, honored our Creator here, and preserved this sacred site. That pride then turned into questions. Why had I never heard of this place? Why was it never mentioned in the scores of books and materials I read about Shawnees, about Ohio? Why had I never seen a video of this place? Don't the people of Ohio know about this treasure? And why is there a golf course on these sacred mounds? Doesn't anyone care? From pride, to questions, to bewilderment, to anger, to disgust—I felt all those emotions in a matter of moments. I felt as if I had been violated. I was no longer an assimilated Eastern Shawnee. I was an enraged Native American. Someone has to speak out against this insensitivity, this wrongdoing, and if no one else will, then I will. I will not be silent. Practicing and believing in both my Shawnee religion and Christianity, I left that viewing platform thinking, "Father, forgive them, for they know not what they do."

From that day in 2007, I have continuously focused upon the legacy of my ancestors in the Ohio Valley. After seeing Newark Earthworks and learning more about them, I realized their complexity and the knowledge their creators—my ancestors—had to possess to construct those earthworks and other mounds. They had to be proficient in astronomy, mathematics, geology, geography, science, arts, construction, spirituality. The more historical sites I visited in Ohio involving Native Americans, the more impressed I became with their accomplishments, their intellect, their understanding of the complexity of this world. Yet the word most commonly encountered in Ohio describing Native Americans was/is "savages." How can they constantly be referred to as savages with the complex, sophisticated, scientific, and artistic treasures they had constructed? Again, I knew I had to speak out.

My visit to Newark Earthworks led to visits to other mounds, led to realizations that my ancestors, in reality, were not savages, but in numerous instances rivaled the brilliance recognized by the slaves who built the pyramids in Egypt, the slaves who built the Great Wall in China. From Serpent Mound to Seips Mound, to Fort Ancient, to Mound City at Chillicothe, I found sites worthy of World Heritage nomination. These sites have outstanding universal values, culturally, scientifically, and artistically. They must be preserved. Too many mounds have been destroyed, have never been recognized, and we must never let that happen again. Wake up, Ohio. Recognize the treasures right before your eyes. There are 1,121 World Heritage sites in the world. Only twenty-four of them are in the United States, including Yellowstone, Glacier Bay, and the Grand Canyon. Newark Earthwork Mounds and others in Ohio should be added to that list. This should be a legacy for my ancestors.

I began my quest by meeting with the Ohio History Connection numerous times, many times questioning them, pointing out discrepancies, inaccuracies, and inattention. How did it happen that a golf club has a lease from the Ohio History Connection, the keeper of some fifty historic sites? And why is that lease so long? Why was Native American access to Newark Earthworks limited to one day a year, and even now only four days a year? What relationship does Ohio History Connection have with federally recognized tribes? Where is the consultation, the talking with us rather than talking about us? What are the sites that my tribe can visit? How are those sites depicted, and who is making the decisions regarding those sites and those depictions? Where are they getting their information? These discussions continued, challenging at times, but ultimately resulting in a close relationship, a relationship where now we work collaboratively, where we listen to each other, respect each other, feel comfortable working through issues, and where consensus is reached.

Discussions began with other individuals and entities as well. Soon, Ohio History Connection took the lead, involved the National Parks Service, approached educational institutions, recruited others, and involved community leaders, and a World Heritage nomination was submitted. Programs were developed and presented. And it was at Mound City in Chillicothe, Ohio, where in 2016 I first heard archaeologist Dr. Brett Ruby describe my ancestors as "geniuses." I wept. At long last, the word "savages" had been challenged. Too often that word had been used in reference to Native Americans only. But as David McCullough addressed this issue in his book, he wrote, "Much blood had already been shed in wilderness battles and atrocities committed by both natives and white men." Yet only Natives were called savages. He continued pointing out other examples of non-Natives acting as savages, referencing the "infamous massacre by American militia of ninety-six peaceable Delaware Indians in central Ohio in 1782—Christian men, women and children who knelt singing hymns as they were systematically clubbed to death, all because they were mistakenly thought to have had a part in the murder of a family of settlers."

As months and years passed, several other critical issues regarding legacy surfaced. Several of these critical issues involve the subject of death. The state of Ohio possesses more than eight thousand human remains of my ancestors. Why? Our culture teaches us that our spirit does not rest until it is reunited with Mother Earth. Why are a minimum of eight thousand of my ancestors' remains kept in museums, in basements, in storage boxes, even on fireplace mantels? And why are they still being tested? They are two hundred or more years old. They need to be buried. Their current status is not the legacy my ancestors should have. Then there is the subject of where those human remains should be buried. We have always believed our people should be buried close to the place where they died. The same is true for human remains. They should be buried in the vicinity where they were found. Those remains, over two hundred years old, belong to people who never lived in Oklahoma. That was never their home. We would hope that a cemetery—a Native American cemetery—could be established in Ohio so those remains might finally rest in peace. They lived in Ohio, loved Ohio, died in Ohio, and their legacy should be to remain in Ohio, perhaps at one of the Native American historical sites cared for by the Ohio History Connection.

The next legacy issue concerns Ohio burial laws. Most are unaware that Ohio has one of the weakest burial laws in the United States. Any person who died and was buried more than 125 years ago is subject to having their graves dug up and burial items looted, with only a small penalty to the looter. It was, and is, common practice for Native Americans to bury their loved ones with personal items meant to carry them into the afterlife. Today those personal belongings, such as pots, knives, jewelry, weapons, and other items, bring high prices on eBay and other auction sites. Unfortunately, because so many tribes lived in the Ohio Valley area, many Native American burial sites are targeted by pothunters and looters who dig, pillage, and remove the funerary objects and, yes, even bones in order to sell them. What continues to happen to the dead in Ohio is deplorable. Grave robbing and digging without consequences is unacceptable; a stricter Grave Protection Act is desperately needed.

* * *

I have several great-grandchildren. My youngest is Beckett, who is two years old. Beckett has no siblings, has lived in a world of adults, and is a thirty-year-old adult living in a two-year-old body. Beckett often makes profound statements. Beckett loves his nighttime bath. He loves sitting in the tub, playing in the water, especially when the water begins swirling around him as it drains. He sits there until every drop has disappeared, then gets up, ready to be dried off, dressed in his pajamas and ready for bed. One evening, however, he continued to lie in the tub after it had drained. His mother said, "Come on, Beckett. The water's gone. It's time to get out of the tub, get dried off, put your PJs on, and go to bed."

"No, I don't want to, Mama," responded Beckett.

"Beckett," replied his mother, "I said it's bedtime. Get out of the tub, let's get you ready for bed."

Again, Beckett responded, "No, I don't want to, Mama."

Clearly agitated now, and in a raised voice, my granddaughter said, "Beckett, this is the last time I am going to tell you. The water is all gone. It's bedtime. Get out of the tub, let's dry you off and get your pajamas on."

Once again Beckett replied, "No, I don't want to, Mama. I want to lie here and think about my life."

Perhaps it is time we join Beckett and think about our lives. Perhaps it is time we think about how Native Americans were forced from Ohio. Perhaps it is time we think about how they were treated. I realize that those of us alive today are in no way responsible for past incidents in history. But we do have some responsibility for current practices. I ask you to think about the Native Americans legacy in Ohio. I ask you to think about respecting sacred places, preserving historic landscapes, labeling people with negative words, being insensitive to cultural beliefs, condoning the number of unburied human remains in this state, permitting graves to be robbed, and not enacting stronger burial laws. I ask for your help in finding that balance between history and legacy. Let's think about our lives and our responsibility in establishing accurate and appropriate legacies for all.

APPENDIX

This table is different from the one in *The Bone and Sinew of the Land*, for it is a snapshot only of farmers of African descent noted in the 1850 federal census. In some instances, data from the 1860 census are included for townships that were created after 1850. Each entry is considered a settlement, even if there is only one property-owning African American denoted as a farmer in the township, because this farmer represented more African Americans in the area. For example, in Liberty Township, Highland County, there are twenty-one farming families of African descent, but only three are noted as owning property, so those are the only three named, even though it is likely those other farmers owned property as well (see below). Also, it must be stressed that the federal census is notoriously inaccurate in the antebellum Midwest for information concerning property-owning farmers of color, especially after 1850. Some, like John Langston, seem to have refused to be counted on a federal document, which represented a federal government that was willing to trample states' rights in the non-slaveholding states in order to uphold southern slavery. Others were just not counted, and we cannot know why. There are many examples of this, including in Highland County and other counties where land deeds and agricultural census records reveal the facts about property ownership among farmers of color. This list is, thus, inherently conservative, for it only shows the African-descended people who were listed as farmers and property owners. It excludes all other African American rural property owners, including mill owners, general store owners, wagon makers, ministers, blacksmiths, and so many others. As Stephen Vincent notes in *Southern Seed, Northern Soil*, the majority of African Americans in the antebellum Old Northwest Territory states lived outside of cities. This list is just the tip of the iceberg, but it offers hints to the diversity that existed in frontier and rural Ohio before the Civil War, and the rich history that still needs to be explored.

County (Township)	Name	Birth year	Birth-place (state)	Race	Estimated worth ($)	Improved acres owned	Unimproved acres owned	Total acres owned	House number
					JACKSON COUNTY				
(Milton) 1850	Noah Nooks	1806	VA	M	3,000	1860: 100	1860: 72	1860: 172	1165
	Will. Woodsen	1822	OH	M					1119
	Jms. W. Stewart	1813	VA	M	2,700	1850: 80 1860: 83	1850: 53 1860: 40	1850: 133 1860: 123	1136
	William Yancey	1788	VA	M	2,000	1850: 56 1860: 35	1850: 56 1860: 35	1850: 112 1860: 40	1120
	Christ. King	1800	VA	M					1137
	Stephen Thompson	1788	VA	M	700	30	40	70	1138
	Arthur Qualls	1820	VA	B	300	1860: 20	1860: 10	1860: 40	1158
	Thom. Woodsen	1784	VA	M	6,750	1850: 365 1860: 315	1850: 88 1860: 55	1850: 453 1860: 360	1173
	Geo. Woodsen	1808	VA	M		60	90	150	1174
	Will. Woodsen	1834	OH	M					1176
	William Qualls	1794	VA	B	232	1860: 25	1860: 4	1860: 29	1359
	John Fullerton	1800	VA	B	700	50	25	75	1360
	William Cassels	1804	VA	M					1362
	Joseph Cassels	1825	OH	M					1364
	Booker Hawks	1810	VA	M	250				1370
(Franklin) 1850	Dennis McArty	1805	VA	B	50				965
	Joseph Harrison	1800	VA	B	100				968
	Benjamin Carter	1792	VA	B	400	15	30	45	969
	Kendall Lee	1791	VA	B	600	28	27	55	970
	Jacob Bell	1788	VA	B	50				972
(Jackson) 1850	Jesse Braman	1796	VA	B	390				224
	Jeremiah Harms (Harris)	1810	VA	M	600				225
	Henry Hams (Harris)	1820	VA	M	500				226
	James Braman	1788	VA	B	120	25	55	80	263
	Flemmon Bryant	1826	OH	M	300				266
	Jesse Arter	1820	NC	B	200				340
	Jeremiah Harms (Harris)	1770	VA	B	50	16	44	60	341
(Liberty) 1850	Jonathon Hill	1816	MD	B	800	20	60	80	351
	Jordon Luckaoo	1814	VA	B	100				352
	Michaus Douell	1818	VA	B	800				353
	Jer. Walker	1790	VA	B	800	30	50	80	492

County (Township)	Name	Birth year	Birth-place (state)	Race	Estimated worth ($)	Improved acres owned	Unimproved acres owned	Total acres owned	House number
	John Beauman	1815	VA	B	400	30	50	80	493
(Lick) 1850	John E. Cassels	1812	VA	M	1,500	60	20	80	893
	John Leach	1820	VA	M	1,000	50	10	70	896
	Benjamin Wilson	1800	VA	M	800	40	20	60	897
	Thomas Leach	1807	VA	M	1,000	20	61	81	897
				PIKE COUNTY					
(Seal) 1860	Isaac McCansy	1818	OH	M					468
	Isaac Brown	1815	VA	M	250				469
	Levi Townsend	1807	VA	M	1,500				625
	Wm. B. Wilson	1787	VA	M	150				661
	Fred. Jackson	1821	OH	M	800				682
(Jackson) 1860	Bethnel Dalby	1784	NC	M	150				723
	Bedord Janes	1807	VA	B	60				725
	Julius Winpage	1803	VA	B	320				726
	Andrew Jackson	1827	VA	M	80				729
	Anthony Hall	1785	KY	B	200				733
	Lewis Reid	1804	VA	M	300				734
	Abraham Cance	1803	VA	B	50				738
	John Smith	1790	VA	M	500				739
	Jos. W. Smith	1826	OH	M					740
	Thomas Jackson	1804	VA	M	800				742
	William Napper	1816	VA	M					746
	William Patson	1800	MD	M					771
	Carter Harris	1806	VA	M	500				
	James Smith	1790	VA	M	100				779
	Julius Johnson	1804	VA	B	400				782
	Pleasant Harris	1806	VA	M	500				791
	George Smith	1786	VA	M	1,000				794
	Tiphaniah Smith	1812	VA	M	1,000				795
	James Lucas	1780	MD	M	1,100				805
	Zacariah Lucas	1790	MD	M	1,900				816
	Abraham Cunningham	1804	VA	M	400				817
	Abraham Lucas	1829	OH	M	2,000				818
	Clifford Smith	1808	NC	M	8,500				940
(Pebble) 1860	James Barnett	1790	VA	M	3,000				1539
	Franic Buped	1797	VA	M	1,100				1555
	Robert Sparrow	1815	VA	M	1,000				1557
	Guck Foster	1795	VA	M	2,200				1564
				BROWN COUNTY					
(Eagle) 1850	Alex. Cumberland	1830	OH	B	200				2322

County (Township)	Name	Birth year	Birth-place (state)	Race	Estimated worth ($)	Improved acres owned	Unimproved acres owned	Total acres owned	House number
	Mer. Cumberland	1806	VA	B	700				2324
	Isaac Parsons	1820	VA	B	400				2327
	Joseph Lows	1800	VA	B	100				2329
	Lewis Williamson	1795	SC	B					2335
	Alexander Cliff	1828	OH	B	20				2336
	Joseph Lows	1832	OH	B					2337
	Glascow Ellis	1797	VA	B	100				2338
	David Anderson	1800	VA	B	100				2339
	Henry Hudson	1790	VA	B	150				2342
	Andrew Toler	1816	VA	B	200				2343
	Emanuel Cumberland	1813	VA	B	450				2346
	Brister Essix	1817	VA	B	100				2347
	Jacob Jones	1805	VA	B	80				2348
	Charles Baylor	1766	VA	B	250				2349
	Moses Cumberland	1825	OH	B	100				2351
	Adam May	1827	OH	M	20				2352
	Lewis Hurley	1800	KY	B	1,100	1860: 60	1860: 20	1860: 80	2360
GALLIA COUNTY									
(Greenfield) 1850	James Coker	1815	TN	M	500				
	Mary Stewart	1817	OH	M	1,000				
	James Cradolph	1807	VA	B	400				
	Pleas. Matthews	1807	VA	M	2,000				
	Wm. A. Stewart	1825	TN	M	600				
	Richard Dungy	1795	VA	M	1,500				
	James M. Stewart	1824	TN	M	200				
	John J. Stewart	1820	OH	M	400				
	Uriah Rickman	1812	TN	M	500				
	William Dungy	1802	TN	M	500				
	Susannah Dungy	1800	TN	M	400				
	Wm. N. Stewart	1825	OH	M	500				
	Gilbert Seaton	1805	VA	M	200				
	Richard Stewart	1800	VA	M	2,000				
	Isham Chaves/Chavis	1793	VA	M	1,200				
	John Chaves/Chavis	1822	VA	B	100				
	Joseph Riggs	1823	VA	M	300				

County (Township)	Name	Birth year	Birth-place (state)	Race	Estimated worth ($)	Improved acres owned	Unimproved acres owned	Total acres owned	House number
	Omstead [Amistad?] Hughes	1809	VA	B	700				
	Michael Coker	1822	TN	B	200				
	Buck Dungy	1820	TN	B	600				
	John Matthews	1814	VA	M	2,000				
	Elisha Coker	1817	TN	B	250				
	John Brown	1821	VA	M	500				
	Richard W. Stewart	1819	TN	M	400				
	John Coker	1815	TN	M	100				
(Raccoon) 1850	John Bunch	1800	VA	B	100				
	Samuel Vires	1815	VA	B	400				
	Isham Howard	1821	VA	B	400				
	Shadrach Ford	1800	VA	B	400				
(Hunting-ton) 1850	Churchville Anderson	1826	VA	M	500				
	Eliza Anderson	1824	VA	M	500				
	Rich. Anderson	1829	VA	M	500				
	Isabel Anderson	1810	VA	B	400				
	Joseph Anderson	1831	VA	M	400				
	Columbus Anderson	1824	VA	M	500				
	Daniel Anderson	1828	VA	M	1,000				
	Chamberlain Anderson	1824	VA	M	500				
LAWRENCE COUNTY									
(Rome) 1850	Joseph Howard	1813	NC	M	350				
(Washing-ton) 1850	D. Brown	1805	VA	B	800				
(Fayette) 1850	Horace Witcher	1780	VA	B	250				
	Noah Twyman	1780	VA	B	7,500				
HIGHLAND COUNTY									
(Concord) 1850	James Martin	1814	VA	M	800	40	56	106	405
(Fairfield) 1850	Ben. Rollins	1828	VA	B	625				897
	Robert Lawson	1810	VA	B	625				898
	Fleming Fowles	1815	VA	B	800				901
	John Menor	1809	VA	B	100				902
	Lazarus Mitchell	1790	VA	B	260				906
	Hannibal Turner	1804	VA	B	100				907
	Monroe Bryant	1818	NC	M	11,010	200	167	367	988
	Andrew Payton	1784	VA	B	9,630	130	91	221	1005

County (Township)	Name	Birth year	Birth-place (state)	Race	Estimated worth ($)	Improved acres owned	Unimproved acres owned	Total acres owned	House number
	Charles Payton	1790	VA	B	2,500	70	30	100	1052
	Thornton McNeil	1801	VA	M	200				1124
(Greenfield) 1850	Solomon Turner	1823	NC	M	50				1288
(Liberty) 1850	William Moore	1799	VA	B					262
	Peter R. Goen	1825	TN	M					270
	Lewis W. Wood	1820	OH	M					329
	Prince Johnson	1810	VA	B	900				335
	Jeremiah Wood	1795	VA	B	500				363
	Thomas Trimble	1787	KY	B					383
	Joseph Trimble	1831	OH	B					383
	Wm. Williams	1814	VA	B					384
	James Jenkins	1791	VA	B					534
	Wm. Rickman	1813	VA	M					612
	James Payton	1819	VA	M					621
	James Gordon	1800	VA	B					622
	Horrace Suthard	1829	VA	M					627
	Andrew Payton	1818	VA	M					629
	Jasper Rickman	1824	OH	M					632
	Jackson Rickman	1832	OH	M					633
	Henry Day	1818	OH	B					642
	William Willis	1780	VA	B	150				644
	James Garnet	1830	OH	M					660
	James Johnson	1834	OH	B					674
	Ephraim Johnson	1830	OH	B					674
	Peter Rickman	1818	OH	M					679
(Madison) 1850	John Stewart	1797	VA	B					1467
	Thomas Lewis	1795	NC	M					1603
	J. Anderson Lewis	1833	NC	M					1603
	Thomas Rickman	1817	VA	M					1606
(Marshall) 1850	Peter Rickman	1814	VA	M					53
(Paint) 1850	Joshua Taylor	1809	VA	B	360	80		80	1633
	Henry Robinson	1815	NC	B					1833
	Willis Clark	1800	KY	B					2060
	Peter Roulens	1824	OH	B					2069
	Jason Newby	1820	OH	B					2072
	Miles White	1824	NC	B					2073
	Jonathon White	1803	NC	B					2074
	Lewis Prather	1820	OH	B					2074
	Stephen White	1831	NC	B					2074

County (Township)	Name	Birth year	Birth-place (state)	Race	Estimated worth ($)	Improved acres owned	Unimproved acres owned	Total acres owned	House number
	John Junes	1785	VA	B					2077
	James Solomon	1802	NC	B					2080
	Green Findley	1831	VA	M					2081
ATHENS COUNTY									
(Rome) 1850	Jerry Sims	1822	VA	B	500				
	William Tabler	1814	VA	M	800				
	Nathan Colbert	1798	VA	M	300				
(Athens) 1850	George Braxton	1794	VA	M	1,500				
WASHINGTON COUNTY									
(Barlow) 1850	Shadrack Whitfield	1810	VA	B	1,200				
	Joseph Holbert	1804	VA	B	700				
	Benjamin Barnet	1821	VA	B	100				
	Peter Barnet	1791	VA	M	200				
	John Holbert	1777	VA	B	1,000				
(Warren) 1850	Amos McPherson	1809	VA	M	1,200				
	Ambrose Asbury	1798	VA	M	800				
	Amos Beaty	1821	VA	M	390				
	Abraham Shafer	1789	VA	M	1,000				
	John Stewart	1811	VA	M	800				
	Jos. Cross	1808	VA	M	500				
(Watertown) 1850	Michael Stephens	1808	VA	M	500				
(Union) 1850	Aynil Norman	1798	VA	M	500				
(Decatur) 1850	Savilla Tucker	1820	OH	M	350				
	Samuel Spars	1824	VA	B	350				
	John Cozens	1797	VA	M	300				
	Richard W. Fields	1827	VA	B	300				
	John Wilkinson	1809	KY	B	400				
(Roxbury) 1850	George Mail	1817	VA	M	210				130
(Marietta Ward 2) 1850	Harry Bartlett	1780	VA	B	800				
MORGAN COUNTY									
(Morgan) 1850	Sylvanus Morin	1792	VA	M	2,800				
(Noble) 1850	Reuben FitzGerald	1794	VA	M	400				
	Anderson FitzGerald	1814	VA	M	700				
MEIGS COUNTY									
(Salem) 1850	Ezekiel Gomer	1784	VA	M	5,000				

County (Township)	Name	Birth year	Birth-place (state)	Race	Estimated worth ($)	Improved acres owned	Unimproved acres owned	Total acres owned	House number
HOCKING COUNTY									
(Ward) 1850	Anth. Mabray	1795	VA	B	162				
	John Hardin	1804	MD	M	700				
	Abraham Gross	1820	MD	B	162				
	Adison Curry	1814	VA	B	162				
CHAMPAIGN COUNTY									
(Urbana) 1850	James Hunt	1802	VA	B	300				239
	Thomas Gibbs	1798	NC	B	600				251
	Henry Griffith	1812	VA	M					9
	Henry Demsey	1766	NC	M	100				32
	Archibald Andrews	1820	NC	B					57
	Lewis Levite	1796	VA	M					110
	Isaac Curry	1800	VA	B					119
	William Boyd	1787	VA	M	200				144
LOGAN COUNTY									
(Jefferson) 1850	Isaac Akey	1815	PA	M	2,500				259
	Solomon Day	1788	VA	M	2,000				260
	Jess Archer	1819	NC	M	500				262
	Micajah Demery	1814	NC	B	1,400				
	Nathan Nusun	1811	NC	B	700				292
	James Hicks	1824	VA	M					296
	George Jorns	1781	VA	M	2,000				313
	Owen Ardis	1823	VA						315
(Monroe) 1850	Christ. Hicks	1808	VA	M	500				76
	Job Pearce	1825	OH	M					77
	John Taylor	1810	VA	M	700				78
	Everett Bird	1800	VA	M	1,000				80
	Allen Taborn	1786	NC	M	500				82
	Deliard Dempsey	1815	NC	B	15				134
	Leonard Whitfield	1818	NC	B	100				168
	Merit Bonser	1806	VA	M	800				174
	Jason Hicks	1795	VA	B	1,000				184
	Wm. Dempsey	1824	NC	B	900				187
	Owen Bird	1803	VA	M	1,000				189
(Perry) 1850	Washington Banks	1815	OH	B	500	15	35	50	156
	David Day	1791	VA	B		30		30	159
	Richard Day	1825	VA	B					159
	Annamas Day	1829	OH	B					159

County (Township)	Name	Birth year	Birth-place (state)	Race	Estimated worth ($)	Improved acres owned	Unimproved acres owned	Total acres owned	House number
	Felix Day	1833	OH	B					159
	Joseph C. Ash	1827	NC	M					160
	Elisha Bria	1790	VA	M					162
	James Bria	1830	OH	M					162
	William Robert	1774	MD	M	1,000	50	50	100	199
	Anthony Banks	1775	VA	B	12,000	100	107	207	206
(Harrison) 1850	Lerdon Waldon	1829	NC	M					118
(Liberty) 1850	Littleton Conner	1833	OH	B					345
(Lake) 1850	Stephen Depp	1829	VA	M					170
	Benj. Dempsey	1817	NC	M	200				175
	O. Dempsey	1832	OH	M					192
	Samuel Taylor	1825	OH	B					227
	James Payne	1826	VA	B					228
	Tobias Moxley	1822	OH	M	500				255
	Wm. Fletcher	1822	VA	M					255
	Moses Paine	1811	VA	M	150				256
HARRISON COUNTY									
(Cadiz) 1850	James Manly	1824	NC	B	1860: 1,000				662
ROSS COUNTY									
(Chillicothe) 1850	William Bierd	1803	VA	B	450				564
	Peter Bunch	1789	VA	B	350				670
	John Eidler	1810	VA	M	1,350				772
	Mark Shover	1811	VA	B	800				774
WAYNE COUNTY									
(Pickaway) 1850	George Adams	1800	VA	B	1,800				42
DARKE COUNTY									
(German) 1850	James Clemens	1781	VA	M	11,000	125	425	550	73
	M.H. Shaffer	1810	OH	M					3
	Gabriel Green	1783	VA	B		20	10	30	19
	Charles Mason	1804	KY	M		15	55	70	28
	Synis Facton	1817	OH	M	24				61
	PC Hollim	1828	OH	M	1,000				74
	Emeline Lewis	1815	NY	M	130				75
	Richard Ross	1815	NC	M	500				80
	Allen Jones	1795	NC	B	150				85
	Stephen Wade	1820	OH	M	100				89
	Janette Stokes	1807	GA	M	600				90
	Isaac Ross	1807	NC	M	600				91
	John Sanders	1786	MD	B	800				92
	Jesse Oky	1817	NC	M	500				93

County (Township)	Name	Birth year	Birth-place (state)	Race	Estimated worth ($)	Improved acres owned	Unimproved acres owned	Total acres owned	House number
	John Oky	1815	NC	M	500				94
	Monids Burden	1816	SC	M	2,000				95
	Ch. Clemens	1808	VA	M	1,200	30	50	80	96
	John Clemems	1813	VA	M	500	20	20	40	97
	John G. Williams	1787	PA	M	400	25	15	40	100
MERCER COUNTY									
(Butler) 1850	Harrison Logan	1814	VA	B	380				580
(Centre) 1850	Peter Johnston	1818	VA	B	350	20	20	40	447
(Granville) 1850	Burl Archer	1790	VA	B	800	30	20	50	492
	Alex. Bowles	1800	VA	B	270				498
	Benjn. Smith	1815	KY	B	300				499
	Squire Knox	1806	NC	B	800				521
	Thomas Tanner	1797	NC	M	200				522
	Peter Newby	1800	NC	B	800				532
	Wm. Kemble	1808	VA	B	500				533
	Harrison Lee	1820	KY	B	400				536
(Jefferson) 1850	Reuben Clark	1805	TN	B	1,350	1850: 30 1860: 110	1850: 250 1860: 50	1850: 280 1860: 160	337
	Peter Banks	1800	VA	B	1,500	1850: 30 1860: 16	1850: 90 1860: 14	1850: 120 1860: 30	
(Macon) 1850	John Dover	1823	KY	B	800	35	13	48	218
	Merid. Simmons	1793	VA	M	300				172
	Jas. Hall	1830	OH	B	63	15	63	78	173
	Monroe Truss	1820	VA	B	174				174
	Chas Moore	1798	PA	B	2,500	30	50	80	175
	Jacob Mortimer	1795	VA	B	600	20	60	80	188
	Wm. Moss	1815	VA	B					190
	Sandy Bush	1801	VA	M	500				191
	Wm. Overton	1800	VA	B	700	12	108	120	192
	Thos. Graves	1800	VA	B	450	25	15	40	228
	Saml. Jones	1797	NC	B	150	30	50	80	229
	Wm. Jones	1822	VA	B	600				230
	Thos. Dixon	1767	VA	B	400				231
	Jas. Hall	1811	VA	B	450				232
	Isaac Johnston	1805	VA	B	400	18	22	40	235
LORAIN COUNTY									
(Grafton) 1850	Gabriel Gunn	1804	NY	B	1,000	35	33	68	1651
(Russia) 1850	John White	1815	TN	M	310	1850: 25 1860: 30	1850: 35 1860: 20	1850: 60 1860: 50	52
	Henry Harris	1816	VA	B	300	8		8	182
	Sylvanus Resley	1815	NY	B	1,400				183
	Thomas Brown	1815	TN	B	1,000	45	45	90	261

County (Township)	Name	Birth year	Birth-place (state)	Race	Estimated worth ($)	Improved acres owned	Unimproved acres owned	Total acres owned	House number
VAN WERT COUNTY									
(Wilshire) 1850	Jordan Evans	1807	NC	M	300	25	15	40	407
HURON COUNTY									
(Greenfield) 1850	Steph. Robuson	1795	NY	B	4,800	60	180	240	2971
MUSKINGUM COUNTY									
(Meigs) 1860	Chas. M. Brown	1801	VA	B	3,000	1860: 100	1860: 60	1860: 160	27
	Allan Guy	1795	OH	M	1,800	1860: 40	1860: 20	1860: 60	38
	Aguira/ Aquilla Lett	1805	VA	M	3,000	1860: 140	1860: 43	1860: 183	54
	William Lett	1810	VA	M	500				55
	James Lett	1812	VA	M	3,000				58
	Purnes Sims	1790	PA	M	1,500				59
	John Calaman	1814	VA	M	1,600				60
	Tobias Hance	1789	DE	B	600				90
	Moses Caliman	1824	VA	M	4,000	1860: 140	1860: 33	1860: 173	106
	Mary Lett	1790	MD	M	3,000				132
WARREN COUNTY									
(Wayne) 1850	Rose Smith	1783	VA	M	2,000	60	53	113	183
	Peter Black	1820	OH	B					184
	Henry Dudley	1790	VA	B	200	25	75	100	264
	Tippor Namion	1801	NC	M					402
	Jackson Stewart	1814	VA	M	160				435
	Paster Stewart	1812	VA	M					470
	Jacob Green	1787	NC	B		60	28	88	476
	William Magee	1822	VA	M	1,500	40	54	94	603
	John E. Moss	1819	OH	B	3,000	25	25	50	613
	James Mumford	1827	VA	B					681
FRANKLIN COUNTY									
(Perry) 1850	Pleasant Litchford	1789	VA	B	8,000	1850: 100 1860: 130	1850: 137 1860: 97	1850: 237 1860: 227	137
	Patterson McReddy	1800	VA	B					138
	William Garnes	1822	NC	M					141
	Samuel Slott	1820	NC	B					142
FAYETTE COUNTY									
(Perry) 1850	Thomas Waldron	1800	VA	M	1,000				634
	Nathanial Williams	1797	VA	B					769
SHELBY COUNTY									
(Van Buren) 1850	Martin Cheston	1785	VA	B					8
	David Bizzle	1810	NC	M	200				13
	Blake Reynolds	1801	NC	M	1,200				14

County (Township)	Name	Birth year	Birth-place (state)	Race	Estimated worth ($)	Improved acres owned	Unimproved acres owned	Total acres owned	House number
	Samuel Bond	1815	PA	M		30	10	40	15
	Thomas Moss	1818	OH	M					17
	Humphrey Clinton	1785	VA	M	800	35	45	80	18
	Solomon Lett	1805	OH	B	250	16	50	66	19
	Wm. Creth	1780	VA	B	300	20	20	40	20
	Isom White	1790	VA	B					27
	Sam. McDaniel	1812	VA	M					30
	Zacariah Lucas	1810	MD	M		40	120	160	31
	Moses Redman	1784	VA	M	2,000	40	120	160	33
	Siphax Davis	1801	VA	M	160	20	20	40	36
	Jas. Hill	1800	VA	M					38
	Wm. Byers	1798	OH	M	250				74
	John W. Jones	1787	VA	M	4,200	50	90	140	75
	William Stuart	1806	NC	B	2,000				83
	Henry Galloway	1806	MD	M					91
	Samuel Collins	1776	VA	M	1,000				94
	Jacob Collins	1814	VA	M	400	10	50	60	95
	Samuel Collins	1812	OH	M	200				96
	A.W. Bell	1799	VA	M	250				97
	Geo. Collins	1808	VA	M	500	55	30	85	98
	Edward Jackson	1789	MD	M	500				101
	Jas. Budman	1808	SC	M					102
	Wash. Williams	1809	VA	B		40	360	400	102
COLUMBIANA COUNTY									
(Knox) 1850	John Lacy	1814	VA	M	400				27
	James Davis	1810	VA	B	400				28
STARK COUNTY									
(Lexington) 1850	Luke Rawls	1790	VA	B	300				255
	John Oliver	1785	VA	B					288
	Jas. B. Holliday	1820	OH	B					332
	Axam Hamlin	1802	VA	B					337
	Chas. Lamaster	1783	MD	B					342
JEFFERSON COUNTY									
(Mount Pleasant) 1850	David Wyatt	1813	VA	B	3,000	18	00	18	41
	Allison Buck	1805	VA	B	1,200	20	10	30	113
	Dan. Robinson	1813	VA	B	3,500	65	15	80	197
	Letti Robinson	1790	VA	B		47	23	70	198
	William Hamlin	1812	VA	B	200				216

County (Township)	Name	Birth year	Birth-place (state)	Race	Estimated worth ($)	Improved acres owned	Unimproved acres owned	Total acres owned	House number
	Henry Ricks	1817	VA	B		20	20	40	366
	Murdock Joiner	1826	VA	B					387
DELAWARE COUNTY									
(Concord) 1850	Abraham Depp	1790	VA	B	7,500	105	295	400	2164
	James Wallace	1822	VA	B					2165
(Radnor) 1850	Thom. Crawford	1803	VA	B	500	15	10	25	202
(Thomson) 1850	James Munton	1814	VA	B	1,500				98
GREENE COUNTY									
(Caesar Creek) 1850	James Green	1815	VA	B	1,000				1169
	Samuel Brown	1820	VA	B	1,200				1170
	Alex. Brown	1832	OH	M					1170
	Jms. W. Brown	1834	OH	B					1171
	Robert Baker	1810	VA	B	1,000	40	20	60	1172
	William Jackson	1800	VA	B	1,400				1262
	Jms. A. Jackson	1826	VA	B					1263
(Sugar Creek) 1850	William Price	1815	VA	B	2,000	40	10	50	1735
(Xenia) 1850	Richard Brown	1800	VA	B	700				599
	William Stewart	1795	VA	B		45	29	74	1204
KNOX COUNTY									
(Hilliard) 1850	Erckel Thompson	1775	VA	B	12	60		60	1500
(Morris) 1850	Thom. Snowdon	1805	MD	B		100	73	173	480
LAKE COUNTY									
(Concord) 1850	Lewis Easton	1800	VA	B					91
(Painesville) 1850	Isaac Stanton	1815	VA	B	500				19
	John Goodenon	1825	VA	B					563
(Perry) 1850	Arthur Morris	1810	MD	B					190
	Simon Morris	1832	OH	B					190
	Isiah Morris	1834	OH	B					190
MIAMI COUNTY									
(Concord) 1850	Alex. Hamilton	1805	VA	B	700				1419
	Joseph Haggard	1804	VA	M	200				1593
(Spring Creek) 1850	James White	1810	VA	B	300				80
(Union) 1850	Simon Gillet	1822	VA	B	200				2366
(Washington) 1850	Nelson Cole	1810	VA	B		17		17	270
	Johnston D. Crowder	1820	VA	B	100				285
	William Taylor	1819	OH	M	50				384

County (Township)	Name	Birth year	Birth-place (state)	Race	Estimated worth ($)	Improved acres owned	Unimproved acres owned	Total acres owned	House number
	Dudley Crowder	1826	VA	B	350				408
TRUMBULL COUNTY									
(Farmington) 1850	Prince Way	1810	OH	M	900				
(Mesopotamia) 1850	Thos. Blackwell	1815	NC	B	1,300				
(Bloomfield) 1850	Wm. C. Jenkins	1805	MD	B	800				
MAHONING COUNTY									
(Smith) 1850	Miles Manzillar	1799	VA	M	3,100				
(Austintown) 1850	David Scisco	1778	PA		500				
(Goshen) 1850	John White	1793	VA		2,000				
(Youngstown) 1850	Abram Brown	1807	OH	M	1,448				
PORTAGE COUNTY									
(Charlestown) 1850	Jeremiah Loudin/London	1799	CT		1,200				
(Atwater) 1850	Alexander Pool	1820	VA		300				
	Newton Thomas		OH		800				
(Ravenna) 1850	Ed. Matthews	1818	VA		150				
GEAUGA COUNTY									
(Bainbridge) 1850	Mack/Mack P. Matthews	1829	MA	M	2,640				
SUMMIT COUNTY									
(Stow) 1850	Jacob Holmes	1802	VA	B	250				
CUYAHOGA COUNTY									
(Independence) 1850	Thomas West	1796	VA	M	2,500				
	Enor West	1820	NH	M	800				
(Middleburgh) 1850	Joseph Peak	1814	OH	M	1,000				
	George Peak	1804	PA	M	100				
	Peter Sherman	1791	NY	M	800				
ERIE COUNTY									
(Perkins) 1850	Isaac Brown	1798	VA	B	1,800				
RICHLAND COUNTY									
(Sharon) 1850	Abrah. Duncan	1806	VA	M	1,400				
MORROW COUNTY									
(Harmony) 1850	Daniel Kenney	1795	VA	M	1,000				
	David Ramy	1795	VA	M	2,500				
(Peru) 1850	Abrah. Simpson	1792	MD	M	425				
(Washington) 1850	Isaac Robison	1793	PA	B	3,500				

County (Township)	Name	Birth year	Birth-place (state)	Race	Estimated worth ($)	Improved acres owned	Unimproved acres owned	Total acres owned	House number
SENECA COUNTY									
(Tiffin) 1850	Archie Waldren	1801	VA	M	400				
	Celia Manly	1800	NC	M	250				
(Seneca) 1850	Daniel Whetsele	1788	VA	M	2,000				
	Felix Whetsele	1807	VA	M	300				
	Elizabeth Prater	1790	VA	M	500				
	Samuel Grimes	1784	VA	B	1,300				
(Big Spring) 1850	Calista Allen	1794	VA	B	700				
SANDUSKY COUNTY									
(Sandusky) 1850	John Hawkins	1804	NC	B	900				
(Crawford) 1850	William Bollin/ Boffin	1781	VA	M	1,200				
HANCOCK COUNTY									
(Delaware) 1850	James Ramsey	1805	MD	M	300				
AUGLAIZE COUNTY									
(Delaware) 1850	Jefferson Wert	1805	OH	M	400				982
	Jane Crowder	1796	OH	M	400				
(St. Marys) 1850	Edward Cook	1798	SC	B	400				622
(Washington) 1850	Pleas. Brannon	1799	OH	M	500				809
ALLEN COUNTY									
(Bath) 1850	James Robinson	1812	VA	B	500				294
(Perry) 1850	Wyatt Stewart	1809	VA	B	2,000				936
COSHOCTON COUNTY									
(Virginia) 1850	Nelson Glede	1797	VA	B	1,700				
(Bethlehem) 1850	David Warren	1778	VA	M	3,500				

Note: M = Mulatto; B = Black

CONTRIBUTORS

Timothy G. Anderson is associate professor in the Department of Geography at Ohio University, where he has taught courses in cultural and historical geography since 1996. Anderson's research interests focus on the historical settlement geography of the United States, especially the production of regional and ethnic cultural landscapes, and the production of cultural landscapes associated with Germanic diasporic movements and communities. He received his PhD in geography from Texas A&M University (1994) and was a Fulbright scholar (Romania) in 2014.

John Bickers is an assistant professor of history at Case Western Reserve University and a citizen of the Miami Tribe of Oklahoma. Bickers's research focuses on Native American history in the Great Lakes region. His current book project, *The Miami Nation: A Middle Path for Indigenous Nationhood,* examines the Miami Tribe in the nineteenth and early twentieth centuries through the lens of Indigenous nation-building and sovereignty.

Anna-Lisa Cox is an award-winning historian whose newest book, *The Bone and Sinew of the Land,* was honored by *Smithsonian Magazine* as one of the best history books of 2018. Cox's original research underpinned two exhibits at the Smithsonian's National Museum of African American History and Culture, where she co-curated the exhibit on African American farmers in the nineteenth-century Midwest. She has received numerous fellowships for her work, most recently receiving an Archie Green Fvellowship from the Library of Congress Folklife Center to collect oral histories from multigenerational African American farmers in the Midwest for the Folklife Center's permanent collection. Her writing has been featured in a number of publications, including the *Washington Post, Lapham's Quarterly,* and the *New York Times.* She is currently producing the Questioning Conversation video series for the NPS Underground Railroad Network to Freedom program. She received her MPhil in social anthropology from the University of Cambridge and her PhD in history from the University of Illinois, and is a nonresident fellow at Harvard University's Hutchins Center for African and African American Research.

Joseph A. M. Gingerich is an associate professor of anthropology at Ohio University and a research associate at the Smithsonian Institution, National Museum of Natural History. Gingerich's expertise includes hunting and gathering societies, stone tool technology, spatial analysis (GIS, analysis of artifact distributions, and human use of landscapes), geoarchaeology, and the first peopling of North America. His current work focuses on human responses to changing environments, changes in stone tool technology over time, and the spatial arrangements of artifacts at hunter-gatherer campsites. Most of his current research is based in the eastern United States and East Africa. His research has been funded by the National Geographic Society, the Smithsonian Institution, and the National Science Foundation.

Kim M. Gruenwald is an associate professor of history at Kent State University in Ohio, specializing in colonial America, the American Revolution, and the Early Republic. She is the author of *River of Enterprise: The Commercial Origins of Regional Identity in the Ohio Valley, 1790–1850* (Indiana University Press, 2002).

William M. Hunter is a historian and geographer who serves as the regional historian for the National Park Service, Interior Region 2 South Atlantic-Gulf region. Working on behalf of the region's parks and their resources, Hunter draws on his professional, academic, personal, and volunteer experience to preserve and protect its important cultural resources and help lead the regional Park History program. An expert on the National Historic Preservation Act and the National Environmental Policy Act, he has been involved in the successful development of projects of all scopes and scales since joining the NPS. He previously served as the planner and environmental coordinator for Cuyahoga

Valley National Park, James A. Garfield National Historic Site, and First Ladies National Historic Site, as well as a historian and architectural historian in private practice.

William Kerrigan is a professor of history at Muskingum University. He is the author of *Johnny Appleseed and the American Orchard* (Johns Hopkins University Press, 2012) and has coauthored several local history works. He teaches a broad range of courses in American history, including courses on the American Revolution, the Civil War, environmental history, and Ohio history. In addition to writing and teaching, he keeps active in the public history arena, presenting talks every year on various Ohio history and Civil War subjects for many Ohio museums and historical societies.

M. Duane Nellis is president emeritus and trustee professor at Ohio University. Prior to arriving at Ohio University, he was president of Texas Tech University and the University of Idaho. Previously, he served as provost and senior vice president at Kansas State University and as dean of West Virginia University's Eberly College of Arts and Sciences, the institution's largest academic college. He is recognized nationally and internationally for his research that utilizes satellite data and geographic information systems to analyze various dimensions of the Earth's land surface. This research has been funded by more than fifty sources, such as NASA, the National Geographic Society, the US Agency for International Development, and the US Department of Agriculture. His research has led to more than 160 articles and reports in a wide range of professional journals, and over twenty books and book chapters, and his selection as a fellow of the prestigious American Association for the Advancement of Science and as a fellow of the Explorers Club in New York City. He is past president of the American Association of Geographers. He received his BA in earth sciences/geography from Montana State University in 1976, and his MA and PhD degrees in geography from Oregon State University in 1977 and 1980, respectively.

Adam R. Nelson is senior associate dean in the School of Education and Vilas Distinguished Achievement Professor of Educational Policy Studies and History at the University of Wisconsin–Madison. He received his PhD in history from Brown University. His publications include

Education and Democracy: The Meaning of Alexander Meiklejohn, 1872–1964 (University of Wisconsin Press, 2001) and *The Elusive Ideal: Equal Educational Opportunity and the Federal Role in Boston's Public Schools* (University of Chicago Press, 2005), as well as two forthcoming works: *Exchange of Ideas: The Economy of Higher Education in Early America* and *Capital of Mind: The Idea of a Modern American University,* both scheduled for publication with the University of Chicago Press in 2023. His research has been funded by grants from the National Endowment for the Humanities/American Antiquarian Society, the National Academy of Education/Spencer Postdoctoral Fellowship Program, the Charles Warren Center for Studies in American History at Harvard, the Advanced Studies Fellowship Program at Brown, and the Vilas Associate Program at the University of Wisconsin–Madison.

Jessica Choppin Roney is an associate professor of history at Temple University. Her current book project, *Revolutionary Settlement: The Colonies of the American Revolution,* examines the two linked diasporas that resulted from the American Revolution: one of Loyalists predominantly to Canada, and one of Anglo-American settlers to the trans-Appalachian West where they founded colonies that might—or might not—one day be part of the United States. Her work asks how these people (and the policymakers who wanted to regulate them!), who had all lived through the American Revolution, drew meaning from that seismic event, and how they implemented those lessons as they created new colonies as parts of larger empires.

Joseph Thomas Ross is an independent scholar. A native of Ohio, he received his BA from Ohio State University and his MA from Ohio University. His research focuses on the imperial similarities and distinctions between the American and British Empires in the early trans-Appalachian West.

Brian Schoen is the James Richard Hamilton / Baker and Hostetler Professor of Humanities and chair of the History Department at Ohio University. His research and teaching focuses on the political, social, economic, and intellectual history of the United States from its early struggles through its near dissolution in the midst of the Civil War. He is the author of *The Fragile Fabric of Union: Cotton, Federal Politics, and* *the Coming of the Civil War* (Johns Hopkins University Press, 2009), as well as numerous articles, book chapters, and coedited collections exploring the early US republic and Civil War eras, most recently *Continent in Crisis: The U.S. Civil War in North America* (Fordham University Press, 2023).

Cameron Shriver is a research associate at the Myaamia Center and a visiting assistant professor of history at Miami University. He is currently building a geographical and historical database of Myaamia (Miami Indian) reserves and land transactions, and also works on intelligence gathering in the colonial Ohio River valley and Great Lakes. Shriver completed his PhD in history at Ohio State University in 2016.

Chief Glenna J. Wallace was elected to the office of chief of the Eastern Shawnee Tribe of Oklahoma in 2006. She is the first woman ever elected to this office. During her many years of service to academia, the community, and the tribe, several organizations have bestowed honors and recognition for her dedication and work, including local, state, regional, and national teaching awards; 2007 Woman Tribal Leader of the Year (Engage Life Program); the DAR Heritage Award; the Governor's Outstanding Teacher Award; and the Soroptimist Woman of Distinction Award.

INDEX

Entries for figures indicated with an *f.*

Abdy, Edward, 193–94
abolitionists, 162, 188–89; Native American, 191; White, 191
Abrams, Elliot, 28
Adams, Samuel, 97
Adams County (OH), 140, 142–43
Adena, 172
Adena Culture, 4, 22–24; conical mounds, 22–24; earthworks, 4, 22
African American(s): churches, 123; discrimination of, 10, 225–26, 238–39; education, 9, 191, 193, 225–26, 238; erasure from history, 193–98; "exceptionalism" and, 192–93; farmers and farming communities, 121–23, 187, 189, 194–95, 198, 238; "impermanence," 196; lifepath of, 123f; manumitted, 123; military service, 191–92; monuments to, lack of, 195–96; Native Americans and, 190; pioneers and settlers, 5, 7, 9–10, 121–23, 140, 142, 186–98; population, 1850 census, 113, 122; preservationists, 193, 196–97; taxation of, 226; violence against, 193–94; voting rights, 186
African Europeans (Otele), 192
Age of Discovery, 43
Age of Enlightenment, 43, 100
agricultural societies, 181
Algonquian: language family, 51; western, 49
Allegheny River, 41, 151
Allegheny-Ohio River, 38
Alligator Mound, 30
Alumapees, 51
American Sunday School Union, 226

Ames Township (OH), 223
Ancestry.com, 124, 126
Anderson, Benedict, 197
Anderson, David, 29
Andover Theological Seminary, 226
Anschutz, George, 160
Appalachian Mountains, 2–5, 54, 99, 102, 108, 117, 121
apples / apple culture, 6, 168–82; class inequality and, 10; commercial production, 181–82; grafting, 169–70, 174–82; Native Americans and, 169–71, 182; orchards, 170, 180–82; picking, criminalizing, 181; plant origins, 169; Roxbury/Putnam Russet, 174; seedlings, 168, 175–78, 180–81; seeds, 169, 176–77; winter, 181
Aquanishuonigy, 44
architecture styles: Cape Cod, 125; churches, 131; folk, 142–43; I-houses, 120, 126–27, 143; Pennsylvania bank barns, 126; saltbox houses, 125; transverse crib barns, 120
Arkansas, 244
Armstrong, John, 89–91, 94–95, 102, 104
Armstrong Station, 104
Articles of Confederation, 203
Athens (OH), 227
Auglaize County (OH), 128–29
Austria, 53

B&O railroad, 146
barges, 161–62
Barnard, Henry, 219, 225
Battle of Fallen Timbers, 66, 208, 222